Finding
(My) Self
(Love)

One Girl's Journey of 17 Countries
Across 4 Continents in 6 Months

K i m   O r l e s k y

authorHOUSE®

T0365024

AuthorHouse™
1663 Liberty Drive
Bloomington, IN 47403
www.authorhouse.com
Phone: 1-800-839-8640

Published by AuthorHouse   02/19/2015

ISBN: 978-1-4969-5967-6 (sc)
ISBN: 978-1-4969-5966-9 (e)

Library of Congress Control Number: 2014922402

Print information available on the last page.

Any people depicted in stock imagery provided by Thinkstock are models,
and such images are being used for illustrative purposes only.
Certain stock imagery © Thinkstock.

Print information available on the last page.

Thank you to everyone who was a part of my journey, near and far.
This is my love letter to you.

Feeling the Fear...

I woke up yesterday with incredible anxiety and the paralyzing fear of what I am about to do.

I thought "what if I cancel the trip?", "what if I just went and found myself a new job"? I know that's not the right answer. I will forever regret not taking this step. Maybe the fear is here to remind me that this is a big step. Not everyone can do it. I will appreciate myself that much more for what I am capable of doing.

Six weeks ago I hit my breaking point with my boyfriend, who I still love. For two years he has been travelling back and forth, out of town six days a week, partial weekends for me. Occasionally we missed our limited weekends because he would be invited for a weekend away, or worse yet, the upcoming 10-day boy's vacation. I didn't even get 10-day vacations. My heart could no longer handle loving him as much as I do and feeling like I can only spend such little time with him. I called him up and told him I couldn't do this anymore.

I cried in the shower the next day. What did I do? What next? Like divine intervention I heard the words in my head, "sell your house. Go travel". I called my mom thinking she was going to commit me. My world trip. The one I have been daydreaming in my head for years. It's time.

As the trip came closer I started doing more self-reflection and I started meditating. One of my sessions told me to keep myself open to possibilities. Say yes to the things that will come. I would love to come back to my unfinished love story, him ready to say yes, to fully commit to us. But I also need to take this opportunity to learn and grow from others too. After all once I am back, and even more importantly during my trip, if he wants to be a part of my life he will be. We will make mutual efforts. I will meet people on my travels that may change my life, and no matter what the distance, we will remain friends. The world is small and the people and experiences will find me.

The movers came on the weekend and moved my belongings into storage. As I sat in my car, watching them shut the truck, I texted my now ex. I wanted to see him before he left out of town again. It was potentially our last time ever seeing each other. Whether it was by coincidence or design we couldn't arrange our schedules.

> Me: I do love you. I always will. That will never change. But now I think it's time for me to let you go.
>   I will miss you tremendously. You have no idea. I will probably contact you again in the future, but hopefully I will be in a better place where I am no longer holding onto the hope of us. And we can laugh about ourselves, and reminisce about all the great memories we had and when I tell you I love you it will be in a place of friendship and not of passion. I will do my best not to contact you before then.

Everything I own is now in a garage, not to be seen for at least six months. I wondered how much of my belongings I will forget about and how much I will even care about.

I came back to the house the next day I walked through each empty room remembering the day I moved in. All those memories I said goodbye to. I thanked it for being my home for four and a half years. I wished it the best for the new owners. I held back the tears.

I left Calgary in the morning. In the event I needed some extra encouragement to get on a plane I woke up to freezing rain and snow.

I was surprised that I wasn't nervous, anxious or overly excited to leave, just really calm. I was ready for everything that I was about to do, or maybe slightly in denial.

Sydney Has Stolen My Heart

Sydney, Australia
March 30

After a fourteen and a half hour flight and an 18-hour time change from LAX I arrived in Sydney at the ungodly hour of 6:30AM on the first day.

I spent the day excited about being somewhere different. I kept myself busy. Busy to beat the jetlag and busy to avoid the heartbreak. I spent the whole weekend exploring the city. I went to the Aquarium. I went shopping and explored the famous Paddy's Market, the city's largest flea markets. Of course I explored around the Circular Quay one afternoon and just sat and enjoyed a glass of wine while I stared at the iconic Opera House. That same afternoon I walked through the Botanical Gardens and sat on a bench or the grass and read a few pages from my book. I just took it all in.

The final day that I was in Sydney I explored Manly Beach. I never considered myself to be much of a beach person, but with nothing but time, and my overactive mind, I needed to start to chill. The one thing I asked for the most was more patience and calmness in my life. I may as well start learning.

From Sunset...

I started my 3-day Uluru safari tour today. The day started off with a 6AM pickup. However I was up earlier than that because of the jetlag.

I hadn't heard anything from him. I thought maybe I would send his mom a message through Facebook, asking how he is, whether she thinks I should contact him, but when I went to find her contact she had already deleted me. I had this strong sensation that he deleted me off Facebook a couple of days ago, but it turns out it was her. My broken heart felt like I was shattered more.

Uluru national park is four hours from Alice Springs, so I got comfy and allowed my brain to start exploring heavy thoughts.

Our first stop was the Stewart Camel farm. The night before I had met a couple of men who said they were former camel racing champions. At first I thought it was a joke, but sure enough I was confirmed when I arrived at the farm. Unfortunately the camel I rode didn't go nearly as fast as a racing champion, but the guide did allow her to move at a fast trot when she saw her home base again.

At this stop I also had the option of buying a fly net for my face. No joke. The flies are so bad here that I could double as a child in a charity commercial. I decided to tough it out, "live like a local", and go without the net. I learned the "Aussie Outback wave", which is a constant swatting of the flies off my face. Constant.

After having a laid back lunch at the campsite, we headed off to go see the cultural centre and Kata Tjuta, a series of 36 domes that cover the Australian outback. Unfortunately the day was too hot to enjoy the full hike, but even the short

3km walk was enough to take it out of me. I separated myself from my group on the way back down, sat down and found incredible calmness in the mountains and the wind as I looked out to the desert. Please help me find peace in my head and my heart.

Afterwards the group headed over to Uluru in time to watch the sunset send its colours over the red rock. As the sun set I drank champagne and snacked on the appetizers provided. It was lovely.

I sometimes feel that I am in a transitional phase for my travels. I love the excitement and fun atmosphere of the backpacking groups. I get the opportunity to see them throughout our stops, but I prefer the luxuries of the more expensive tours. For almost double the price of the backpacking tours I get champagne, wine with dinner, permanent tents with a cot, and 6 German-speaking tour-mates.

After a dinner of kangaroo and camel we headed back to our individual campsites for an early bed. I stayed up a little longer to have an evening shower and do some sink laundry. As I got back to my tent the stars were fully emblazoned throughout the sky. I could see the Milky Way above. I laid on a bench and just stared up. I wish my camera could capture a picture. But then I probably would have spent more time staring at the camera screen than up at the sky.

...To Sunrise

Yulara, Australia
April 2

We were having an early day in order to catch the sunrise viewing of Uluru. Unfortunately my jet lag hasn't completely left me yet, and my body naturally woke at 4AM. I took advantage of the early morning wake-up by packing my bag, doing some tent yoga, and updating my blog over a cup of coffee at the outdoor picnic table.

Breakfast was a continental spread. With my Aussie-land experiences, I'm trying all things local and new, because why not? One of the breakfast options was toast with vegemite. I don't think it gets more authentic than eating vegemite in the outback. I took one bite and threw it in the garbage. It was terrible! It was salty and gritty, and an aftertaste that lingered even with sips of coffee. It was not the Australian answer to Nutella that I was expecting.

Uluru for sunrise was as to be expected, busy. Fortunately they have so many viewing areas that everyone can easily find themselves a front-row seat among the many levels of trail and platforms. It was still very pretty, but I preferred the sunset.

Our tour followed up the viewing with an opportunity to walk the entire 10.6km of trail that surrounds the rock. Normally I would walk with purpose, but this time I decided to go at a slower pace and try for a walking meditation. I was successful in snippets, and when I was in that moment, I could feel just being. No thoughts. No mindless narratives that typically run through my head. I was fortunate enough to see a couple of wild dingoes scurrying along. I was startled at first, but realized they were harmless as long as they didn't feel provoked.

The walk was nice for the most part, that is up until that last 1.5km. It was so hot today, and I'm already a water fanatic,

I had to pee. Bad. I would have had no problems squatting on the edge of the trail, but by this time more tour buses had unloaded and there were people to be seen in every direction. There was no hiding from them. And there was no way I was going to head into the grasses. Chances are the second I go for a squat a python would bite my ass. I kept telling myself at a fast walk it would only take 10 minutes, but 10 minutes I really didn't have. I had to run. I ran so fast in 37 degree heat I think people thought I was training for a death race. And in my head I was. "The finish line is just up ahead", I told myself. "Push! Push"! Finally I saw the car park, but no bathrooms. To throw insult to injury the designers of the walk placed the toilets another 250m away. I almost didn't make it.

After finishing lunch back at the camp we were off for another three hour drive to our next destination, King's Canyon. Tomorrow another walk is planned, but this one promises to be an oasis among the desert.

King's Canyon or
Missing Love and Finding Love

Petermann, Australia
April 3

King's Canyon
It thunder stormed and rained all night, and continued to drizzle rain right through the morning. Half of my small seven person tour group decided to back out of the three hour, 6km, King's Canyon walk.

We left the camp to arrive just as the sun was rising. King's Canyon is very remote and has no services, so they do not allow walks to start after 9AM to prevent people from being stuck in the canyon and suffering from dehydration. Thankfully the rain stopped as we started our walk and the all-day cloud coverage made it a cooler day, and a much more tolerable walk.

King's Canyon is stunning. It is a tear in the rocks allowing for spectacular views, and a natural walking trail. The walk goes from the highest peak to the deep low: a watering hole with vegetation and animals, romantically named The Garden of Eden. We stopped there for a bit and enjoyed nature before finishing the last leg of the walk.

After, we headed back to the camp for lunch. We picked up the remaining group members and made the five hour return bus ride back to Alice Springs. I have a flight tomorrow back to Sydney, and the start of my East coast tour the following day.

Missing Love and Finding Love
Twice this week I've had dreams that have caused me to wake up crying. My dreams have been conversations with my lost love. Or not so much conversations as me trying to have him talk to me while I sit and wait to hear his thoughts, but they are never expressed. The only things he tells me are of pain

and frustration and nothing of love and healing. I wake up crying because I feel his pain, but until I know more there is nothing I can do.

It also hurts because I have had a maternal ache in me for a couple of years. I soften with every sight of a baby or a pregnant woman. My heart doesn't tell me "want" anymore, it tells me "need", yet I'm further away from it now than ever.

I miss companionship. I miss kisses and hand holding. I miss hearing "good morning, beautiful" and saying "good night, darling".

I also know that if I was to do this trip with someone else I would be missing out on a massive part of my emotional education. I wouldn't be chatting with as many interesting people. And I certainly wouldn't get to spend as much time lost in my thoughts or, even better, completely thoughtless.

I've had a lot of conversations about love and travelling alone on this trip. I've met a few people that want to hear my life story, particularly about the part of my making this trip by myself.

I would be lying if I said that I wasn't seeking love during my travels. Not the love of a companion but instead the love of myself. I do truly believe that one day I will be married, and one day I will have "the little prince" or princess that I ache for, but right now is not that time. My focus is on myself and finding true joy in solitude. One day I will be 87 and my husband of 50+ years will have finally passed on, and for the first time in decades I will be alone again. I am doing this for that elderly woman that needs something to reflect on and pull her through those dark days. She can relive the love of being solo and reflect on memories of youth and travelling.

Even though it's only been a week, I have started to find this joy in solitude that I am seeking. I have had great conversations with a wide variety of people and learn something new from every one: the deaf man at the Sydney bar, the Swiss couple who think Canadian English is just terrible, the Aussie who lived in Banff for a couple of years, the woman from Singapore travelling with her husband and kids that dreams of a life different from where she is now, and the two small town former camel racing champions. I know this trip will just continue to get better. And I know that old woman will look back on these days and be so happy I took this time out for myself.

Learning to Slow Down

Sydney, Australia
April 4

Somewhere someone has a list of words used to describe me. I'm sure the list is plentiful, but I would not be surprised if on it one of the words contained "high-strung".

I have always been a person in a hurry. I speak with rushed enthusiasm. I'm in a hurry to get to where I'm going, even if I don't know where that is quite yet. I have goals and timelines that cause me stress and anxiety if they aren't met exactly how I have them planned in my head. Oprah has said to be careful what you pray for because you will be challenged with it. I was hoping to learn more patience, but as a part of that learning to slow down is the first step.

I've had a few opportunities where I had to focus on slowing down. The woman in the retired Swiss couple group during my last tour was deaf. She had a device surgically implanted in her head so she could hear. She spoke fluent German and English, but her English was still challenged. When I spoke in my regular enthusiastic pace she could not understand me. I had to learn to slow down my speech as to annunciate each word. I was told this is going to be even more challenging as I travel into many of the Asian countries where English is not widely spoken, and those that do speak have a limited vocabulary.

I've also practiced my patience with many of the shuttles and bus tours. Normally I would become incredibly anxious, constantly staring at my phone and the time, calculating time to the airport, time in the airport, and time left to boarding. Aussies are an island-time version of the western world. For the most part everything has to be on time, but if it isn't then "no worries". Just go with the waves.

The shuttle on the way to the airport included many delays. I haven't had a phone in over a week. Without a phone I have stopped looking at the time as often. I just continued to read my book, and when I got bored of that stared out the window. It was calming, and I forgot about how to let it go. When we got to the airport there was a mass of schoolgirls heading home from a two week class trip. I became nervous thinking I wouldn't get through check-in in time for cutoff. Then I talked myself out of it. Of course they were going to get us all through check-in. Once I had that conversation in my head I slowed right down.

I'm going to try to slow it down much more throughout this trip and hopefully bring back a more relaxed persona with me. I'm starting to like this version of Kim. I have far too much anxiety for no reason. That anxiety has actually cost me a very important part of my life. Today has been very heavy as I have reflected on the fact that had I slowed down more in life I may be in a different place, but then again lessons in life come when they need to. I like to believe that events happen in a deliberate way to take us on the journey and not straight to the destination. So says my favourite book, The Alchemist.

As I rode on the plane from Alice Springs to Sydney I wrote my ex a long letter.

Me: I made a huge mistake. But you already know that. I dream of a future with you, but I was so short-sighted I couldn't see past the pain of missing you all the time. I was frustrated and angry and gave up far too soon. There are so many things I wish I could change. Most of all I wish I was able to talk myself of the ledge before I jumped. But now I am here and further away from you and any glimmer of a life we had together than ever before.

Yet I still see that glimmer. In the short amount of time that I've already been here I've learned a lot about you and myself. I need to slow down. That's a big one.

You tried to show me that on so many occasions, but I was so focused on the end goal and getting there as quickly as possible. I notice that now. Some of your traits that I never understood I get now. I was in such a rush for everything and I don't even know why. I'm sorry for that.

I also need to see more love in my life. You loved me so much. I hope you still love me. But I need to notice it more and appreciate it. I needed to give you more kisses. And hold your hand more and just be. I'm sorry I wasn't always present to your presence nearly as often as I should have been. There was a day that I was and I forgot how to be there.

I would love more than anything in the world to receive an email from you, or better yet skype with you. Hear your voice and see your gorgeous face. I hope you come and see me. I hope you accept my apologies. It was all me. I was mad for all the wrong reasons and I took it out on you and on us.

I miss every part of you. I miss your eyes. I miss your lips. I miss your arms and how they would hold me so tight. I miss being in love with you and being loved back. And I'm not missing just general companionship or love in general, I know what that pain feels like. I'm missing you.

I'm so afraid that I screwed up beyond repair. And I will have to live with the pain of knowing that no one else in my life will fill the void that you left behind. That I will never love or be loved by anyone else the way we were, and I pray hopefully will be again. Sooner rather than later… but there I go, being in a rush again. I still need to work on that.

I need to continue this journey for me and for us and our future. I hope you think about me as often as I think about you. But I hope you aren't brought to tears on a daily basis like I am. The pain is so unbearable some days that I literally feel nauseous.

Your mom deleted me from Facebook. That really hurt. I was going to reach out to her and see if I should contact you, but when I saw she deleted me I felt that our relationship may be fully over and that it's just a matter of time before everyone from your family is gone from my life. Then there is no coming back.

I don't know if I will send this to you. Maybe I'll take a bit of time to re-read it to myself then delete it. However I feel better putting down the pain.

I love you. With all my heart. I was a complete idiot. I see that now. I need to finish my journey but I hope I have a home to come back to. Because I consider you home, and without that I feel hopeless.

I cried all day for you. I miss you so much. It feels like my heart is being crushed from my chest. I never wanted to leave you. I don't know why I did. You are everything to me.

I filed the letter away. I wasn't ready to send it.

Coach up the Coast

Crescent Head, Australia
April 5

Today was the first day of my 14-day East coast tour. Since being in Australia some of the laid-back lifestyle has started to rub off on me and I've not been doing my typical Type-A traits such as double, and triple, checking items. This means that I was checked out of my hotel only to realize my tour bus doesn't leave for another 90 minutes

The bus is fairly full, and with a lot of 20-something year olds. I was the oldest one in the group at 31. We played an icebreaker game, like speed-dating where we took the time to meet a variety of people five minutes at a time in order to choose bunk mates to share a room with. Many of the people were the expected University student on gap year, but I found a few that were on gap year between high school and University. I don't even know if they were old enough to drink! But maybe just barely, since the legal drinking age is 18. Maybe that's why they chose to come to Australia.

Our first stop on the way to Byron Bay was Blue Tongue Vineyard. The Hunter Valley has vineyards well over 120 years and most specialize in the Shiraz and Semillon grapes. We had a quick winery introduction and then the "tasting" started. When with a group of younger peers the goal is to drink your sample as quickly as possible so that more wine can be poured in your glass. I tried to sip and appreciate the wine, but noticed quickly that I was missing out and losing this game.

It's a beautiful drive up the coast. I was able to see a few kangaroo in the field on the way to the vineyard, but we were already passing them before I could take a photo.

There are quite a few Canadians on the trip; one girl from Edmonton, another from Winnipeg, and quite a few from Ontario. It's an interesting mix of characters. I'm sure I will have plenty of stories to tell, assuming I can stay up as late as them. I can't party like I'm 23 but thankfully it's a 6AM wakeup and no one will be able to stay up late anyway.

From the people that I met so far I believe there is a lot to be learned. When it comes down to it many of us are searching for the same unknown finish line and I think we will all help each other learn what needs to be done for us to all get there.

Dear Future Kim

Byron Bay, Australia
April 5

Dear Future Kim,
Your trip is now over. Six months just flew by.

Right now, I am on a bus heading towards Byron Bay. Most of the people on here are much younger than you, and that's okay because you are in a place that you will take so much more out of the trip. Embrace that.

Hopefully you no longer live with the pain of a broken heart that you have felt over the last two months. I know it hurts a lot right now, and maybe it forever will, some days seem like they are worse than the ones before, but it does get better. I hope you do get the love that you are praying for every night. Please know that it hurts a lot for him right now too, and he will reach out when he is ready, if he ever is. And if he doesn't, that's okay, because then it wasn't meant to be. Life is too short to have one person for everyone, and sometimes that's just how it is. Thank the universe that he was brought into your life to begin with. He helped bring you to a place you didn't know that you needed. You will have love in your life again. I promise you that.

I hope you look back on this trip with no regrets, because you shouldn't. If you took time out for yourself, focused entirely on what you want in life and come back as a calmer, slower, more relaxed person then you did everything right. Everything will work out in the end.

Future Kim, please know that you didn't have to change. You were perfect the way you were before you left. I'm glad you wanted to though. Please hang onto those feelings that make you a better person. Look back on this letter and remember how distant it seemed when you were writing it. Think about how different you can be within six months. Anything you want to change in your life from this moment forward will only take a very short period of time. This will always be the truth. Think about the simple ways that you are different than you were before you left. Live your life to the fullest to ensure every single day continues to be everything you've always dreamed of.

Please know that although some days you are homesick, lonely, and missing certain people, including your dog, including him, you are really only gone for a short amount of time. If it makes you feel better they are missing you too. But know more than anything else your memories from this trip will never be about homesickness, unless you focus too much on it. Don't let homesickness be your focus.

I am so proud of you for taking this journey. You inspire yourself, you inspire others and you are greater than the single days. Your life, somehow, will once again be everything that you've ever imagined and more. You are amazing. Everything works out in the end.

Love,
Kim

Let's Catch the Big Grey

Byron Bay, Australia
April 6

Today was our surf lesson. I had tried surfing before, years ago, in Maui. I was very excited for my chance to try again. I was determined that no matter what I wasn't going to give up. I was going to take advantage of my time here, and have no hesitations to try to get up on the board. If I went the entire lesson and couldn't get up, that would be okay, at least I put in a true and full effort.

We had to go to a second beach, as the first one we arrived at was not the right conditions. Since most people in the group had tried surfing before we were given a quick refresher on getting up on the board, then we were off to hit the water. No better opportunity to learn than to try. It took me a little while to get up on the board but eventually I was able to stand and ride a wave. I think my yoga experience helped me out a lot. It was like moving from chatarunga to warrior one. Once I had that down I was able to catch a few more waves. I took more nose dives, bails and wipeouts than I did getting on the board, but when I popped up, it was awesome!

While all the young kids slowly worked their way out of the water to suntan and rest, I pushed through my exhaustion and kept going. There was time to rest on the bus on the way to Byron Bay. Now was the time to surf. The only way to get good was to keep practicing. I wasn't going to go in until they called me in.

As I caught more waves I became more confident. Then one of the instructors asked me if I was "ready to catch the big grey"? I was! The big grey is the bigger wave; it looks grey just before it crests. Let's catch the grey wave! The instructor helped pull me further into the surf, turned my board around and told me to start paddling. My arms felt like they were going to fall off. "Up! Up!" I heard them calling from behind. I slowly lifted my body, steadied myself and nose planted. I was exhausted and so happy with my efforts.

After six hours of driving we finally made it to the hippie town of Byron Bay. There's lots of free love, free spirits and a go with the flow mentality. It's also an expensive place as many people from the surrounding cities try to capture the real estate market for a vacation spot.

A few of the ladies and I went out for dinner at a little Italian restaurant then headed out for drinks. The bar we went to had a drum and DJ set called Afro Moses. We danced the night away in interpretative dance as all the locals wanted to come and meet the group of ladies with all the different accents. I ended up chatting with a cute man for most of the night. He had me laughing with photos of yet another thing that can kill me in Australia, because everything is out to kill you in Australia, the horrific Drop Bear. It looks like a koala, but will wait until a person, and preferably a tourist is in the area. The Drop Bear will then leap down on its victim and attack. Tod told me that the Drop Bear is also the only natural predator of sharks. It was the first time in a while I was feeling attractive and sexy. Tod and I continued to laugh and chat, had a couple more drinks and literally shut the place down, at midnight. Tod then asked if I was interested in going back to his place.

Diving Deep

Byron Bay, Australia
April 7

Before leaving for the East coast tour I sent my unfinished love story a message. I remembered from his stories that he worked at a bar in Surfers Paradise back in his 20s.

> Me: It really is beautiful here. I could see why you would never want to leave. I head up the East Coast tomorrow. One of our stops is in Surfers Paradise. I will have a beer in your honour.

He read it, but had no response. I was angry and upset. He doesn't care about me at all. He's already done with us. He doesn't even want us to work out.

The morning was a struggle. I woke up at Tod's vacation rental. As I flirted with Tod all night I knew what I was doing. This was not casual flirting, this was focused. Maybe a new guy would shake the cobwebs out. If I slept with someone new I would realize I really wasn't missing my ex at all, what I am probably missing is some good sex, and if I got that I would feel cured and much better.

I laid in Tod's bed still in a half-drunk haze. "What time is it?" I asked him, "I have a diving lesson today". He was disappointed that I had to leave; he thought that we could enjoy the morning, have breakfast, and take our time before he flies back to Sydney.

I arrived back at my tour group's campground. My ex had responded to my message finally. "Enjoy!" was all it said. Are you kidding me? I waited days and all I get is "Enjoy!"? The only thing I've heard from him since our text message exchange in Canada. And coincidentally enough it is the morning after I have a one-night stand. Did he feel his heart breaking? Did he feel that I was trying to get over him? Or maybe it is a pure coincidence and I am reading more into it than is there. I do have a tendency to overthink.

I made it to my diving lesson and was scared when on the medical form I had to fill out if I was hung over which, without question, I very much was. Thankfully because it had been several hours since my last alcoholic drink it wasn't a big deal, I just needed to power through.

After a quick pool training session on diving basics and skills, we headed out. We got in the van and headed to a beach spot where there was nearby coral. The boat took us out, and I prepared myself for the anxiety of strapping on the heavy equipment and falling into the water, prepared to head 10m down. I was so nervous. I tried descending a couple of times and both times resurfaced because I couldn't handle the fear. After my second time resurfacing, I talked myself down, and became prepared to descend. Slowly I went deeper and deeper. It was amazing. There were so many fish. I was glad we were in a smaller group, because the instructor was able to hold my hand as we dove until I felt comfortable enough to be on my own. We stayed down for a bit, but the day was windy and the water was still choppy even deep below.

We took off the tanks and continued with snorkeling for the rest of the morning. I saw three sea turtles. The first one was a small one that surfaced within touching distance. There was also a massive one that I saw at the bottom of the ocean. I saw a couple of leopard sharks, which are not dangerous. They are bottom feeders. I also saw a school of squid, eels, various fish of all sizes and colours, and many sea urchins.

I was so glad I did it. I want to go diving again when we get to Cairns, and now I won't feel nearly as nervous to head down.

Brisbane Bound and
Back to the Billabong

Brisbane, Australia
April 9

Yesterday we arrived at Surfers Paradise, which could be described as an adult playground, or as many locals call it "a dirtier version of Vegas". I was going to head to the beach, but I was distracted by shopping. Lots and lots of shopping. I bought a super cute romper that I had to wear out. Thankfully it wasn't a late night at Sin City.

Today we were heading to Fraser Island after a bit of time in Brisbane. We only had a couple of hours to enjoy everything that Brisbane had to offer, and after being pretty shopped out from Surfers Paradise I thought it would be great to take in the relaxation of South Bank.

We left Brisbane for another four hour bus ride towards the ferry to take us to Fraser Island. As we sat on the bus I felt compelled to send my unfinished love story a message. I wanted to hear from him, but I wanted to be loose and flakey in my note.

> Me: I hope you're doing well. I'm having a good time on this trip. I'm really glad I'm doing this. I'm learning so much about myself. In my reflections I've also noticed there was a lot of things I didn't understand about you and things I didn't take notice on.
>
> I don't know if you are reading my blog, but I decided to change direction. I'm going to be heading to Japan next and working my way down. I'll probably be in Thailand and Indonesia area by end of May beginning of June. If you are going to be in the area for your own vacation, let me know. It would be really great to see you. Maybe if things go well we could

continue on for a bit together. But we don't have to decide anything until after we meet.

Don't feel compelled to decide or even reply to this. I know sometimes the right words are difficult to find. And that's okay. I know they will come eventually.

I hope you are finding happiness. I really wish the best for you always. You are in my thoughts constantly.

By the time we got to the ferry terminal it was already sunset. The days are getting cooler and darker faster as Australia moves to the winter season. By the time we caught the ferry it was already completely dark. We were so remote from everything that the starry sky was comparable to what I saw in the outback.

Seeing the Forest
from the Trees

Fraser Island, Australia
April 10

When I was in university I applied for a job as a business analyst for one summer. During the interview one of the questions asked was to rate my Microsoft Excel knowledge on a scale from 1 to 10. I told the interviewer it was an odd question because a year previous I would have rated it an 8 out of ten, but since learning more about the program I realized how much I actually didn't know about it and now rated my level as a 6. I loved the idea that the more I learn the more I realize I actually know less.

After arriving very late at Fraser Island, we woke up in the morning and had a full day planned. Our first stop was Mackenzie Lake. It was so pristine and beautiful. The weather cooperated so well: sun, warmth and little breeze. We spent a couple of hours swimming, trying stand-up paddle board, and I did a little bit of yoga practice on the white sand.

We were then lead on a bush walk through a rainforest area. I spent the walk separated from the group just to listen to the sounds of the forest. I kept my eye out for flying squirrels, but didn't spot any.

We then hit the sand highway. You are allowed to drive up to 80km/hr along the entire bank. We stopped a couple of times to collect clams and watch for dingoes. We stopped again when we came across a beach plane. I had to take the opportunity to see Fraser Island from the air. The island is so beautiful. There were untouched lakes, massive sand banks and some of the clearest, bluest ocean I've ever seen.

The plane landed next to a sunken ship site and we moved on to Eli Creek, where I crawled along the creek bed as the water pulled me along to a pool of water.

Before the day was done I started to realize that there is more to me than what I was anticipating in learning about. I came out here hoping to learn patience and I was open to anything else that came my way. But since being here I realize that there is more. I feel like I am just turning around and realizing that there is a complete forest just beyond the trees. My scope of what I thought I knew about myself was just the beginning. I don't yet know what is out there, but I feel like I am just scratching the surface.

There is so much love and appreciation in Australia. It's like no place I've ever been before. I'm so glad I started here. I feel like my heart is open and everyone I encounter is an opportunity to have a grateful experience. It is proper etiquette to ask everyone about their day. You also have to just ask for whatever you want because it always comes back to you and then some. Here I feel more open to possibility and people. I truly do love it here.

Hold Your Horses

Emu Park, Australia
April 12

I woke up with the sunrise around 6AM. It was nice to wake up before everyone else. The day was calm; the staff were having their own breakfast and offered me a coffee before everyone else. I made a seat at the breakfast table to finish the last of my blog entry from the day before.

I really like calm mornings. I was starting to get into the habit of them before I left. I would work out or meditate, or both if I found enough time, make myself a cup of coffee and read the news. Since being out here I sometimes find the same calmness in the mornings, but without the hectic nature of reading the news and prepping for my day. Mornings sometimes took on a pre-anxiety to the day without anything even starting yet. Since I've had no reason to read the news, I haven't. Facebook isn't nearly as important as it once was. I don't seem to have the fear of missing out that I did. I'm now afraid of not finishing my blog entry, and therefore not capturing what I've done. I love everyone around me, and I am generally interested in their stories, but I don't feel that need to know and compare as I did when I was home and fully connected.

The day before our tour group arrived at a farm, or more like a dude ranch. The day was full as we learned how to lasso, snap a whip and participated in a goat rodeo. Goats are incredibly strong for their small size and the put up quite the fight. I don't think there is anything funnier or more nightmare-inducing than hearing a small kid scream as a couple of petite ladies lasso one and work to have it wrestled to the gate so it may run off to the field to play with all its friends.

In the morning I was off to do some goat mustering. Everyone in the group was given a horse and then we had to go find the goats grazing in the field. We rode the horses behind the goats and using some solid "Oy! Oy! Oy!" or "bastard, bastard, bastard" yelling we pushed the goats into another pasture. Like typical Australian life, this was not a fast job. The horses move slowly because they can't go faster than the goats and goats just pretty much do whatever they want. It was a two hour job for us to get all the goats into the new pasture.

We then jumped on the back of a flatbed truck and were shipped off to another field where we could learn to trap shoot. I was given five targets, and missed all of them. The gun was heavy and it kicked back quite a bit after each trigger pull.

After a hearty lunch we were on the road again for another few hours. We need to make it to the coast by tomorrow night to hopefully hit Whitsunday. Unfortunately there is a cyclone that just hit the area, and we're all crossing our fingers that the worst of it passes by the time we get there.

Weathering Cyclone Ita or My Unfinished Love Story

Emu Park, Australia
April 13

Weathering Cyclone Ita

Last night as we arrived into Emu Park we were told the unfortunate news that Cyclone Ita made landfall just South of Cairns and we would not be taking the following day to drive to Airlie Beach to get to the Whitsundays. Thankfully the storm was downgraded from a category four to a category one, but the rains and winds are expected to stay for at least the week. Nobody knows at this point if we will get a chance to see the Whitsundays, but there's nothing else that can be done at this point but to sit and wait out the storm.

Our Plan B for the day was to check out a local crocodile farm, try their meat, and then finish the day off doing a little bit of shopping.

At the crocodile farm they had a few eggs ready to hatch and we gathered around to watch the baby break out of its egg. We then walked around the farm as the owner fed each croc a quarter of raw chicken. Back inside everyone had a chance to hold one of the older babies.

There was no avoiding being drenched. The rains just kept falling and falling all day. I don't know if I will ever be caught in an actual tropical storm, but if this is just the tail end I hope to never have to endure the full event.

There are only a couple of things in my life that I would say I have an unfinished love story with. One of them will be Australia. I have had such an amazing time here, and have seen some of the most beautiful countryside and met some absolutely amazing people. It will be incredibly unfortunate if the storm prevents our group from seeing the Whitsundays, but if it's not meant to be, that's okay. I will have a reason that I must return to Australia. But for now we go with the waves.

My Unfinished Love Story

The thing about unfinished love stories is there is no point in overthinking the days. I have always been an over-thinker. I will allow my thoughts to spin out of control and cause me to see the worst case scenario of situations as the likely outcome. I will then act on my worst thoughts despite the likeliness of it actually happening or not. That's when things can really get messy for me. Once I get to the point where I've spun my thoughts into the worst it can be incredibly difficult to talk myself off that ledge. I compensate by making large decisions that will dramatically change my life. Some of these decisions are for the best, like coming on this trip, but others lead to unfinished love stories.

My second unfinished love story is the one I think about daily. I have had every thought under the sun about it, and the best answer I come to is to let it be. A lot of things can change and develop while I am away. I've recently had so much anxiety about all the things that could be possible: maybe he meets someone else, maybe he gets into a relationship, maybe I never hear from him again, or maybe I will always have the regret of travelling over being in love, maybe, maybe, maybe. It gets so bad sometimes I want to cry and get sick. My stomach turns in so many directions that I don't even know where to start. And since being on this trip, a new answer starts to come. The first step is to talk myself off that ledge. How can I react to something that is not even determined to be a fact? I need to learn to react to only what I know, and then take it as each day.

I need to remember that an unfinished love story is just that - a love story. There will be an ending. Maybe it will end with us never ending together. He does meet someone new, and he is happier than he's ever been, and that would warm my heart because he deserves that. Or maybe I will learn and grow so much that when I get back I am in a much better spot for the love that he gives me. I am ready to accept the life we build together as opposed to trying to move it in a direction that is forced. I am better prepared for a lifetime with him. Or maybe it's a combination somewhere of the two. But it's all maybes. And I need to learn that all possibilities are likely, not just the worst case scenarios. And if it wasn't meant to be, then that's okay. There will be some type of ending to this love story; I just need to go with the waves.

Embracing Australia's Natural Beauty

Mount Rooper, Australia
April 14

The rain finally stopped this morning. As the group gathered for breakfast we all held our breath for good news. There was a collective cheer as our guide told us that in the morning we would be driving to Airlie Beach and hopefully will be catching the ferry, assuming the roads weren't flooded, the rains didn't pick up again, and there weren't any delays. There were no promises that we would actually make it to the Whitsundays, but there was hope, and we were going to be moving forward as much as we could.

The entire day we drove. It took over six hours to get to Airlie Beach from Emu Park. As we drove further up the coast the grey skies slowly turned to sunny, blue ones. The only evidence that there was a cyclone in the area two days before was the amount of flood waters on the side of many of the roads. We made it to the ferry launch just in time to catch the last ferry to Long Island.

The entire drive became more and more beautiful as we moved further up into the tropics. Although the sun was setting by the time we hit the Whitsundays, I know it was well worth the wait.

Many places in Australia are shoes optional. It's part of the way of kicking back and relaxing. The last couple of days I have been embracing this. I try to wear my shoes as little as possible, which includes the easy parts of walking along beaches, but sometimes down the road or through a small town.

I've always been a very up-kept girl. I love getting my nails done. I have hair appointments every 6-8 weeks. My wardrobe includes multiple dresses, jewelry and dozens upon dozens of shoes and 5" heels. I miss dressing up, flat-ironing my hair and putting on my makeup. But I knew when I was to come on my trip all of that would have to go. The only makeup I carry is mascara and eyeliner, and I only have put it on a couple of times when I've gone out on the town. My clothing options here are incredibly limited, and although I have bought a few items, specifically from Lorna Jane, Australia's answer to Lululemon, I don't have anywhere near the variety that I do back home. Almost all the pieces of clothing that I wear here are some type of athletic wear.

I was told last night that going shoeless is really embracing my inner bogen, an Australian slang for a blend of a hippie and a redneck. I think I'm okay with that. If being natural makes me feel a bit more free and relaxed, I will embrace that. After all I can always put shoes back on, cut my hair and get my nails done again, but it takes longer to embrace the natural.

Sailing the Whitsundays

Long Island, Australia
April 15

Wow.

This place is by far the most beautiful and romantic place that I have ever been. There are no words to describe the beauty, but I will try.

When we arrived last night I was already blown away by the beauty. I love arriving at resorts late, during sunset or the early evening. It is early enough to take it in a little bit; enjoy a few drinks and everything the resort has to offer. Then when I wake up in the morning I get to experience that same shock and awe but this time in a different light.

I started off with my traditional glass of champagne upon arrival, sat down at the beach bar and took it all in. I imagined being here with my unfinished love story. We would hold hands, drink our champagne and when we weren't staring at the stars and the moon and the Southern Cross we would be looking deep into each other's eyes and still see the exact same things.

I have been to many beautiful resorts: Mexico, Cuba, Dominican Republic, Hawaii and Jamaica. By far this one tops all of it. Looking out into the ocean there are nothing but more mountainous islands, white sand beaches, turquoise waters and so much wildlife.

I woke up before sunrise. Our room is ocean front and to look out made me want to get out and experience the day. I went for a run down the beach and followed it up with a bit of Sun Salutation Yoga. After breakfast our former racing yacht was ready to pick us up for the day. Because it was a small crew, they gave people the opportunity to help set up the sails and man the helm. I jumped at the chance to do both. I have always dreamed of sailing. I wanted to do it all. I loved every minute of it. Both raising the sails and steering were incredibly difficult and took a lot of upper arm strength.

We sailed directly to White Haven Beach. Considered one of the top ten beaches in the world, it features pure white sand, turquoise waters, coral reef, and rainforest bush walks. The sand is something incredibly special. It is so fine that it feels like flour or icing sugar. It has a 99% pure silica content which makes it so soft, and it squeaks as you walk on it. The beach looks like someone took white and blue paint and made swirls in the islands.

I took one of the short bushwalks to a lookout. I stood there in awe for a couple of minutes because I was stunned by the beauty. I could not imagine that something this astonishing exists in real life.

We followed up the time at the beach with a little bit of coral reef snorkeling. It was cut short because despite everyone wearing stinger suits, there were a few different types of jellyfish in the water freaking people out, including me.

The waters were still really murky from the cyclone the days before, and I was told that it might stay that way for at least a month until everything finally settles. My quitting early did not disappoint. As soon as I got back on the sailboat I saw dolphins swimming in the water just in front of the boat. I could die today, and this would be the best day of my life. Almost.

I fell asleep on the sailboat as we made it back. I was in complete bliss. I never want to leave. I will seriously contemplate moving to Australia once this trip is complete.

We made it back to the resort just in time to participate in the lorikeet feeding. They wild birds are trained to come around 4:45 every night for a nectar feeding. It was the perfect ending to a perfect day.

Not Going Home

Today was a long day on the bus. We had an eight hour drive up to Cairns for the last of our tour, and for me, the last couple of days in Australia. It's hard to imagine that I have been gone for almost three weeks already. I think the longest trip I have ever been on before this was 16 days when I went to Europe, and the longest time I have ever been travelling by myself was five days to Seattle in my early 20s.

I had a few small bouts of homesickness already on this trip. The first one was the day I was flying back to Sydney from Alice Springs. I woke up and felt the bruises on my heart. Everyone told me that I had to have no contact with him while I was out here, but I wanted so desperately to hear from him, to skype with him, or the ultimate act of love and he comes and visits me.

That same day I reached out to many of my friends and family just to hear about their days. Everyone wants to ask about all the fun and amazing things that I am doing and experiencing, but sometimes it is nice to hear the everyday actions of everyone else. It makes me feel like I am back at home and we are having the same conversations we do every day.

My second bout of homesickness was embarrassingly enough during the tour group on Fraser Island. We had such a great day, so it wasn't brought on by boredom or the feeling of missing purpose or everyday habits. But when I took notice of the Australian coins, I asked my tour guide what the names of the coins were and when he told me skippy it came on fast. I will admit that participating in the drinking game "flip cup" probably helped to heighten me to a more sensitive level. Yes, I was "that girl". But just hearing that the coin was called a skippy because locals nicknamed the kangaroo skippies made me relate the way Canadians call our coins toonies. Our $2 coins are toonies, because a loonie has a loon and a toonie is worth two loonies. We don't call it a bearie, which is the animal on it, because that would make too much sense. And it's spelled like loonie with a "t" as opposed to its value and spelling it "twonie".

But yesterday night as our group drank and sang karaoke on the beachfront my homesickness compelled me to send him a message before going to bed.

> Me: I like to believe that you read my blog. I usually put little hints (and sometimes very overt ones) that you are always on my mind. You always are. I hope you are doing well. I want that more than anything.

When I checked my email on the bus I was shocked to see a response from him. I responded back right away.

> Him: I'm doing fine. Miss you but that is something that I've managed. As usual, I'm extremely busy, so that helps. Going to San Diego with a friend for some good times.

> Me: Thank you for responding so quickly. Sometimes I don't know what to think. I'm working really hard on controlling my anxiety and my thoughts that spin so quickly.

> It's good to be busy. I am so proud of you
> The trip sounds fun. I've always heard great things about San Diego. Do you have any other trips on the horizon?
> I'm glad you've managed missing me. You've always been a really strong person. I'm still working on it. Like I said before you are constantly on my

mind, and that is no exaggeration. But if you can manage, I will try harder too.

You are so incredibly amazing.

It's hard to come to the realization that I am not going home. I am sure that I am going to have more bouts of homesickness. As long as I stay active the time will go by fast. I don't want it to fly by, but I do want to take full advantage of every waking hour. If this is my one-shot I don't want to look back and regret wasting my days.

I know I will continue to miss home, but maybe if I'm lucky some of home will come to me. Or maybe this is part of the journey to help find the home that I am looking for in myself. I am really lucky to be here, and I'm very grateful that I am taking out this time.

Diving the Great Barrier Reef

Cairns, Australia
April 17

How do you describe checking off a bucket list item? Diving the Great Barrier Reef. That sentence alone brings on a sense of awe and pause. It is one of those things that is completely incomprehensible. I always imagined it to be huge, beautiful and perhaps something built up in my head that would never deliver. It was huge, beautiful and beyond my expectations.

It was a two hour boat ride to the reef. There were going to be two stops, one before lunch and one after. We had the option to snorkel, dive or take the glass bottom boat. They provided options for everyone to experience it in one way or another. The boat out was fast and the water was choppy, so unfortunately out of a group of about 40 there were a few seasick people. I was not one of them. I've never been a motion sickness person.

I was amazed that with no diving experience, only a willingness to go, you could dive in the middle of the ocean with no training beforehand. The instructors even told me that they have taken people diving that didn't know how to swim, but wanted to go desperately. Granted we didn't go very deep, and if there was a problem we could always resurface very quickly. But the experience itself was absolutely amazing!

Those that chose to dive were given a crash course in diving, skills and signals. Our first reef was just outside a turtle habitat. The sandy island was known to be a frequent breeding ground for turtles, and therefore turtle spotting would be quite common. I was in the second group of divers, which made me glad. I was still quite nervous despite my Byron Bay diving and told the instructors as long as I was holding onto someone the entire time I would be fine.

When we jumped into the water the instructor noticed that my mask wasn't sitting on my face properly and insisted on switching it out before we went too deep. My anxiety started up. I didn't know how I would be able to complete the dive knowing that the mask they gave me initially wasn't tight enough. I focused on counting my breath and slowing down, and after the new mask was on, we descended.

Slowly we made it deeper and deeper. The coral slowly came closer to my body, and I was so afraid of making contact with it. Then I started to slow my body down and enjoy everything that was being pointed out to me. There were so many fish! There was beautiful coral everywhere. My instructor ensured I was holding onto either his arm or his hand the entire time, which kept me fairly relaxed. At one point he pointed out a purple sea anemone and when we came close it sensed that something is coming and it collapses into itself in the fastest way.

Out of the many fish I saw the only ones that I recognized were the clown fish in the coral. Just like in the movie, they hid there. They would come out, and go back in, go out, go back in, and maybe a fourth time they would go out and maybe go back in.

When we finally resurfaced they asked us if we wanted to do a second dive. If I wanted to get over my nervousness about diving, I had to do it more. We headed out to a very random open water area.

If I ever thought I was speechless in my life I had no idea. I ensured I was paired up again with my first instructor, Simon. He kept me so calm and focused on the first dive that I didn't want to mess up that flow.

We descended close to a coral wall. It reminded me of the scene from Finding Nemo where Nemo goes out past the drop off to touch the boat. This was it. As a novice diver I am limited to 12m, but that was deep enough, and I could see the coral wall continued deep into the blue abyss. The coral was all around and it brought all the fish. Schools of fish: super tiny fluorescent ones, translucent medium sized ones, ones longer than my legs that looked like a rainbow explosion. There were ones I could barely see because they looked identical to the rocks until they moved and took shape. Ones that looked like leopards, or had pieces that looked like single horns, or various stripes. There were so many, in every direction, in every colour and size.

We resurfaced after 30 minutes. This was by far the coolest thing I have ever done in my life.

The End of Oz

Port Douglas, Australia
April 18

Today was my last full day in Australia. In my three weeks here, I have accomplished almost everything that could be possible in Australia, minus hugging a koala, so today was the day. I rented a car, and with four other ladies we headed to the Wildlife Habitat Sanctuary about an hour North of Cairns in a town called Port Douglas.

The car I was given was a very rundown Hyundai Accent with over 205,000km. We joked that it was the rough car given to North Americans that don't have experience driving on the left. For the most part I did alright, when I was able to think about signaling, but there were a few times that I hit the wiper instead of the indicator.

The wildlife sanctuary had no cages for the animals, but rather large open spaces where the birds were allowed to fly wherever they wanted to, the kangaroos hopped in their defined areas, and the koalas had plenty of space in Eucalyptus growths. The ladies and I all squealed like school girls while we were having our photos taken hugging a koala. The money raised goes to help cure the koala's most deadly disease, chlamydia.

We then decided to explore more of Port Douglas. It is a stunningly beautiful resort town. It would be the type of place that I could come back to and easily spend a week shopping, golfing, boating, sunning and everything else Australian.

Back home I would occasionally write my unfinished love story a card with words of love and affection. While I was shopping in town I saw the perfect card: A woman washing hearts and hanging them outside of her travel trailer while looking out to her city. That was me. I need to be away but I can't wait to come home with a new clean heart. I wrote him a love letter and then sent him a message asking for his forwarding address. I can't wait to mail it to him. I still love him so much.

It was a calm day and a perfect way to end my time in Australia. I am very sad to leave, but last night I dreamed of Japan, and started to become excited again. There is so much left to see and do, and I've just completed one country.

Continental Reflections

As I write this I am on an eight hour plane ride to my next amazing destination, Tokyo. During the flight I listened to my Australian national anthem, "Riptide" by Vance Joy, sat back in my seat and reflected on my last few weeks and what I've already learned about myself.

Over the last three or four years I found myself becoming less extroverted and more introverted. Although many people still saw me as an extrovert I didn't feel the same. About four years ago I was in a dark place, in a job I hated, dating a man that I thought was the one, but later found out he was scouring online dating sites. My ambitions and dreams were crushed and I found that I just didn't want anyone to know that the life I had built up in my head wasn't going to come, at least not at this stage.

A couple of years later I found myself with a new job and new man but I still didn't feel like I had recovered fully from my original crushing blow. Without the full recovery I felt myself slipping again into an unnatural mix between extroversion-introversion that made me feel like I struggled to place myself in the right context at the right time. When I needed to be extroverted I couldn't. I knew I was off, but I didn't know how to fix it.

Australia brought that love of being around people out in me. I originally booked my tour group as a way of having someone else take care of the logistics of planning. I wanted to shut off my brain for a bit. I felt indifferent if I met some people that I could have conversations with on the group. The people I met were all wonderful, and it felt so good to have some of the same soul-searching conversations with so many people.

However my biggest take away was from the local culture. I forgot how something as simple as asking a person how their day is going, and being sincerely interested in the answer, can change the mood of both me and the person I am speaking with. Something so simple started to pull me out of my uncomfortable introverted funk. I wanted to engage with all people, not just those I already knew. I became lifted as I had these brief conversations. I felt like I was touching more people, and I allowed them to connect with me.

There is so much beauty and so much to see in Australia, I just found myself automatically walking slower. I wanted to stare at the trees, listen to the birds, feel the sunshine, and still get things accomplished in a day. I even reconsidered the number of cities and countries that I want to hit. I cut out a couple of the places that I was planning on seeing because I am starting to like the slower pace of life.

I've had moments, and sometimes full days, of weakness where I was so focused on what may or may not be waiting for me when I get home, if my unfinished love story will be there for me, or if he won't. Stuck on thoughts of the future, him, or heartbreak took my focus away from me and why I am here. I am sometimes so focused on what the future has in store that I lose the beauty of the journey. I felt like the line in Riptide: "I just want to know if you're going to stay. I just gotta know. I can't have it any other way". I felt like not knowing what the future had in store prevented me from enjoying the journey that I am on now.

In my head and in my heart I know I have done everything to let my unfinished love story know that I love him, I miss him, I want to be with him, and I am so sorry my actions caused us both so much tremendous pain. I need to be confident that he does know all of that. There is nothing more that can be said or done. My journey with myself is not finished. I still feel like I am not the completed version of myself, and I need to focus on that right now. Like being on a plane when they run through the safety procedure: I need to ensure I am fine before being there for others. I need to focus on everything that is happening each day over the next few months before looking too far into the future. Everything will work out. It always does.

The Exhilaration
of the Subway

Tokyo, Japan
April 20

I arrived in Japan late evening. I was exhausted after the flight and just wanted to get to my hotel. My options were to take a metro line with two transfers or a shuttle that will drop me off at a nearby hotel with a short walk for three times the price. I decided on the shuttle because I didn't want to think about memorizing Japanese characters at 9PM.

Although Narita airport is only 60km outside of Tokyo, it took us 90 minutes to get to our stop. There was so much to see along the way: a replica of the Eiffel Tower, plenty of bridges lit up, Ferris wheels, and lots of fluorescent signs.

I had Google mapped where my hotel was in relation to the Hilton that I was dropped off at. Google said it would only be a six minute walk. That's assuming I was walking in the right direction. I knew I had to walk past a park and my hotel would be on the other side. After 40 minutes of walking, zigzagging directions, staring at street maps, I decided to give up. I would find a taxi and pay to have him take me the two or three blocks to my hotel. With a "konnichiwa" I got the attention of a cab driver sitting in his car and showed him my map and my address. He pointed in the direction I needed to go and I think he said it was only a block away. I walked in that direction for probably longer than a block. I finally spotted a McDonalds and was ready to quit and find Wi-Fi, when I saw my hotel right beside it. For future reference I will always book my hotel next to a McDonalds, because everyone knows where those are.

My room was super impressive. Everything is extremely automated in Japan, and they provide you everything you will need to have a good stay. Realistically I didn't even need to bring luggage. They gave me a toothbrush and paste, pajamas, and laundry detergent with a washer/dryer combo in the room.

I had morning tour group to see Mt. Fuji, Lake Ashi, with a boat and gondola ride just outside of Tokyo. I was ready to try the efficient Tokyo subway. After a bit of stumbling over the ticketing machine, I figured out the line that I needed to catch. The trains stop at the exact minute they say they will in the exact gate opening spots. With each train stop musical tones play, which remind me of a child's video game when the player chooses that "Apple" starts with "A".

The tour started at 9AM. Our tour guide was very knowledgeable and helped us out with some of the Japanese culture and signs on the road. We were supposed to arrive at Mt. Fuji by 10:30, but when we were faced with some construction our guide apologized profusely that we will be 30 minutes late.

As we left Tokyo the landscape started to become more mountainous and lush with trees. We passed gorgeous little towns that surrounded lakes, and there were still a few cherry blossom trees that that hadn't lost all their blossoms yet. It is hard to believe an hour outside of the world's largest city, at over 13 million people, it could suddenly get so sparse.

By the time we arrived at Mt. Fuji the weather was really foggy, grey and cold. The guide told us that Mt. Fuji is a woman; she is shy and does not like to be exposed too often. There is an average of only two days per week that people get any viewing of her, he said. Unfortunately, today she was being particularly stubborn. The heavy fog prevented us from getting higher up Mt. Fuji, and even sadly enough, seeing it. But now I have a reason to come back.

We visited a couple of little towns, but my favourite by far was a town called Hakone. We then took the bullet train to return to Tokyo. What took us an hour to leave the city took us 20-minutes to return. Our tour guide then navigated us through a very busy Sunday afternoon metro station.

By the end of the night my brain was numb, I was tired, and my unfinished love story had sent me a note saying, "There is no forwarding address. bye. Bye".

At that moment I just wanted to be home so bad. I picked up McDonalds, headed back to my room and rented Les Miserables on the TV to get my English fix. The best thing about sleep is it fixes so much. The morning is a brand new day.

Sushi and Beer for Breakfast

Tokyo, Japan
April 21

I woke up feeling a lot better than I did last night. When I went to bed I was feeling like my wounded heart had salt thrown into it. I'm getting better at calming myself down and not carrying the weight of the negative thoughts. I'm not ready to go back. I know whatever will happen, will happen, but I need to be on this journey right now. When I read my unfinished love story's email I wanted to immediately react, send something nasty back, but I talked myself off that ledge this time. I took a deep breath and allowed the acceptance that I need to be here right now to become more important. I'm happy I did that. I still live with hope, but if I'm not ready to go back, he may not be ready to forgive. Until I'm ready to return I will try to put focus on the individual days as I am being introduced to new areas of myself.

The fish market opens around 4AM with a tuna auction and I caught the subway around 5:30AM to see all the excitement. The market itself was fairly easy to find. The fish portion though took a bit more persistence. I asked a few people that looked like they were tourists as well, and no one knew where the fish were, so I decided to go deeper into the mad rush of cars, trolleys and commuter buggies. My perseverance paid off. When I went in I saw so much freshly caught fish. They were being sliced and diced and presented for restaurateurs to purchase for their fresh catch of the day specials. The aisles were cramped and usually there was just enough room for one motorized buggy, which meant that I would be run over if I stood in the way. I saw what I needed to, and decided as a celebration of all the fishy excitement it was time to eat.

The queues for each sushi restaurant were long, despite it being 7AM. A woman shared her umbrella with me while we stood in the sprinkling rain. After 30 minutes I was guided to an outside menu board where I chose a salmon, tuna and sea urchin meal then continued to wait outside until a seat at the sushi bar became available.

I sat down and one of the restaurant staff let me know that someone at the other end of the bar wanted to buy my meal. I was flattered and accepted out of fear of coming across rude. I asked if I need to do something to return, and the server said to buy the gentleman a beer. I ordered the beer and my offer was returned to me. I shared it with a Japanese couple sitting next to me that spoke a bit of English and helped me with my proper Japanese dining etiquette. The beer is always poured for others first and when it was my turn I had to hand it to another person to pour for me.

On the way to Ueno Park, I jumped off the subway early. Rojoku was the neighbourhood where all the sumo stables were, and I knew there would be some training with the upcoming matches in May. If I was lucky enough to find one maybe I could peer into a window. As I wandered the streets I was excited to see a sumo wrestler outside getting some air. I pointed to my camera, and he nodded yes, but his friend turned and walked away at that moment and I ended up getting a nice photo of a sumo ass.

When I arrived at the park I didn't know what to expect. I was hoping to see a few cherry blossom trees still in bloom, but was not expecting to see the number of shrines and temples around the massive park. I loved all of them. I took part in the meditation and the prayer ceremonies that each one recommended. By the end of the afternoon I had never felt more at peace with my life, and my decisions.

I realized at that moment that I was grateful to be here. I am happy to be doing this alone. I am pushing myself out of my comfort zone. I am talking with people that I wouldn't be engaging with if I was here with someone else. I have the opportunity to just do, as opposed to plan it all out. And most of all, as much as I like all-inclusive vacations from time to time, I'd much rather be doing this. I want to be learning new languages one word or phrase at a time, not staying in English speaking tourist zones where trying the language brings back English responses. I want to have the fear of being lost on a subway and having faith that I will actually make it to wherever I am going, not catching a taxi because it is easy. I want to dine at local restaurants and be immersed in the culture. I want to order the house wine, not because I can't afford more, but because I want to experience a different way of life when I am away. I want to be a traveller, not a tourist.

In the evening I headed out to the young and generally odd Shinjuku neighbourhood. There were karaoke bars and peep shows on every corner. There was a wide variety of stores and restaurants, including the notorious Robot Restaurant; a cabaret show that has no purpose or function, just a bunch of half-naked girls dancing with robots. The pinnacle was a shark eating a robot while being ridden by a mermaid.

After wandering Shinjuku for a while I decided to head to the Harajuku neighbourhood. I started to walk and loved the idea of being lost, but not really, in the world's largest city. I was here, by myself, but never alone. When I got to Harajuku I couldn't have been more disappointed. It's no wonder Gwen Stefani sang about it. It was in her comfort zone. It is all high end designer stores, all in English, and the Harajuku girls are all trying to be American, with bleached hair and labels I could buy in any Canadian or American store.

I was tired by this point and made it back to my hotel, but not before stopping in another local restaurant for dinner. There is something to be said for a kind smile and nod that can transcend language. Even though I could speak no more than a handful of words and phrases, all learned over the course of a couple of days, by necessity and determination, and the people in the restaurant knew little English, I was still able to enjoy a beer and an excellent tempura meal cooked right in front of me. I love this country.

Finding Tranquility
Among 13 Million People

Tokyo, Japan
April 22

I woke up this morning in an amazing mood. I had a dream that was so wonderful there was no way I was going to allow it to leave me. It involved my unfinished love story. He and I were together and we were overhearing his friend and my mom on a phone call conversation. They were arguing between them on whether my unfinished love story and I should be together. We were both interested in listening to find out what others thought. When the call cut out, I just turned to him and asked him what he thought.

"But what about your work?" he asked me.

I smiled and said, "Lucky I don't have a job right now. I can find one anywhere".

"And what would we do about our living arrangements?" he followed up.

I quickly responded, "We will live anywhere in the world you want".

Then he smiled at me. I know this smile so well. He smiles first with his eyes and then with his mouth, but there is an undeniable twinkle in eyes when he looks at me. It warms my entire body and I smile back. Then I woke up.

I could have allowed that dream to make my day sad, knowing that it will be a long time, if ever, before I see that smile again, but instead I decided to hold onto the moment I woke up to. That warm, full-body, loved feeling.

Maybe it was a sense of peace that my mind and body decided to give me. I've been down, always thinking about him. Or maybe with all the meditation and praying I did yesterday at the many temples that I stopped at, my mind decided to reward that peace with a simply wonderful dream.

Whatever the case, after that dream I wanted it to be a good day, and it was.

I had to check out of my hotel room today. I originally only booked it for a couple of days, and when I went to check in they were fully booked tonight. I ended up booking a Ryokan, a traditional Japanese room in the district of Asakusa, very close to the Sensoji Temple. A traditional Japanese room has no bed, but rather a wicker mat on the floor. They provide a kimono and slippers to wear, traditional tea in the room, and the traditional bath, all which I will take part in before heading to bed.

Before checking into my new hotel I stopped at another park that surrounded a couple of temples and ponds. The park was huge and it was so tranquil walking the pathways, sometimes noticing that there was no one around me.

I stopped at the main temple to place a prayer and participate in a prayer writing tradition. The written prayer was very specific in how a prayer would be received. First there needed to be gratitude for what you already have or had, secondly the prayer you are asking for, thirdly you had to place a promise for what you will do until it comes to you.

I thanked my unfinished love story for entering my life to begin with. He taught me what a love that encompasses my entire self felt like. It was because of him that I am currently on this path, and for that I am grateful. I am grateful for having the means, support and opportunity to be here. I am thankful for the people that enter my life during this journey, even if they are only there to take a photo, bring me conversation during dinner or a tour, or even better become a friend when I am finally back. I asked for a continuous open mind and the faith that whatever is given to me while I am on this path is all part of the soul-searching journey that I am here for. I asked for safety while I travel and for love to come to me when the time is right. I promised that I will work on keeping my mind open and be ready to accept the many possibilities. I promised upon my return that I will use my learnings to help others and make the world that I touch a better place.

I left the park to arrive at the Asakusa district. There were little shops, and very traditional Japanese restaurants and coffee shops. I bet that you could live in Tokyo your entire life and not experience all the different districts and neighbourhoods that the city has to offer.

After visiting the Sensoji Temple, I decided to make my way to Shibuya Crossing, Tokyo's version of Time Square. The ride was about 30 minutes, and I found myself falling asleep on the train, but I guess that puts me closer to really experiencing Tokyo life.

I walked up and down the streets of Shibuya and found a small store where I bought myself a bracelet that has stones linked with self-awareness. When I picked it up I thought it was beautiful and the meaning behind the few stones made it much more relevant to my journey.

I absolutely love Tokyo. I did not give myself enough time here, but then again I'm already exhausted and am really looking forward to the relaxing atmosphere that Kyoto will bring tomorrow. After all of the hustle I could definitely use some additional time to reflect on the many things I have taken in over the last few days.

Faith

There are many things about Tokyo that have left me astounded, but the biggest one would have to be what I've learned about faith. There are so many ways a person can place their trust in faith, and Tokyo has really opened my eyes to many of them.

Travelling in a country where English is rarely spoken, it's not completely out of daily life but, it can be challenging to get through the day. I see many other travellers that have that look of frustration on their face immediately in the morning because they feel that can't order a coffee. Free Wi-Fi is surprisingly difficult to come-by in Japan, but with a little preparation there are many free apps that can be downloaded that have vocabulary for the basics, and they will even speak for you if you feel uncomfortable trying the words of out for yourself. With at least two free apps, I've been able to go from no Japanese to a vocabulary of about 30 words and several more at the touch of a button. But even if I was to pronounce it wrong, if I say as much as I can confidently, I can have faith that I am close enough to be somewhat understood. I tried. Eventually the words start to roll off the tongue, and that's really the beauty of the Japanese language. The words start to sound like a song of soft tones said in smooth, quick succession.

Then there's the faith of getting the answer and then holding on. The subway and metro lines are so vast there is no way I could memorize the many stops that I need to get from point A to point B. I've relied heavily on Google Maps for many of my days. It will tell me to go to a station, buy a ticket on one line, ride it for 12 stops, go to another platform for another line and ride that for another two stops.

I'm a super analytical person. I need all the information before I can make a decision or act. However, in times of stress I can act on limited information as long as I know my next move. I do believe the saying that I don't need to see the entire staircase, only the first step. For me one of the scariest things to do is ride a foreign subway system for the very first time.

I've learned a lot about faith in spirituality and religion. There are so many temples and shrines throughout Tokyo. It's amazing to see a commuter on a bicycle stop, do a quick prayer and carry on their way. So many Western religions require the devotee to practice regimented schedules. To know that a person can still be religious or just spiritual in a brief moment of their day is so inspiring to me.

Since I have nothing but time on this journey, I've made a point of stopping to do a brief prayer at each temple that I come across. I go through the local custom and then sit to myself and clear my mind. Today I practiced gratitude for being here. I thanked the world for putting me here in this moment. I said to myself that every day is a gift, and I truly believe it. I prayed again for life to bring me exactly what I need.

On my way to Skytree I was stopped by a woman that asked if I wanted to meet Buddha. There was a practice going on upstairs. I've always been interested in Buddhism, but have never taken the time to learn or practice it. I agreed to join her and we went upstairs. We did a joint chant before I had to leave.

I feel like every day I'm going a little further down the rabbit hole to finding out more of who I am. One of the girls on my Australian tour, Claire, told me to buy myself a ring. I did yesterday. It was a bit of a splurge; a rose gold 10K diamond band. I didn't think about it at the time that I tried it on, but only later realized I bought it to fit my left hand ring finger, my wedding finger. My right hand ring finger is a little bit chubbier, and it is too tight of a fit. I'm really happy with my choice though. There is only one other person in the world that I would want to be doing during this journey with and still then he comes second to me experiencing all of this solo. I'm slowly learning about everything I really am, and I really love this girl.

Releasing Expectations

Kyoto, Japan
April 24

I arrived in Kyoto close to dinner time. I checked into my unique airline cabin hotel. They have a bed and a TV, separating the units by curtains. I'm working my way down to the capsule that I will be spending my last night in.

I found an area of small bars, bistros and restaurants walking distance from my hotel. I decided to pick one at random. Between my minimal Japanese and the bartender and waitress's very limited English we were able to have a fairly good conversation. Mostly me showing them pictures of different places I was considering visiting in Kyoto and asking their opinion with either a thumb up or down.

I still hadn't had a Japanese karaoke experience so after dinner I found a karaoke bar around the corner. Unfortunately something was lost in translation because I was given a karaoke room all to myself. I laughed, decided to make the most of it, and sang all four of the English songs available until my hour was up.

In the morning, based on the feedback from last night's bartender and waitress, I made my way to a district called Arashiyama. I've seen so many pictures of the bamboo forest and always imagined it was a thin path weaving through dense bamboo, almost mystical in feel. As I walked the car path, I realized this was the bamboo forest that is in the pictures. I was disappointed at first that my expectations of the place didn't quite match what I built up in my head, and then I stopped and looked all around me. It was a beautiful place. I decided to accept and not hold onto my original expectations. That's when the mystic that I originally hoped for started to appear.

After visiting the forest, and the adjacent temple and garden, I wandered a bit more and found a monkey park. The

60

park promised some of the best views of Kyoto, and I would be able to see monkeys! The climb was tough, but once I made it to the top, I was rushed into an area where tourists are in the cage and the monkeys are free. I fed a few monkeys from the inside of the cage, laughing as they would grab the banana pieces out of my hand.

I made my way to Fushimi, known for its orange beams and crossways. The paths led all the way up a mountain. The pillars changed in sized and depth, but they were always the same. They were pure orange on one side, prayer writing on the other.

After doing the monkey walk I didn't know if I was up for another hill climb but I just walked. I ended up turning a corner by mistake and found myself in another area of multiple prayer temples. There would be sections within the path where I found up to 80 different prayer areas. I imagined each monk created their own small temple.

The symbol throughout Fushimi is a fox, which is said to bring news to people and their prayers. I bought a small, palm-sized, porcelain fox with a message inside. The message read: "Given time, the cherry blossoms on the hillside, which seem to have been withered begin to bloom and smell sweet. In the beginning my fortune is not good like a cold winter, but later it is getting better and better like spring comes. Be moderate. Wait for my time and surely I will be happy. He is sure to come, even if late". Please let that be true.

My wrong turn lead me down the hill instead of going further up, but this turned out to be a good thing. I made it to the Kyoto Jishu Shrine, said to hold the god of love and matchmaking. You are supposed to walk with your eyes closed from one love rock to another, and if done successfully your love will be realized. As I was doing it I had a Korean gentleman offer his assistance to help me, as long as I helped him. We're all looking for love. We both completed the walk successfully, and hopefully our wishes will come to us in the future.

I followed up the walk with another prayer ceremony where I used a large, outstretched cup to catch water from a waterfall. The water from the cup is then poured on each of my hands and placed in my mouth. I gently allow the water to flow out which cleanses my hands for prayer and my words for truth. I placed my prayer and said my goodbyes to the man I had just met.

I am glad to have just released the day to what was to come.

Past the Chatter

Kyoto, Japan
April 25

I had another dream about my unfinished love story. We were having a conversation that felt so incredibly real. I could tell that we weren't yet married, there was either intention or commitment but nothing fulfilled. We were discussing the possibility of starting a family, by allowing whatever will come.

I haven't heard from him in almost a week, and based on the fortunes and messages I feel like I am receiving, it won't be for a while, but it's best for him to reach out first. I doubt I will hear from him for at least a month, and I'm okay with that. I have a lot of ground to cover in that time. While I'm travelling my days seem infinite, but back home they feel mundane and a month will pass by faster there than here. I need to remember that.

My dream reminded me of a Japanese belief, stolen from the Chinese, about soulmates. It is believed that two people are tied together by an invisible red thread by the fingers. It is said that this thread can stretch and tangle, but it will never break. Two people will always be pulled together again. Despite everything around them they will always find each other.

I woke up super early this morning, packed my bag, walked over to the capsule hotel, dropped off my bag, and went out for all the remaining things I needed to see in Kyoto. It wasn't until I went to check into the capsule hotel that they couldn't find my reservation for tonight. I started panicking. I needed a place to sleep tonight. I fly out tomorrow. I double checked my itinerary. An entire day disappeared from my mind. I was a day ahead of myself.

Once I realized what I had done it worked out to be such a relief. I feel like since I've arrived in Japan my days have been filled and I've had little time to relax. The buildup of busy day after busy day would normally drive me, but after being away for a month I find it to be too much. I need to relax. I'm excited to have tomorrow with nothing planned. Before coming on this trip having no agenda would drive me crazy, as if I'm not taking full advantage of the day. However, now I no longer want to fill my day with "stuff". I want to take out the time to spend an afternoon in a park or just sit in a café to people watch.

This morning I took the bus to get to Ryoan-ji, a Buddhist Zen rock garden. I had to really stretch my limited Japanese to find the right stop and bus, since there are no English translations, like there are on the subway. I got on a bus that a local assured me was the correct one and at the next stop a tour guide sat next to me. He was helping a group of eight people navigate their way through Kyoto and I was able to get some great advice from him.

Ryoan-ji came hugely recommended with caveats. A beautifully stunning and peaceful rock garden filled with crowds preventing the full Zen-effect. The garden is considered the purest form of Zen garden, and all others try to mimic the purity and perfection that Ryoan-ji has built. I sat there for a while just staring. Staring at one set of rocks, then moving over and staring at the next set, and sometimes turning my head to see the previous set in a new perspective.

There was so much noise but as I sat there I thought to myself, this is life. My stillness and clarity needs to rise above that. I need to focus past all the voices heard and listen for my own message.

I finished the day visiting a couple more temples, and then feeling like I was being hit with death by shrines and temples, I decided to walk. I walked until the only thing I could think of was I need a haircut.

I wanted my fringe back. I missed it. I loved the way I looked. I loved the sassiness and youthfulness that it made me feel. I walked into the first salon I saw and more or less asked for a cut.

Looking at the Pieces
on the Path

Kyoto, Japan
April 26

I wasn't expecting to be in Kyoto for another day; for whatever reason my days slipped from my mind. I wanted to take some time out for reflection and I thought the perfect place would be the suitably named Philosopher's Walk.

I thought about a lot of things while I made my way down the path. This wasn't my first planned trip to Japan. When I was in university I dated a guy that lived here for a year. We dated about a year and a half. I was close to marrying him. He asked my mom for her permission. We looked at rings. We were planning a couple of weeks in Japan, and with less than a month before our trip he broke up with me. I never saw it coming. After I moved out of his place, I never heard from him again. Still haven't.

I thought about the number of times I've been in love. Four times. Four guys I've lived with. My longest relationship was three and a half years.

Between most of those relationships I would allow a few months to pass and get right back on the horse. Join an online dating website and just start going on dates. I always liked online dating, for a short period of time. It was a great ego boost. I enjoyed first dates. I would learn a lot about people. I always looked at dating as a way of finding out more about myself through other people's eyes. It was through all my loves that I was able to learn about myself, what I like, what I didn't, what I'm looking for in a partner.

My first love taught me about the importance of taking care of my own future and dreams. No partner, no matter how much in love I think I am, will provide the same foundation that I can create for me.

My second love, my previously cancelled Japanese vacation, taught me a lot about love for culture and language. He introduced me to love at first sight. I remember meeting him for the very first time and feeling dizzy. I could hardly stand when I would try to talk to him. But as time went on our differences increased and we were both constantly trying to change each other.

Love number three allowed me to plan everything, to the point that it drove me insane. I realized that although I was happy to do the planning, I wanted someone else to take charge from time to time. I wanted more balance in my life. It also took me a year to break up with my third love. I wasn't in a strong enough place at the time when I knew it needed to be done. Like the straw that breaks the camel's back, it was a simple request to make dinner after I had been travelling back-to-back on work trips the entire week that made me say it was enough. Despite the fact that he was my longest relationship, he was also the easiest one to move on from.

As I continued to walk down the path I realized why I am on this journey. After the first year of my career I thought I had it all figured out, and in a way I did. I was on this ridiculous high of having finally finished school, excelling at my job, and making enough money to finally start affording the life that I thought I deserved. My life was complete. All the pieces of the puzzle were exactly where they needed to be, and every morning I would wake up happier with life. But somewhere along the road, as time moved on, and life slowly became slightly more complicated, more pieces to the puzzle were being added. I convinced myself that my puzzle was still complete; I just needed to fit those extra pieces around the edges. I managed that way for years. Then everything snapped.

When I made the decision to leave I thought it was because I was a broken person that needed to be fixed. Today I realize that isn't the case. I am a puzzle that needs to have all the pieces pooled together and shaken. There is a different picture than the one that I had started to create. It will probably look similar to the original, but I will know that it is not the exact same. The pieces are all there, they just need to be re-arranged.

This brings me to my fourth love, my unfinished love story. The path did exactly what it promised to do. I walked and the answers started to flow to me. I looked down into the canal and realized that even though it was nice to look at the water ahead, the water directly in front of me showed me the beauty of the fallen flowers from the trees as they floated in the stream. I am usually so future-focused that if I took the time to look at the things closer to me I would realize the details in the beauty, and actually find myself more engaged and enjoying the path instead of trying to reach the end.

I stared at the cherry blossom trees. Even though many of them lost their blossoms, I knew they were still beautiful, and when the spring comes again so will a fresh set of flowers. In the meantime the blossoms that once graced the trees now added colour to the path, so that there is still a memory of what was and what will be again.

That's when the ultimate answer came to me. Love is patient. Before I came on this trip I asked to be taught more patience. I still believe in my unfinished love story. I believe when he is ready he will come back to me. In the meantime I need to be patient. I need to believe and then wait. If I can't wait then I don't deserve his love, and if it is not him, then my potential fifth love.

I have always been impatient in the ways of the heart. I have always actively been searching for "the one". Right now I have to wait until my puzzle pieces have been rearranged. Then, for once, I will take the back seat and wait for love to come to me.

Newer is Always Better

I couldn't figure out if Shanghai's growth was outpacing the people or if the people were outpacing the city. I took an hour-long cab ride to my hotel and was stunned by the number of cranes and construction sites. Housing developments created in cookie-cutter fashion. Complexes of 10 to 20 towers all looking identical, built at the same time.

Between the construction and the factories Shanghai is in a constant state of haze, preventing what could be a beautiful sunny day to come through. It blankets the sky and hides many of the buildings from the amazing skyline that so many people flock to enjoy.

I was excited to be meeting up with a friend from 10 years ago and his wife, whom I have never met. They now live in Italy, and she is finishing her PhD research in China. Shaune told me how proud he is of me for taking this journey. I told him that I am still in love with my ex. He then looked at me and said I may always be, but love should also be easy. Both sides should be willing to compromise to make it work. He said to look at him and Natalia, he was willing to live in Italy for her.

I laughed about that. I doubt there are many people who would turn down an opportunity to live in Italy.

Shaune then told me to take this time to explore everything the world has to offer. There are new people to meet all the time.

When we were ready to eat Shaune asked a group of people for directions on a good restaurant he had heard about it. The group said they were heading in that direction already then asked us to join them. We were suddenly a group of seven people that had just met and having laughs, drinks and dinner together. It was the best Hunan Kung Pao I have ever had.

The Road to Beijing

Beijing, China
April 29

After an incredibly long day in Shanghai, I couldn't wait to get out of the city. Shanghai has left me exhausted. For the first time I reached a city that I wanted to just get out of. I'm not disappointed that I went. I can't fall in love with every place that I visit. I don't want to.

Maybe part of my dislike for Shanghai came from my emotions. I have been gone for a month now, and in an odd way that makes me a bit sad. I know nothing much has changed in that time, but I still miss the everyday.

It was Shanghai's people and traffic that I found most exhausting. There are two types of people. The first group is rude, aggressive and pushy. They have no problems cutting in front of me in the queue. They pushed their items, advertisements and begging cups. They ran me over with their bike, motorcycle or car. They are in a massive rush with no destination.

The second group is super friendly, they want to chat, offer a seat, and their overall demeanor surpasses language barriers. Thankfully these people always showed up when I needed it the most. When I felt like I was ready to give up on the day, someone would appear and bring a smile to my face with their kindness and generosity.

I was determined to leave Shanghai and get on a train to Beijing today. Month-ago Kim would have never in her mind thought about buying a ticket day of, and subsequently booking a hotel the night that she arrived. She was more prepared, and the anxiety of not knowing would have thrown her for a loop. However, in a month, I have forced myself to ride with the punches easily and become okay to go with the flow.

The train station was intense: lines in every direction, and half the time I didn't even know what the people were lining up for. They had plenty of tickets left, but only first class. Fine, just get me out of Shanghai.

I sat on the train and watched the beautiful Chinese countryside. At one point the smog lifted and I saw blue in the sky again, but unfortunately it was for too brief a period of time. The grey coverage came back, and Beijing is in the same haze.

I thought about how lucky I am to be here but how I am really glad to be here solo. I would love the company, and in my head I still have the sweet face of my unfinished love story to remind me of home. His face comes to me daily, but even more so when I am frustrated, especially days like yesterday.

I imagined calling him and saying that I'm done, I'm ready to come home, and he tells me he would love to have me back, but I'm not ready, it's not time yet.

The people I met, the places I stay at, riding subways and buses, are all things I would never do if I was with someone else. I would be in the same locations, but on a removed level. This is all part of the journey, and in many ways so much more important than the sightseeing. The sites are a destination, but how I get there, how I navigate, ask for directions, chat with others and remove myself from my previously pretentious lifestyle is the root of all of my growth.

I always felt grateful for the life I had, but I did become accustomed to it. It became too ordinary for me, and I felt like I was in a competition with myself every year to gain more stuff, more clothes, fancier dinners and bottles of wine. I knew I was lucky compared to my peers, but I am really starting to fully appreciate everything I had compared to the rest of the world. I feel now like I truly understand.

I walked around looking for a restaurant to eat at for dinner. I saw a pub that was offering Long Island ice teas and pizza. Oh, god, yes! I am allowed to revert to my comfort foods every now and then.

I thought of the Friends episode where they ask "what do they call Chinese food in China?" I think they just call it food. Here they have Western food restaurants specializing in the types of dishes I would get back home. And just like walking into a Chinese restaurant and seeing Chinese people there and thinking "this must be a good restaurant, Chinese are eating here", so goes the same for Western restaurants here. They sat me at a fairly big table against the window. I was their free advertising.

Anything Broken
Can Be Fixed

Beijing, China
May 1

Today was a terrible day. It was terrible from the moment I woke up. Despite my best attempts to smile and force myself to feel that I was doing okay, it just never got any better. When travelling alone, the hardest thing is that there is no one to give a pep-talk but me. I can't call my friends or my mom or a significant other just to vent out the day. Thankfully writing has given me that venue. With writing I feel like I absorb my thoughts and feelings before putting them out there. I have been known to talk faster than my thoughts, and if I'm in a really heated mood I will immediately wish I could take it all back.

My anxiety woke me up this morning. Yesterday I was stuck in a thought about my unfinished love story, and then found myself dreaming about him last night. We were talking on the phone about how we will never be able to see each other again. The overwhelming emotion shook me up far earlier than I should have wakened. I couldn't get back to sleep as my anxiety moved from thoughts of him, to visions that I would miss my flight out of Beijing, to just general anxiety that China is not my place.

I had an enjoyable time on my Great Wall tour the day before and spent the time chatting with another Canadian.

I was warned that Beijing can be hard to handle but there are so many amazing things to see in the city, I headed for the Imperial Palace and Forbidden City. I rented an earpiece but found the information to be bland, in the few times the earpiece worked. As I walked around the palace grounds there were many chambers and exhibits that were blocked off for no reason. The military men kept people moving along blocked corridors and after walking around for two hours I enjoyed about 50% of grounds.

On my walk to the Temple of Heaven I had to pass through Tiananmen Square. I wasn't surprised when suddenly the sidewalk was blocked to one-way foot traffic. The people were then guided towards the entrance of the Museum of the People's Hero, which was decorated with massive posters of Mao.

I pushed my way through the people and through a series of crisscrosses, underground walkways, and security checks, I eventually made my way to the other side of Tiananmen Square. I was spent after carrying my bag all day and having not eaten in the day. I told myself the next rickshaw driver I saw I would take. From my lips to angel's ears a man drove up to and offered to take me to the Temple of Heaven.

We jetted in and out of hutongs and he brought me right to the gate of the Temple of Heaven. He then insisted that I pay him more than what I paid for my flight from Beijing to Xi'an. No way. I offered him a couple of very generous amounts but then he started getting aggressive and threatened to call the police. I couldn't even make eye contact with him. I was so angry. I wanted to spit in the bills as I handed them to him. I was embarrassed that I was so widely taken advantage of. I should have negotiated before stepping foot into his rickshaw. Heavy sigh. Lessons learned. Never again.

I found it hard to really enjoy the Temple of Heaven after that. I saw the part of the temple that I wanted to see, and decided to get to the airport, despite the four hour early arrival. Get me out of Beijing.

I found my terminal and never in my life have I felt as much like an inept traveller as I did today. When I went to use the auto-check-in machine, I inserted my passport into the area that looked like was meant for scanning and pushed it so far in it was inside the machine. My passport! My brain switched to panic. I was immediately relieved that I bought a language app. The phrase "I lost my passport" in Chinese was worth every penny.

As the perfect evening to my horrible day the cab driver from the Xi'an airport decided to take me on quite the ride. I showed him the name and address of my hotel all written in Chinese and we set off. We took a U-turn after 10 minutes of driving on the freeway and another 20 minutes later I saw signs directing us back to the airport again. 40 minutes into the ride he pulled over and asked for the hotel phone number. He spoke with someone, drove for another two minutes, and dropped me off at a hotel that was not mine.

I was livid! I threw him a bill, I was not paying him the rest; this wasn't my hotel. I walked into the hotel in a fury of emotion. A very nice English-speaking hotel manager came to my rescue. The cab driver ran in after me, screaming at me to pay the rest of my tab. The hotel manager knew that my hotel was walking distance and offered to walk me over. I was so grateful to have someone so kind after such a rough day. I got up to my room and had a very long cry.

It was a terrible day. But as I write this, and reflect, there was nothing about the day that was broken beyond repair. It was tough to have no one to talk me through it, but that might be a good thing. There are going to be many broken days in my life. If I can fix them before getting to a point that I am spun out of control, then days like today are one of the many reasons I am here.

It also doesn't make me miss him any less.

Second Chances

Guilin, China
May 4

I only spent one day in Xi'an. See the Terracotta Army; fly out to the much calmer Guilin. I grabbed a fancily dressed female cab driver wearing lace gloves, the cab decorated with Hello Kitty seatbelt covers, and made it to my hostel.

The day I arrived I rented a bike and rode to the Reed Flute Caves. Imagine the busiest street you've ever been on. Now half the cars are scooters and bicycles, and one-way streets and streetlights have no meaning. And I want to ride a bike in this? My anxiety couldn't be higher. But if it is done on a daily basis by so many others, I can do it too.

I tuned out the horn honking and worked hard to not react when I saw another bike, or worse a car or bus, coming my way. I find an old man and I follow close behind him. I may not be fast, but I ride.

When I made it to the cave it was simply amazing. I separated myself from the group and enjoyed the mystic in peace.

After the cave I explored the beautiful hillside. I stood and stared. I wanted to meditate but couldn't find myself in a position to concentrate on the things I needed to. My mind has been a jumbled mess since coming to China and I have been desperate to clear it, focus it and find some new answers. I am so happy I finally found a town that I can slow down in. Before I came on my trip I thought I would be focused on the cities, but since being away I find that I really enjoy the nature, the stillness and calmness that the smaller towns provide. Maybe deep down I am a small town girl.

I woke up in the middle of the night from a very elaborate dream. I was at a party, when suddenly I saw my unfinished love story walk in. My heart skipped a beat. I had to talk to him. Earlier in the dream someone had told me that he had moved on and was now seeing a new girl. This information made my head spin and I decided to retaliate by hooking up with a new guy. I found out afterwards that he actually wasn't seeing anyone, someone lied to me, and now my unfinished love story was devastated because he thought I was moving on. I needed to explain to him and ask for forgiveness. Everyone was blocking me for speaking to him at the party. When I finally got in front of him, I asked for two minutes of his time. I woke up as I was being kicked out of the party, before I even got to ask for my second chance.

About three hours away from Guilin is the Longji Rice Terraces. It is a spectacular sight along the mountain side and filled with layers of greenery. The entire horizon is a painting of lines of green grass, brown soil, grey water and clouds.

Today was not ideal for doing a four-hour mountain climb. It rained the entire day, up until the moment we left. There are stone pathways that lead to the top of the mountain for different lookouts. I wanted to do the trek alone and tried to separate myself from my small group at a kissing fish spa in the first little village. I have never tried it but wanted to experience it. The kissing fish felt like little tickles all around my feet. I was surprised when the other six people I shared a van ride with all waited for me to finish.

We continued on as a group meandering pathways with no clear direction. Eventually we made it to the top and ate at the first restaurant we saw. I shared several dishes with three siblings from France. One of the items we ordered was whole chicken in spring water. It sounded better than it looked. We were given a bowl of water with chopped up chicken pieces. The sound of the chainsaw just before our meal made us know that at least the chicken was incredibly fresh.

At this point I was cold and decided I would enjoy the gondola ride to the bottom instead of more walking. I knew there was a café below and I could sit and relax away from everyone with a pot of tea. A young woman from Israel asked to join and we had a great conversation about travelling and current events.

I'm glad I gave China the second chance that it deserved.

Breaking Up

May 5th. It's officially been 3 months since I ended things with my unfinished love story. It's been 15 days since I've heard anything from him. It's been seven weeks since the last time I saw him, kissed his lips, held him close and told him that I still love him and still dream of a future with him.

One of the hardest things I've ever done, and still struggle with to this day, is ending a relationship with a man that I am still madly in love with. I felt I had no choice. I had to be fair to us.

We were together for two wonderful years. Everything about him I loved. And even though we did have our own challenges, I would never change one minute of any day. He is sweet, thoughtful, makes me laugh, ambitious, and caring. The best part about him was that I knew he loved me so much. So why break up?

For our two years we were apart the majority of the time. He had a job that required him to be out of town six days a week. I understood this when we started dating, and I told him I could hang on. I said we would do it for two years. Anyone can do anything for two years.

He worked hard and he was always generous with the money his hard work brought in. My 30th birthday present was the entire bar tab my friends built up. Every anniversary, Valentines, or occasional weekend, he would bring flowers home or have roses delivered to the house. He bought me diamond earrings for my last birthday, and a ruby necklace for Christmas the year before because the red reminded him of my lips when I put on my lipstick.

We moved in together after a year and a half to give us a few more hours together in our already limited time. And things were good but then I wanted more. I missed him when he was away. I found my entire week was a waiting game until I would get to be with him again.

I did my best to keep busy. I trained for a marathon, I started learning websites, I studied Spanish, and I would fill my weekdays going out with friends. But I grew tired of keeping myself busy for busy's sake. I then found myself at home alone, wishing I could be like other couples and eating my dinners with him, as opposed to almost every one by myself.

When he did come home I was overjoyed. I would have everything prepared so we could just focus on each other. He would come home Saturday afternoon. We would cook dinner together. We would drink wine and cuddle while watching movies on the couch. On our Sundays we would have coffee and take our dog, Tila, for a walk. We would go to Home Depot and all the home stuff that I couldn't do on my own throughout the week filled our day. He loved to repair things or make house improvements. Our first Valentines, we had only been together for a couple of weeks, he bought me dimmer switches for my house, and wanted to install them.

But then, all too quickly the day would be done. The final hours before he would leave again we would eat dinner by candlelight and I would try to not think about the fact that it would be another five nights until we were able to do this again. He would sometimes leave so early on Monday that I wouldn't even be up as he kissed me goodbye. He always kissed me. He always sent me a text telling me good morning once he knew I would be up.

I found myself looking forward far too much to our next vacation, because then I would get to see him for a whole seven days. It meant for one full week I would get his company and conversation at dinner. It meant falling asleep beside him and waking up to his warmth. We would always come back more in love than we could ever imagine. I loved holding his hand and seeing him smile, and when I saw it daily I felt my love grow.

But it's a terrible thing to only look forward to the next vacation, and the one after that. When the vacations aren't planned, there's less to look forward to. This year we planned to do a larger African vacation which meant we wouldn't have the occasional week for me to get excited about. I had to wait seven months for three weeks with him.

I could feel myself starting to crack. I needed to be with him more than what we were. It wasn't something that came on suddenly. For months I brought up how much I missed him. Before our second anniversary I was finding myself in a sour mood. We would be having petty fights for no reason. I knew I needed more. I knew even a small change would help, but I needed a step in the right direction.

I asked him if he could start taking off an extra day once a month to be home, especially before or after his planned boy's trips, which meant that I would go 14 days before I would be able to spend a full day with him. My capacity was ten days. After ten days I found myself in terrible moods because I missed him so much. Unfortunately he couldn't take any additional time off. I asked if it would be possible for him to work one day a week, or every second week from home. Then at least we could be together one additional night. That wasn't possible either. I offered to go to him, I would bring our dog and we would spend Thursday nights, or Friday nights in his work town. I had the flexibility to work away from my office. We just needed to find a hotel that accepted dogs, since I didn't want to be unfair to Tila and kennel her every weekend. Unfortunately he didn't think sleeping in the same room as our dog would work for his allergies. I finally offered to make an ultimate sacrifice. I was willing to quit my job and I would move with him to the towns he had to work in. I could rent a house, find temporary work from town to town, but then we could be together. This plan would mean less money to him, and that was not an option either. I asked him for any other suggestions, and he had none.

There was no end in sight for our situation. Once this project was completed there was going to be another project, and one after that. He said this was going to be the case for at least another year, maybe longer.

So where am I left? I want a future with a man that I need more time with. I want to be his wife and have his child. I want to be pregnant and have him there with me through that journey, not be surprised by how big I've been growing week after week. I want to have a father present, and not feel like I am a married single parent. And I started to focus on the pain of missing him while he was gone too much.

I made my decision. I probably should have slept on it. I love him, but our timing was off. That would be very fitting for the story of us. The first time we met I wasn't ready for him. I was too young, and I know I would have never appreciated who he is and everything he had to offer our relationship. It took five years before the next time we would meet again. And after being together for two years, we now know what we have to offer each other, but either he isn't fully ready for me, or I still am not ready for him.

I choose the pain of being by myself over the pain of waiting for him week after week. I came to the realization that if this is how our life is going to be then I need to change my perspective. I need to learn how to be better alone. I need to be okay with the ups and downs of my day by myself. I need to learn the joy of solitude. I could stay and be miserable day in and day out as the pain of missing him continued to grow, but I already knew my sour moods were becoming more frequent. Our petty fights would continue and maybe get worse. I was afraid if I hung on eventually there could be so much damage done it would be beyond any repair for us.

I had no desire to date anyone else. I wasn't in a position to find love. I had already found it. I needed to make it better. So it was time for me to live one of my biggest regrets. I needed to go travel. I never took the gap year between university and my career. I never wandered for months on end with no direction and only my head to keep me company. Maybe that's what I'm missing from our relationship. Maybe that's why I miss him more than the other women miss their men in the same work.

My decision to travel also came far too quickly - the day after breaking up with him. Maybe I should have slept on that one too. But not for one instant, even in the bad days, do I regret making it. I am doing it for myself. I am doing it for hopefully a future again with him. I am doing it for all the answers that I didn't even know I had questions to. Sometimes life doesn't give us what we want, it gives us what we need.

Once I made that decision, I knew that was the right one. Not the breakup. I asked him if we could still be together, or maybe he could wait for me to return. But six months is a long time. Many things could happen in that time. I didn't want him to feel guilty if he met the real girl of his dreams, and maybe I was just the stepping stone to her. I love him so much that I don't want to stand in the way of his happiness. He deserves only the absolute best things and people in his life.

I don't know what the future hold for us. I know I have to be here right now. I don't know if he, or his family or friends read my blog. No matter what the answer, it is the perfect one. If he reads it, it means he is genuinely curious about me. He still cares and wants to know what is going on. Maybe he has hope that we will be together again. If he doesn't read it, he has no desire to know what I am doing; he is in the process of moving on. This blog now becomes my medium to deal with the pain of a breakup, just like any other. But if he was to contact me, if he was to want to come meet me on my travels, my heart would flutter and I would know that he wants us to be as much as me.

For now I will carry on each day. Take it all step by step. Learn what I need to while I am out here. I will always think of him. That will never, ever change. Even if we aren't meant to be, he will always be in my head and in my heart. The best part about life is it loves to surprise us. I know there is a wonderful surprise at the end of this story; I just have to wait and see what it will be.

Bamboo River Raft Princess

There are a couple of ways that you can get to Yangzhou from Guilin: a bus ride or a bamboo river raft. How could I turn down a river raft ride?

The bamboo river raft wasn't a traditional raft, it was made out of plastic, but it was a fun way to see more of the Guilin to Yangzhou countryside. The entire area is covered with mountains that seem to appear out of the Earth in single mounds, without intersecting into one another. As we boarded our boat there was a woman selling flower crowns. I didn't know how much they were, but I offered a fair price and she was more than happy to take that. I put my crown on and became a bamboo raft princess.

There was an optional second river ride on a much narrower raft. Our raft floated down a couple of "waterfalls", which were dips in the river for a fun experience. I was paired up with Gabe, from Chicago. The night before, Gabe and I had a long conversation about taking the time to travel extensively by oneself. He said our conversation started to inspire him to really think about it and start putting a plan together. I love feeling like I have inspired people. I love telling my story, and hopefully people connect in one way or another. Our conversation continued on the raft and we started chatting about love and soulmates. He loved every part of the story that I told him about my life, my past, and hopes for the future.

The end of the night was capped off by attending a show called Impression Sanjie Liu. It was highly recommended by a woman I had met in Xi'an. She said the director of the show also directed the Olympic Games ceremony. Before the show I met a couple of university ladies and urged one of the ladies to travel solo after her course was completed. I received an email

83

from her months later telling me she did, she was so happy about doing it, and it was because of my encouragement that she found the strength to be able to do it.

The show was a masterpiece. The stage was the river, the backdrop was the mountains, and it was an impression of lights, colours and contrasting tones that literally made my jaw drop several times throughout. Entire mountains lit up, the river turned red as layers of cloth rose from the water and moved like waves, and I then lost count of the number of people used for a flickering light display of bamboo rafts. It took my breath away.

I walked down a very bustling West Street, thinking about life giving me what I need, and not what I wanted and asked for. My company would have given me a ten week sabbatical and with six weeks already in I know I still need to be here. I am just starting to really get to know myself.

Temporary Love

I woke up early, as I always do. The day was cloudy and looked like it could rain at any moment. It was perfect for a quiet contemplative day.

I wandered the shops until I heard water running. I made my way over to a bridge overlooking a small waterfall, river, mountains and lush green trees. This is exactly why people love it here.

The area was filled with photographers, painters, and writers. My body told me to stop. I cleared my already calm head and felt nothing but love. I felt what reminded me of a soft kiss on my lips, and a whisper in my ear of "I love you and miss you". I felt in my heart all the love for everyone I had ever met. I missed everyone, but not in sadness, instead in gratitude for where I am and my continued growth.

I felt like a child, who every day looks and feels the same, and yet has been growing so much my clothes no longer fit. That instantaneous look of "when did that happen"? I felt inspired, like I had heard the crack in an ice cube to confirm it is actually melting.

Then the moment was done. I felt it and realized I was somehow already on the path. I don't remember seeing the entrance.

Controlling Anxiety

Yangzhou, China
May 8

Anxiety is a funny thing. Without knowing what it was I suffered from it for years. I would be kept up all night consumed by thoughts and unlikely potential outcomes. I would play series of events that hadn't even happened yet in my head to come to the most extreme best and worst case scenarios. I would worry about timelines and feel that if I wasn't exactly where I thought I was supposed to be by a certain date, there must be something wrong with me, and I need to throw away everything and start all over again. This, of course, would create more anxiety.

I had two major anxiety attacks without knowing what they were at the time. I remember having one so bad that I went to the emergency room. I thought I was having a heart attack. I was short of breath, my heart felt like it was going to burst out of my chest, and I felt dizzy and nauseated. The doctors took my blood pressure, which was extremely high, hooked me up to an EKG to watch my heart rhythms, and then sent me on my way a few hours later telling me there was nothing wrong. For me that just made my head spin worse as I was convinced I was somehow misdiagnosed.

My anxiety controlled my career and my personal life. As a salesperson, it actually worked to my benefit. When things didn't go my way I would persevere, always trying something new. I would knock down doors. I didn't take no for an answer. But what works well in my career did the exact opposite in my personal life. I had timelines and applied pressures to ensure my dates were met.

I wanted to be married by 30, or at least engaged. I am a good catch. I have a steady, successful career. I own a house and a rental property. I live a healthy lifestyle, I am fit and I own a great dog. I had everything going for me. I had no lack of interested prospects. I could actually be choosy.

I had a two-year dating limit. I made this well known. There was only one guy that I dated for more than two years, and I allowed that to slide because I thought if I gave him enough time I would get what I wanted. In turn he had a different agenda and I found out after two and a half years that he was scouring online dating sites. I stayed with him for another year. I was more interested in the ring than the relationship. When I eventually ended things, I decided never again would I allow my two year limit to pass.

In hindsight part of my sour moods as my unfinished love story and I approached our two year mark was my anxiety creeping up. In the back of my head I heard "see? Yet again... another guy not that serious... you'll never be married..." I knew he wanted to marry me. We talked about it at length. We talked about it before we hit our first anniversary. I wanted to marry him too. Still do. But I don't blame him for not proposing. As the two year mark came closer, my mood became worse. I didn't even like the person I was. I was bitter and jaded. I was focused on wanting to be engaged, and feeling like if it didn't happen by the time we hit two years it was never going to happen. I applied so much pressure, that if my relationship was a sales cycle the client would have just signed the papers just to stop the feeling of harassment. And despite the fact that I wanted to be his wife and partner for life, not just a fiancée and a bride, I let the anxiety and determination of a ring before a certain date consume me. However, all that said, I feel like my life deliberately lead me here to this moment.

If I was engaged before the two-year mark, which at one point was a very real possibility, I wouldn't be here. I wouldn't have ever left to explore on my own. I wouldn't be sitting in a café overlooking the Li River, writing, drinking a cappuccino, waiting for the rain to stop, and reflecting on how my anxiety has controlled my life. I wouldn't be six weeks into a trip where I have never in my life felt so calm, so accepting of life as it comes, as opposed to driven and determined for a destination, whether or not having decided if that's even where I want to be, or even open to changing direction along the path.

Had life not put the pieces in place for me to need to be on this trip, maybe I would be engaged right now, but I would never have the opportunity to look critically at my life and figure out what needs to change in order for me to live a happier life. My future would still consist of dates and timelines and overly determined goals. I don't think I would be the wife that someone would be proud to have, and I want to be that woman.

So here's the funny thing about anxiety. I've enjoyed the last few weeks. I've reflected so much on the things that I have wanted to change in my life. I have reflected on my career, my friendships, my family, my relationship and my love story. And I woke up this morning with anxiety because I felt guilty that I haven't dreamed of my unfinished love story in almost a week.

Midnight Bus to Hong Kong or Audience of One

Hong Kong, Hong Kong
May 9

Midnight Bus to Hong Kong
I needed to get from mainland China to Hong Kong today. I looked at a variety of flight options but decided on a 10-hour sleeper bus ride to Shenzhen with a local bus to the Hong Kong border. Part of this trip was to enjoy unique experiences and a bus with bunk beds would definitely be included in that.

I arrived to the bus station after a 2km walking detour. I was waved over by a group of rock climbers done for the day. I crossed the road, and through broken English they asked me where I was heading. I showed them my bus ticket and pulled out my iPad. I completely bypassed it.

When I arrived at the bus station I realized the ticket I bought the day before was issued for the same day and no longer valid. My heart dropped. I really didn't want to have to buy another ticket. Thankfully the woman at ticket counter allowed it to pass.

While I sat at the bus station waiting in nervous patience a UK woman, Fiona, came in. She had met a guy from Winnipeg a few weeks ago in Indonesia. She said it was a strong and instantaneous relationship. They decided to try and make it work, which meant she was on her way to Hong Kong to catch the first flight to Vancouver and make it over to him. I told her the best guys are from Winnipeg. They are down to earth and super chill.

The bus had three rows of bunk beds, about 12 beds per row. Each bed measured slightly less than my height at 5 foot 5 inches. When it arrived at the station Fiona and I were the last ones to get on. I grabbed the first open bed I saw. The bus was playing a Brendan Fraser mummy movie spoken in both English and Chinese. I quickly set myself up with the included fleece blanket and what are now my two most valuable possessions, earplugs and an eye mask. I fell into a solid and uncomfortable sleep for almost the entire trip.

Fiona and I met a Belgium guy on the bus who was also on his way to the Hong Kong border. The three of us were trying to figure out what bus to catch when a man from Shenzhen offered to walk us over to the temporary bus terminal and showed us the bus we needed.

The cross from mainland China to Hong Kong was easy. There were no lineups, no questions. A river separates the two sides, and the border entrance opens directly into a subway station.

I arrived at the station where my hostel is located and found myself trying to navigate myself on my map again. A young man walked up to me and offered to walk me right to my hostel. My heart was overcome with the amount of friendliness and offers of help today

Audience of One

I read two articles posted by Fast Company, both were very relevant to my situation. The first article was about how travel inspires more stories. It's not the miles travelled, but the fact that they were travelled in the first place that inspires.

However it was the second story that really had my mind in motion. It was about the creator of my personal favourite cartoon, Calvin and Hobbes. Bill Patterson only did two interviews in his 10-year career but in one of his interviews he gave advice about being creative. He said to always create for you. No one else matters, except maybe one. In his case his goal was to make his wife laugh. If he did that then he succeeded. People will choose to read or not to, but he never felt creative when he was too busy censoring and thinking about other people.

I love writing for myself. This is my story, good and bad, and the first person I'm writing for is the woman in her 80s showing these entries to her grandkids and saying "look what grandma did". I feel I have been authentic with my writing, minus one element. There is one other person that I want to write for. I want to tell him all about my day, every day. I want to thank him for allowing me to do this, and I want to say "see? I am becoming a better person. I will be home soon. And if you thought it was good then, I promise you it will be better than ever. Better than you could ever imagine". I write for him.

It may not make a difference in my day to day stories, but some people will either love it more or hate it, and I don't care. I don't even know if the person I write for reads it, but I think about him always. Every. Single. Day. My heart is still filled with love and I can't even imagine ever breaking it. In my heart, although not in name, we are together. My heart won't accept it any other way. Maybe one day that will have to change, if it has to. But for every other day I am here I write for him and to him. I believe in our love story so much that there are no other options than me finishing my personal story and then being fully ready to continue ours together.

Dreams Becoming Reality

Hong Kong, Hong Kong
May 10

On the way to my hostel yesterday I started having super strong feelings of missing my unfinished love story. This is not the first time I've had intense feelings or thoughts about him, and the more I get them, the more I'm convinced that him and I are supposed to be together. Each feeling is something different, but in this case I was convinced it was him missing me intensely and I was feeling it.

Once I finished writing my entry for yesterday, no sooner after I published it, my unfinished love story sent me a message. I was shocked. I hadn't heard anything from his since his "bye. Bye" message my first night in Tokyo. I wasn't expecting to hear from him so soon.

Him: Please do me a favour and delete him as a friend

I didn't know if it was a typo and he meant "me" or if "him" was someone else. I was afraid of breaking down in the pub before I had a chance to pay my bill. My heart was not ready to have our story end here. Not this way. Maybe my entry about writing only to him crossed a line. Maybe I was wrong this entire time. Maybe he really wasn't the one I was meant to be with.

Me: delete you as a friend or someone else?

Him: please don't forget what I told you, at 3 months it will be a rough patch, but it will go away, hang in there.

Me: who's him?
I'm hanging in. I miss you so much. I love you.

I need to be here. But I still dream every day of having you in my life. That will never, ever change

He said his friend, my mom, and my sister started fighting on Facebook. I don't have this particular friend on my Facebook, but he is the same one I dreamed was fighting with my mom over whether my unfinished love story and I should be together. I didn't know anything about anything. I was just so thrilled to have my unfinished love story chatting with me in real time.

Me: I think about you always. I would love to FaceTime with you whenever you can. Please let me know.
Meet me in Athens in August. We can do all the islands together.

Him: Apparently August is really busy there. I was told Sep is better because everyone is back in school and the weather is still nice.

His answers were short. He said that he was driving. I didn't know the next time I would hear from him again so I threw my entire heart out there for him.

Me: Okay. I want you to know that I love you with all my heart. I miss you every single moment of every single day. I dream about us always. And my only wish is to kiss your lips and be in your arms again. I look forward to when I am done my personal journey. I will be more of a partner, supporter and lover than you could ever have imagined. I have never in my life said to someone that I love them and my heart fills with so much emotion that it feels like my chest can't contain it. When I say it to you that's the feeling I get. So, literally I love you with all my heart.

I left the pub to go back to my hostel. After an hour I still hadn't heard anything back. I sent him another message thanking for today. I said that although he didn't say he loves me back it was still so wonderful. I told him that I would wait for him to contact me again.

However now I was confused. What could everyone possibly be fighting about? Was it something I posted in one of my blogs?

I didn't get a chance to talk to my mom until the next morning. If only I didn't ask her. I went from feeling the hope that my unfinished love story was ready to forgive me for breaking up with him to do my personal journey, to overwhelming sadness with what she had to say.

My unfinished love story's friend posted a status and tagged him in it. It said that he was seeing a new girl, who was everything I wasn't, and his friend can't wait for them to get married. There were many lines in the status that my mom and sister took as a personal attack against me and decided to come to my defense, which is where all the drama came in. I would have never found out about any of it had I not been contacted by my unfinished love story and then felt the need to ask.

Then I remembered my second dream. I dreamed that someone had lied to me about my unfinished love story moving on and being in a relationship. If I truly believe that he and I are meant to be there is no way he could be in love with someone else so quickly. And if he is, then our relationship was not at all what I thought it was, and therefore not worth fighting for. I don't know for sure if he is involved with a new girl, but I will act as if not, because acting as if he is will just create more uncertainty and unfortunate drama.

I sent him a message in the morning when I woke up.

Me: Mom read me the posting that was deleted. She took a screenshot. I'm glad I didn't see it first hand, it would have hurt too much. Don't feel bad if you feel you have to move on. I will always love you and think about you and I will miss you more than my heart can contain. I will be home in four and a half months. I am still open to seeing you any time throughout my journey and would be more than happy to change direction and locations for you. I will continue to blog every day.

One a side note, I think I sometimes feel you feeling me, and I don't know if it's true. I felt your mom delete me off Facebook. It was right when I arrived in Australia. I felt that you read my blog once. Maybe one entry around the last week of April. I felt last week you were home on a Friday, and maybe with a blonde girl. And around 9PM last night for you I felt you missing me really hard.

But if any of that is true I hope you feel me too. All those feelings of love and happiness and warmth that's me sending to you.

He replied back that he didn't see the post, but it was pretty far-fetched from what he heard and that people should delete other people that don't make them happy.

I told him I understood. I was still really hurt by the posting. I said some of the things it said, but then I let him know that part of the reason I am on this journey is to become more secure with myself and to not let other people's opinions affect me, especially when they are so far away, but I'm working to improve all of that.

I did have a third dream last week. It told me to not lose hope. So I will not. I will still believe that we are meant to be. I will still love him and try to make us right again. I will work on me and make me a better person so that if he does ever come around again I am fully ready to give him my entire self.

I couldn't wait for any additional potential responses from my unfinished love story. I needed to make the most of the day. I had two things I wanted to see in Hong Kong, a certain temple and Big Buddha. I went to the temple first.

Wong Tai Sin Temple is known as the temple "what you request is what you get". People come for a spiritual answer in the practice of kau cim. The person will light incense sticks as they pray and express gratitude before the main alter. Then you move to the back alter where you kneel while concentrating on a question and shaking a tin of numbered bamboo sticks. Once a stick falls out you record the number and take it to your choice of soothsayer who will read your answer for you. The soothsayer also read my palm.

She told me that love is coming. This is a big year for love for me and I need to be patient. I have to stop overthinking too much, because all I do is think. She told me that my love is flying and he will come to me by August. I already had a feeling about August. She told me I will be married next year, and my boyfriend and husband is a very good man who will be with me for the rest of my life. She said that I will transition my job when I am 35 and I will make very good money until I am 55 and then I will stop caring about work. She told me I have an immigration line in my palm, and that part of this journey is to realize that. Finally she said that I would benefit not living so close to my mom.

I continued on my way to see the Big Buddha. Unfortunately the weather started to take a turn for the worse and the rain and wind started picking up terribly. I wanted to complete the wisdom walk after speaking with Buddha, but decided it would be wiser to turn around.

Letting It Go

I love that I can go from one extreme to another in my emotions.

This morning I woke up and broke down, literally. I had a dream that I was chatting with my unfinished love story and confessing my love. He didn't respond. He was stoic. He stood there like a wall. I didn't think my posting yesterday was so depressing, but when I woke up to messages from friends concerned about me I started to see it from the outside looking in. It was a tough pill to swallow. My love wasn't being reciprocated. I broke down again. I sent my unfinished love story an ask: "do you still love me at all"?

I left for breakfast, and after a couple of hours I saw that he looked at my question but didn't respond. I didn't have the words for anything more. I decided to send him the email I wrote and never sent when travelling back to Sydney from Alice Springs. I sent it off saying that I love him and I just want to hear it back. I figured it wasn't going to make me seem any less desperate or crazy than I was already coming across. Then I let him know that if he is ever having a bad day there is someone in the world that loves him so much and would do anything he asked of her.

I walked around in the morning just wishing I was home. I wished so badly that I was home. I needed a hug.

As I walked around a smile slowly came to my face. I did have hugs. So many of them! All those messages, all that contact, even though it wasn't a physical hug, I was receiving more than enough love that I needed to get through the day. I had so many virtual hugs, and that really was what I needed.

Today was a surprise day in Hong Kong. This has happened to me before throughout the trip that I'm either thinking I am inherently forgetful or my life is purposefully giving me "extra days" as a way of helping me slow down and enjoy. I never have a plan for my unexpected days and I end up just being. These in turn become my most memorable and favourite days.

I switched to a hotel on the other side of the harbour. A new neighbourhood brings on new experiences. I LOVE this side; it is hillier, more internationally-influenced and topographically unique. I tried to find Hong Kong Park, but when I came to the botanical gardens that was enough for me. I decided to meditate near a fountain. This may have been one of my longest meditation sessions, despite the fact that my mind wasn't entirely empty; it was focused on one single thought at a time. By the end of it my thoughts were very focused on letting all my other thoughts go. Just let them go. I do overthink. I drive myself to stress. Just let it be. Suddenly the day became happier. Like amazingly happy.

I walked through the park and remembered my Kobo e-reader died. I needed to find some books over the next few weeks to keep my mind interested. I made my way to a bookstore where I picked up a variety, and maybe a bit too much weight.

I then decided enough was enough. I needed to get my hair dyed and I was in desperate need of a haircut. I decided to not mess with my hair. I thought if I had it done in Hong Kong, I could speak English and get what I want. Despite my rationale I still had more cut off than I originally wanted.

I started reading a book that I picked up at the store that I didn't think I would be super impressed with, but ended up falling in love with right away. Many years ago my friend Sarah told me once that we don't choose books, books choose us. Maybe that's why my Kobo died. I would have never have picked this book out if I still had my e-reader. It's a book about calming the mind. It reminded me on how I used to be and think when my life was so much simpler. I used to inspire people with the way I thought. I'm grateful that those same people I used to inspire now inspire me with their clarity. I also want to be that girl that I used to be: calm, focused, and Zen. I remember her. I forgot about her.

The night ended on a great note. I met a couple of IT salespeople from California, and then when the rain became too much on my way to my hotel I ran into a bar and chatted with a semi-retired Australian couple as I waited for it to stop.

Thank you all for your hugs today. It was an absolutely amazing day.

Goodbye Hong Kong, Hello Vietnam

Hanoi, Vietnam
May 12

The morning was raining again. I couldn't sleep. My unfinished love story sent me a response. He told me that what others do is not a reflection of him. He thought my feelings were coming from a place of too much emotion. He said I gave up on us and I cannot take that back. Both sides of a relationship are meant to hang on, which is what makes a relationship strong. That's why he doesn't see a future with us. He is trying to heal his broken heart, he doesn't know if it can be healed for someone else, but how does he know if he doesn't try? He knows that I am trying to find myself, but when I come back I will still be me. He closed by saying he does and will continue to miss me but hopes he can be a better person from the experiences we shared.

It had no desire to get going, so I played Jack Johnson. I opened the curtains, sat in bed, enjoyed the rain coming down and wrote back a long response.

I thanked him for writing back, it's the most I had heard from him. I told him that I used to take his lack of communication personally, but since being away I've learned that it just takes him longer to articulate his feelings.

I told him that I also have a broken heart. I never wanted to give up on us but I needed a break from our situation; from missing him all the time. I wanted to be closer to him and I was feeling rejected after every suggestion I brought up to fix our situation was dismissed.

Then I told him broken hearts heal. They get stronger. The reason we love to begin with is because we have trust that this time around our love will be strong and then we take a leap of faith. But if our hardest hurdle we ever had to get over is two-years of distance and then six-months of travel that's pretty amazing.

I told him if we are both birds, we need to find our happiness. If another girl will help him find his happiness then he needs to do that. I begged him to please don't jump into a relationship just to be with someone though.

I apologized. I apologized for hurting him. I was sorry because his pain is because of me, but I was ready to help him heal. I told him that I would be there for him in the blink of an eye. But if he never saw a future with me I couldn't repair that. I was still dedicated to him and I wasn't going to leave that yet.

I promised our love would be stronger than ever. I promised that I would never leave or break his heart again. We could live anywhere in the world that he wants. I would find a new job, maybe my writing would take off. Because when we were together we were really good together. Like, amazingly good. I still thought only extreme happiness and love when I thought of him, and if I didn't feel that he would never be hearing from me.

I then closed by telling him I love him. I believe he is my true love. I am proud of him. I think he is amazing. He can get any woman or job he wants. And I've heard beautiful things about Greece in August.

I didn't know the next time I would hear from him or would reach out to him again. I said everything.

It's always difficult when I have a flight anything other than early morning, because I have to pack and carry my bag around the city to either catch in a few last minute sights, like I did in Beijing, or just arrive to the airport ridiculously early and wait for my flight, like I did in Kyoto. However Hong Kong has this problem figured out. I walked to the station to catch the commuter train directly to the airport and there they have airport check-in counters. I checked in my bag and had the option to shop in the mall directly above, and then catch the train to the airport when my flight is ready to board. What a relief off my back, literally.

I didn't have any more shopping to do, so I decided to grab a Starbucks, read and sit in quiet contemplation. I've been getting better at quieting my mind and focusing on being in the present. I still have moments that cause me anxiety about the future or the past, but I am learning to refocus my energy on the here and now.

I left for the airport thinking I would walk around, maybe go to a restaurant, but most importantly exchange my currencies. I had plenty of time, and that's when I saw directions to the prayer room in the airport. I've never had any interest to use one before, but since being on my trip I've spent more time meditating, and I'm slowly making it into a daily habit. I have no excuses to not start this new habit. I have a new level of focus and the time to practice. I am becoming better and more effective with each practice. I sat and focused inside myself again. I've had so many questions and concerns about my future; I needed an answer. I heard, "keep doing what I'm doing. Focus only on the now".

As I sat in my taxi from the Hanoi airport to my hotel I felt him again. It was strong. I looked at the time and did the math. It was the middle of the night for him. It felt like he was having a sexy dream about me. I closed my eyes. I wanted to be with him. I felt him all over my body. I felt him run his hands all over me. It was his kisses on my lips. I felt the intensity of one of our love-making sessions. I bite my lip to hold back the sounds I wanted to make. I was still in the back of a cab. Then I felt that explosion of passion as if we were both climaxing; fiery pulses of electricity shooting through my body.

I kept my eyes closed and imagined telling him I have to go, but we will be together soon. In my mind he was still in bed. He grabbed my hand and pulled me back. "Not yet", he whispered. I imagined that I laid down in bed with him for a moment again. I kissed him. Then I broke away from the vision.

In Hanoi there is a blend of new and traditional throughout the streets. Like many Asian cities, my new found love of slowing down benefits me here. For someone that just landed here walking across the street could seem like a daunting task. But now, for me, it's to my benefit. My new slower pace is the perfect way to walk across the street. Only focused on myself and my pace, and not allowing myself to become phased as a scooter zips around me.

It's incredibly easy to become lost in the streets. They lead down narrowing paths and many of the stores look the same. Making turns in new directions left me feeling lost in a short period of time. Thankfully Wi-Fi is easy to come by in the many cafés, and the drinks are delicious and cheap.

Boating the Bay or
Being Kind to Myself

Ha Long, Vietnam
May 14

Boating the Bay
While chatting with the receptionist at my hotel yesterday she booked me for Halong Bay today and Sapa rice fields after that. After a full day of exploring and walking around Hanoi I needed something different. I was starting to feel like I was going through the motions just to get through my trip. Visit my countries, get back home. The enjoyment was almost superficial. I needed some water, beach and boat therapy.

The weather was perfect for jumping on a boat. The temperature was hot, the wind was mild and the air smelled of a light salt. The perfect compromise of sea and fresh water melded together. We took our baggage and jumped onto "small boat to go to big boat", as the locals so wonderfully put it. Once we were on the larger boat we steered our way to one of the caves.

After the cave tour we were taken kayaking to an area that had a low mountain tunnel shallow enough that you could steer with a kayak, but not enough with a ship. On the other side was a cool, calm basin. I jumped out of the kayak when I saw a few Australians wading in the water. Unfortunately my boat captain didn't allow that sort of unplanned behaviour and I guided my first-time kayaking partner how to position so I could jump back in without capsizing us. We kayaked around for a bit as my partner asked me questions about my six-month travel excursion. I never underplay the amount of courage it took to decide to break away from everything and go. I feel so fortunate that I come from a country where taking time off for significant travel is seen as a benefit in one's career, not a hindrance.

We came back to the boat and had an exceptional dinner. The sunset was spectacular followed up with and equally beautiful full moon. The night was capped off with squid fishing, which is done best at night with a beam of light shining onto the sea. I missed my first squid by inches, but caught my second, allowed it to ink itself and then pulled it into the boat.

Being Kind to Myself

All it takes sometimes is one sentence from someone to put everything back into perspective. One sentence. I've heard it many times from many friends, but sometimes it's suddenly one time and everything sticks. Yesterday my friend Jenna said to me, "Kim, remember, if he had given you what you wanted and asked for you wouldn't be there". She was right. I broke down again and then suddenly the pain stopped. It just stopped.

When I woke up in the morning I started writing. I needed to be kind to myself. I needed to stop taking the burden of all the blame. I am a rational person and I really wouldn't be on this trip if I was happy every day or at least most days.

I wrote an angry open letter to my ex. One that I will never send and I will never post. It felt good to write it. Not the anger part, but putting it out there. Reminding me why I am here, why I felt this was my only option at the time, and mostly to take all the weight of the blame off myself. I needed to release all the negative emotions and start bringing myself to a better place. I think a part of me was holding onto all the pain as a way of holding onto him. If I lost the pain, he was no longer a part of my everyday anymore. I know this is false. I have so many wonderful memories of the two of us. I feel like I am a better person just for having him enter my life to begin with. I am richer in experience, and understand a deeper love than I have ever known before. I could talk endlessly about how wonderful I think he is and all the dreams I have of the two of us, but at the end of the day I need to remember why I am here.

I didn't wake up one morning and decide I was unhappy. I didn't hold my feelings in and spring them out of nowhere. And most importantly it wasn't as if I didn't try. I tried really, really hard. I can sit back and know that I did everything I could think of at the time to keep him in my life.

Love is like an ox and a cart, both of them have to be willing to get to the destination, and the same destination, for it to work. The ox can't pull the cart if it's weighed down too much, and the cart can't move on its own without the ox to help pull it along. I was a weighed down cart and I couldn't continue moving forward until some of my pain was released.

I am releasing myself of the pain of holding onto the entire blame. I am no longer going to feel guilty for my feelings and my emotions. I've said that before, but hopefully this time it will stick. I will know when it does because when I go back and reflect on our relationship I will think of it from a place of compassion, understanding and tolerance. One where I can look back and be more aware of what I missed. What I could have done differently, whether that is my actions, perception, or communication style.

I already know one thing. I should have reached out to his family. Not in a way of complaining but in a way of support and a new perspective on things. In all my time, I've never done that before, and that is something I will change going forward. They've known him far longer than anyone else and their insight could have helped me in so many ways. Lessons learned. But in the end, I hope my biggest lesson will be to be a far better and kinder person to myself.

Homesick in Halong Bay

Halong Bay, Vietnam
May 15

This morning I had one of the worst feelings of homesickness that I've had since being on this trip. I am in one of the most beautiful places in the world and I can't stop thinking about how I wish I was back. I wrote my unfinished love story another unsent letter.

> Me: The day should be perfect, but it's not. Not nearly enough. While I lie on my bed in a gorgeous cabin on a cruise ship in the Vietnam harbour I can't stop thinking about you. I wish you were here beside me. I wish you were enjoying all of this with me. I wish when I asked you to come on this tour you would have said yes. Was there something wrong with me or with us? I don't understand why. I don't understand any of the whys.
>
> I had a dream last night that you were with a girl. She was falling in love with you. You felt indifferent towards her. I'm sorry. I did that to you
>
> I hurt you so bad that as much as you want to move on you can't. I'm so, so sorry. I love you. I don't want to hurt you. I would take away all that pain if I could.

I seriously considering getting back to Hanoi and jumping on the first flight back home. It took a lot to break me of it. My inner dialogue was having a debate between all the things I will miss seeing, that four more months not being a long time in the bigger picture of my life, and yet my head was strongly convinced that home would be the best place to be. I've said it before, sleep can help a lot. On the way back from Halong Bay I took a nap on the bus, and felt better about staying.

Back in Hanoi I took a walk around the lake and went into a nice restaurant. After yesterday's post about being kinder to myself I decided to go for dinner at a decently romantic place. It was the type of place that I could see myself staring into my partner's eyes and laughing the night away. If I could do it with someone else, I should be able to do it alone. It was a lovely dinner, despite the laughter.

I was exhausted by the end, eventually making my way back to my hotel, but not before looking at a few beautiful dresses in the stores. I realized that you can take the girl travelling, but travelling won't take the girlie from the girl. I wear a lot of dresses back home. I didn't bring many with me, and have bought three since being on my trip. They're not entirely practical for wearing a backpack, or hiding a money belt, but they sure are pretty. And I feel beautiful in them. Sometimes we have to be what we are and not fight it.

Caught in the Moment

Sa Pa District, Vietnam
May 18

I arrived in Sapa yesterday to spend the day enjoying the Vietnamese rice fields. Instead of a hotel, I chose to spend the night at a homestay, have dinner with a local Sapa family, and learn more about their daily life. The house was spacious, little furniture, minimal lights, and one bathroom, for three generations of family. After working in the fields all day, they all help make the meal, and cook just enough for the night, since there are no refrigerators. We drank rice wine by the shot glass, had a couple of beers, and were served chicken, pork, fish, potatoes and plenty of rice. There was one light bulb per room, all CFL. As I laughed and ate with the family I questioned why I work so hard in my career. Everyone here seemed happy. They had more than enough to survive and plenty of time together.

As the evening rounded out, I sat outside with the French couple. We chatted and listened to music. Andy told me that Caroline was feeling a little drunk, and as he looked at her, I recognized that look. He looked at her like she was the only woman in the world. I could tell that he loved her just with his eyes. I missed having someone look at me that way. The way the entire world disappears when you are truly in love.

I went to bed early and awoke shortly after sunrise. No one else was up. I walked over to a boulder sitting outside the house. It had a perfect sitting platform and overlooked the mountains and terraces. There was a little stream that ran past the house, and as the morning started to glow and the sound of the water flowed past, I found myself in the perfect moment to meditate.

I was thankful for everything that is and was. I contemplated change. Everything changes and nothing is constant. Nothing in life should be taken for granted and attachments need to be weak. This is one of the Buddhist teachings. Not to be taken in a cynical view, but rather one that helps to appreciate the things that are in our life more. If nothing stays the same, everything, every moment, needs to be appreciated for exactly what it is while we are here.

My dreams and my daily thoughts are always on my single thought, whether it is about the past, the present or the future. But today I tried much harder to enjoy the moments that I was currently in for exactly what they were. We hiked the entire day along the rice fields, many of the paths quite tricky. I spend a majority of my time watching my footing on the ground, but had to constantly remind myself to look up and really enjoy the view. Be thankful that I am here. Remember this exact moment. Breathe deep. Let my eyes just absorb what my mind couldn't yet.

I feel like today my concentration on just being and being right here started to take hold. It may be like any other skill and with continued practice I could end up being right here, right now, more often.

My Angel, Anjulie

I had an angel come to me in the form of a 27-year old UK woman last night. I had boarded my train and in walks this woman who is full of personality and immediately starts venting about her bad day. She apologized then says she is so happy to get things off her chest. We immediately start talking.

She told me about her travels and how she was meeting a boy in Hong Kong for the weekend. He was someone that she's been best friends with for years. They suddenly decided they both love each other. He confessed to her at first, but she didn't feel the same way, so for six months he spent the time trying to get over her. She then decided she did love him in return, and another four months passed while he was too bitter to have his love reciprocated. She decided to go travelling and left in February. Last week she received a message from him saying he was coming to get her. Her story touched my heart. I told her I hope the same thing happens to me.

She said before coming to Vietnam she went to Australia to meet another former boyfriend. They had been together for a long time and she ended things with him about a month before he was going to propose. She said she loved him, but felt like he wasn't making her a priority. He cared too much about money and when they had conversations about children she didn't feel confident that he would be around nightly to help her raise them. She said she also was a career woman, and believed both sides have to give a fair amount of time, not just weekends for the man. I told her I understood that concern.

She has the same concern with this new guy, despite loving him so much. He works in finance, makes a crazy amount of money, but with it, a crazy amount of hours. Yet he still doesn't feel he makes enough to raise a child. She told him his bigger concern should be deciding if he's in a career where he has the time. Children can be raised on little money as long as two people have enough time and love to give each other and their children. I breathed deeply. I told her I knew that feeling too.

I was inspired by her story about her new love coming to get her. Before she left she told this man that they were to have no contact except for once a month. They agreed to send each other an email saying 1) how they feel about each other and 2) what could they give to the relationship. She said even though someone feels they are in love with the other person, if they don't feel they are in a position to be there or give what the other person needs, they need to be fair to each other, upfront and honest about it.

For months she's felt incredibly in love with him and couldn't see herself with anyone else in the world. I know that feeling. But she said last month she had a really good day and realized she didn't think about him until about 3PM. She wrote in her last email that she still loves him, she still wants to be with him, but for a moment she saw a glimmer of her life without him. She thought she could actually get over him. Especially since the last few months he wasn't reciprocating any love or interest back. I felt a pull at my heart strings. I know that feeling too.

Then she asked about me. I told her everything. She started out by saying she didn't like him. She said she believed that a two-year relationship in one's 30s feels longer than a two-year relationship among 20-somethings. She could tell I was still in love, but it concerned her that I haven't heard the words from him in months. She said that if in his last email to me he said he didn't see a future with me then I need to take that for exactly what it is and try doing the same. If he really wanted to spend his life with me, I would be there and not here. He would have decided on me already. Then she promised me that one day, too, I will have that day, with that glimmer of hope that tells me, I'm okay to be alone. Everything will be okay.

Everything is exactly where it needs to be. She said I should feel like a priority in his life, it doesn't have to be all the time, but sometimes he has to choose me over everything else, especially work. I would know if I was that priority because I would hear from him, he would do what he needs to choose me. I had a hard time holding back the tears.

We chatted a lot about traveling and trying to improve areas of our lives. She explained that she has gone travelling before and when she came back she was the exact same person she had always been, the only difference was that now she was completely okay with that. She said there will always be parts of herself that she doesn't like, that's life. Like being in any relationship there is always something you wish you could change about your partner, and that's the same about yourself. You just need to be okay that it will never change. Instead find out the reason why you do it, and focus on why it makes you happy instead of wishing you could change. She told me her biggest flaw is being too much of a giver. She will give everything. She will drop what she doing flat to help someone in need, but then finds no one is there for her in the same way. But instead of complaining about it, she understands that she is there because it makes her happy to be there, and that's it. It's about focusing on the areas of your life that make you happy, understanding why you do the things you do, and then end it on the happiness. Not to bring it forward and turn that happiness to bitterness by overthinking too much.

For such a short conversation, it is definitely one that will stick with me forever.

Let it Be

Today was a test. A pop quiz. It's almost been eight weeks since I've been gone and I've done a lot of soul searching. I've had countless conversations with people, I've said many prayers in many temples, I've pushed myself out of my comfort zone, I've done a lot of reading, and I've looked inside myself daily for answers to questions I didn't know I had.

There are so many people that I meet that touch me in amazing and unexpected ways. The man I met a few days ago that just celebrated his 50th birthday and 10-year wedding anniversary, that made me feel that full body smile as I thought he could be a version of my future husband 10-years from now. The many other couples that I have mentioned in various capacities that remind me daily about the love I had and strive for again. I love just watching them and reminding myself of real, true love. There are individuals I talk to and tell my story to and it's always so interesting to hear people's perspectives on five-minutes of dialogue. How does my story really sound to an outsider hearing it for the very first time? Then there's the angel, Anjulie, I met last night. Her timing ended up being more incredibly appropriate than I would have ever imagined. It makes me believe in fate all the more.

I am more convinced that my entire life has created this accumulation of events to now put me in this exact moment this year, and how I choose to live after my trip is done will be the result of what I take out of it.

I did a lot of reflecting on what Anjulie and I talked about last night. Travel will not change who we are, but it could allow us to be more accepting of ourselves. There are some things I do feel differently about. I do feel like I am a much calmer person than I was before. I feel like when I start to feel overwhelmed or anxious I am more capable of pulling myself back and instead just focus on what is in front of me. Expressing gratitude for what I have. Then the anxiety starts to subside.

There is another part of me that some people would consider a negative, and it was something that I tried in the past to curb, I am an emotional person. I wear my heart on my sleeve. I can be brought to tears by a commercial. My heart will ache for someone in need, and I feel it is my responsibility to do what I can to help. Today I decided to accept it and embrace this part of me. It is who I am. Instead of trying to curb the emotions I am learning to recognize them for what they are then choose to feed them or let them pass. I don't want to curb the tears that fall when I am touched by the love in a commercial. I do however want to be more aware of anxiety and sadness. I want to reflect on it. Understand what I really am anxious about. Is it something that I can change right now, and if not I have to let it be. Move on. Focus on what's right now. What can I be grateful for instead? I don't want to walk around with rose-coloured glasses, but I do want to have my days unaffected by a single anxious thought that spins me out.

I decided to skip Hoi An and go right to the beach community of Nha Trang. I caught an afternoon flight and arrived just in time to see the sun bathers start turning in for the late afternoon. I checked into my hotel and logged onto the internet briefly. I don't even know what I want to say about what I saw on my Facebook news feed. Something neither expected, nor completely unexpected. Part of me felt heartbroken and another part felt empty. My dreams prepared me for the moment. I stared at the photos. They were pictures of my unfinished love story and a blonde woman. She was sitting on his lap. He was looking into her eyes. Every caption was one of how much in love they are. I made commentary in my head what he was really thinking, hoping that it wasn't what it seemed. I looked at him and it looked like he was only looking at me, the thoughts in his head saying, "I'm trying".

I closed my iPad. I sang the song "Que Sera Sera". Recognized I was feeling anxiety and I could let it spin me out right there, or I could go for a walk. It was still a beautiful day.

I walked along the beachfront and made a small plan for tomorrow. I need to buy a proper beach towel, or a sarong to lie on the beach tomorrow. I also need to buy some extra sunscreen because I'm close to out. I've learned one other thing about myself: never drink if I am on the edge of negative emotions. I walked to a café and ordered an iced coffee.

As I walked back to my hotel I felt dizzy and a stabbing pain in my heart. It felt like guilt. It felt like him. I closed my eyes and concentrated on the pain, saying in my head, it's alright. I concentrated on telling him that I still love him and letting him know that it will all be okay. "You need to do, what you need to", I said to him in my mind.

Whatever will be, will be.

Goodbye, Calgary

Nha Trang, Vietnam
May 20

I had a terrible sleep. I woke up crying. I called my mom.

If she can push her emotions out of the way, this is where I get it from, she can sometimes give solid advice. I told her I didn't know what I was doing. My head and my heart weren't aligned. I know I need to release my ex, he has obviously moved on, but my heart still felt like it was calling out to him. During the day, when I focused on the moment I was okay, but my dreams were having their own agenda. I cried to her saying, "I just keep dreaming about him. Why won't it stop"?

She told me to draw out my perfect future. It was good advice. I had been so focused on my love story and the short term of maybe/maybe not that I lost focus that there are other parts of my life that I want. What do I want in my career? Where do I want to live? And if I'm not open to enough possibilities of my love life in the short term, at least what does it look like 5 or 10 years in the future?

I am so fortunate. How many other people can truly say they had the chance to reconstruct their entire life, if they wanted to? Maybe all my choices will be the exact same as what I had before, but now I will know that they were deliberate decisions, not a product of circumstance.

One of my Facebook friends, who studies astrology, sent me a message letting me know that I am close to the end of my Saturn in retrograde time, which meant between the years of 28-32 I was going to experience life altering changes. These changes could be very positive if I am open or I would have 10 years of mediocrity if I fought them.

I believe in this stuff. Although I didn't know what areas of my life were parts of my growth and which parts would hinder it. He told me in my meditations to focus on the phrase "maximum clearing for maximum pleasure please".

I wasn't expecting an answer so soon. It told me Calgary was no longer my city. It was time to move. I kind of already knew this. I really fell in love with Australia. I felt I was the most authentic version of myself there. But if not Calgary, I could stay in Canada and live in Kelowna. I am really enjoying the loose way of life. Calgary was a great city for me at the time, but I now realize the areas that appealed to me at one point now make me exhausted. It's no longer the youthful, energetic city I was drawn to. I find it tiring and constantly moving. I used to love that I could make lots of money and live a fabulous life, but now I feel like I'm keeping up with the Joneses and always in competition. It is a constant race to make more, get more, and show off more.

I'm happy my meditation brought such a dramatic change unrelated to my constant love story focus. I get a chance to absorb this change, mourn the loss of my home city and focus my brain on the positivity that will come.

I spent the day in Nha Trang lying on the beach, walking the boardwalk and sitting by a hotel pool with wait staff. I relaxed my overly busy head by tanning, reading, napping and doing purely nothing. Then I treated myself out to dinner at an overpriced restaurant on the beach and enjoyed the sound of the ocean waves.

Remembering to Have Fun

Nha Trang, Vietnam
May 21

I had been putting a lot of pressure on myself that I should feel and come back different, or have some life-changing epiphany while I am out here. There have been a lot of eye-opening moments where I realized changes I will make in my life but I've placed such a focus on self-reflection that I forgot about just having fun.

Last night, after probably too many glasses of wine, I walked past a tourist agency and asked about a bus ride to Dalat then to Ho Chi Minh City, former Saigon. As I booked the bus ride I saw some pictures on the wall of the various tours they have around Nha Trang. One of them was a day-long boat tour of four different islands nearby. It sounded lovely, so I signed up.

The boat had tons of young tourists all there to just have a good time. The male staff on the boat dressed up in grass skirts and coconut bras and entertained us with their "lady-boy" band as they sang a selection of songs from all the home countries of the people on board. Then after lunch we all jumped from the boat into the water and drank some unknown alcohol from 2L soda bottles. We continued to dance and sing and I felt freer than I have in a while. When we made it to our last island I grabbed a beach chair and felt joy for the moment as I stared out at the ocean.

Since deciding on the trip I had been receiving a lot of feedback from family and friends that I need to be open to the possibility that there might be someone else in the world for me. The whole world. Imagine that. I'm travelling everywhere and have unlimited options. There would have to be someone else, right? I really thought about it.

Everyone is well intentioned, and I know all the advice, especially in the realm of relationships, is coming from a place of love. But as I sat there and looked out at the stunning, turquoise sea I thought what all my options are, if I was open to all of them.

My mind became clear and it was my love. It was my unfinished love story. My heart belongs to him. The possibility of anything else made me sad. He makes me excited. He makes me everything. He is the glue that sticks me together.

I wrote him an unsent letter saying all of that. I hoped he really hadn't given up on us. I hoped he still did see a glimmer of love and life as us. If not, I knew I needed to keep doing what makes me happiest, and that continued to be him. It's what makes my heart sing. I no longer wanted to fight or pretend that there were other options. I released my heart to him. It was his. It was my gift to him. I still love him. I will still wait.

That decision may have to change at some point, if it has to, but for now, and the foreseeable future, that's where my happiness lies.

On the day I stopped searching for answers and allowed myself to have a good time, my bliss came. I need to find more of the balance between fun and focus and I think within that middle ground more of my happiness will be.

Premium Service in Dalat

Da Lat, Vietnam
May 22

When I booked my Ho Chi Minh bus ticket I also booked a premium private ride and guided tour into Dalat.

Dalat is a "mini-Paris", French inspired town located at the top of the mountains. The surrounding area is ideal for growing some of the tastiest fruits and producing high quality flowers. I couldn't stop staring out the window of the car as we drove past lush green hills and impressive waterfalls. But as I found myself lost in thought I started daydreaming about meeting my unfinished love story in Athens. I imagined myself so happy I was crying. I could feel my heart ready to explode from my chest. Please, universe, make it happen.

When we arrived in Dalat we had a late breakfast of Pho. Noodles and soup is a common breakfast dish among the Vietnamese. I was excited to spend the day with a couple of locals. My guide taught me the proper way to eat Pho, which included ripping the leaves into the soup, and creating a sauce base to dip the meat into after pulling it out of the soup.

Our first official stop was to a park to see one of the waterfalls. I took an elephant ride, but more impressively I rode an ostrich. The ostrich was restricted to only walking around in his pen. There were two men that stood in the gated area with me because when the ostrich sees his opportunity to bolt he'll take it.

We visited a second waterfall, which was much nicer than the first. It was a low powerful one that reminded me a lot of my vacation with my unfinished love story to Jamaica's Dunn's River falls. This waterfall was far too powerful to walk through, but the memory of Jamaica, us dancing to reggae all night, having romantic dinners on the beach, still brought a smile to my face.

Our third stop was to the Buddhist Pagoda. My guide is Buddhist so I asked her a lot of questions about it and the culture in Vietnam.

It had been ten days since I heard anything from my unfinished love story. As night time came on, despite my exhaustion, I couldn't sleep. I was missing him far too much. I cried. I didn't know the last time I cried. I was still feeling like I dreamed of him, but I couldn't remember any of the dreams. I prayed to the universe that he contacts me soon. I didn't know how much longer I could hold on without hearing from him.

Defining Happiness

Da Lat, Vietnam
May 23

I have meditated every morning for about the last two weeks, and find that my answers are become clearer.

In my recent meditations I have asked what really makes me happy. Unfortunately there is no straight answer to that, so I asked about individual components of my life. I accept that my home city for the last eight years is no longer the right city for me. I have outgrown it. I am no longer an authentic version of myself there.

I asked about my job and career, and the answers still aren't quite clear, but I feel my role will also depend on where I live. Maybe I will take the leftover money from my house and use it as seed money for a business. Or maybe after all of this is completed I will have enough connections that the right role will appear to me through the right conversation.

I asked about time off. I really enjoy the travel that I am doing now. I love absorbing myself in another culture. I was on a half day tour and one of our stops was to a lake. I saw people roasting fish on a fire. I really love camping. I love the simplicity of it. I love the smell of burning wood and having no agenda. I love watching my dog run through the forest and swim in the lake. I like all-inclusives, but they have a time and a place. I love road trips. I loved my vacation last year through the Okanagan wine country.

That was the vacation that my unfinished love story and I decided we were going to move in together. We spent our days either sampling wines at the many vineyards, or boating on the lake, or just relaxing. It was one of the simplest and most romantic vacations I have ever been on in my life. We held hands, laughed, took so many pictures and came back more in love than either of us had ever been in our lives.

I was reluctant to ask about love and relationships in my meditation, but when I did I determined I am a creature attracted to loving and being loved. I thought if I kept asking in my meditations my answer would somehow change. When I ask if I am still happy giving him my heart, the answer always has been, and continues to be, yes.

I don't pretend that he and I are in a relationship right now, when we actually aren't. I don't pretend that I am receiving reciprocated love. I know what is in front of me. It might look like denial to some people, but it truly isn't. When I feel my heart is dedicated to him, I feel full of love, and I am a happier person. I smile more. I feel more open and willing to chat with people. I feel like I have more love to give and I start seeing it more and more around me.

I know my heart and my head belong to someone who I haven't heard from in a couple of weeks, who's last message to me said he doesn't see a future with me, and has not told me he loves me in months. I know all of this. But the feeling in my heart and the hope that he may come back isn't hurting anyone.

The best thing about happiness is I'm allowed to change my mind. I am allowed to say that because today it makes me happy, doesn't mean it will always make me happy. I am allowed to say that I no longer want my home city to be the city I call home. I'm allowed to say dedicating my heart to him no longer makes me happy. And if, or when, that point comes, I will change my mind and decide I will be happier having it just for myself and I will find happiness being alone. Happiness is a moving target and I know it's important to look at it daily. Perhaps if I would have looked at my previous situation as missing him all the time to feeling excited when I do get to see him again, I would still be there. More lessons learned. But I still wouldn't give up this trip for the world.

Realizing my Wrongs

Ho Chi Minh City, Vietnam
May 24

I meditated again this morning, for what I think may have been my longest session yet. In addition to my typical rituals for focused breathing, expressing gratitude, and contemplating change, I added expressing love. There are four tiers of love that I read about: loving kindness, compassion, empathetic joy and equanimity. The goal is to imagine each feeling first inside myself, express it to someone I know and care about, then to someone neutral, then finally to someone that I do not like. Once I complete one tier I go back again and repeat for the other tiers. By equanimity it should feel like a constant glowing aura of love for me and all the people I think about. It truly is a nice way to start off the day.

I was taking a 7-hour bus ride to Ho Chi Minh City. The 1PM bus would give me time to do some morning sightseeing in Dalat but as I sat in bed I decided this was exactly where I wanted to be. I didn't want to see anything or go anywhere. I wanted to stay in bed, watch TV, which is limited to the Disney Channel and Cartoon Network for English programming, and just do nothing.

Despite this morning's meditation I was still having a lot of self-doubt about my future. My head was painting the picture that maybe I never will get married, maybe I never will have my own kids, maybe all I'll be is the crazy aunt that doesn't work, travels, and when she comes home she lives with her parents.

Many women say they admire the way I deal with a break up. I decide it's not working, I give my chances, and then I move on. But I no longer want to be admired for handling breakups; I want to be admired for handling makeups and for having a significant long-term relationship. I want to be the woman that people admire for being with the same man until the day one of us dies, not the woman that can pack it all in and never feel like I've lost a beat in my independence.

As I rode to Ho Chi Minh I contemplated life again, read my books, and that's when it hit me. During the whole breakup I never looked at any of it from his side. I thought I was, but it was always still from my point of view. I realized I did him wrong. Seriously wrong. To the point where I now understand why he would say he does not see a future with me. I had two realizations: pre-breakup and breakup.

When I was at my most frustrated in the relationship I was very vocal about expressing it. I did a good job of providing suggestions on possible changes, and I couldn't understand why nothing seemed to resonate. What I didn't do was outline the potential consequences. He probably knew I was frustrated, but I never made him aware that I was frustrated enough to end us. It makes my heart break thinking about it. Giving him the benefit of the doubt, he may have been more willing to work with me on making a change had he known more about how I was feeling. How truly frustrated I was. That I was feeling I was being left with no other options. He never knew I was close to breaking up leading up to it. Then I hit my breaking point and I ended us. He never saw it coming. For that I am truly, truly sorry. I feel like an absolutely terrible person for what I did. This whole trip is now worth that lesson alone.

I wronged him again when I actually broke up with him. Although, yes, in name and title, the house and dog were mine, in one sentence I took everything away from him. The moment the words "I need a break from our situation" came out of my mouth, I took away his girlfriend, his house, his dog, and everything he probably used to define his "home". I took it all. In his head I probably went from someone he trusted and loved to a horrible human being that crushed every one of his hopes and dreams. And then I was the one who was surprised when he didn't try to fight with me to save us. More than likely he probably didn't know someone that could say that she loves him could have the capacity to do something so dramatic and insensitive. I had no idea that's what I did. And for that I am unbelievably sorry.

What was supposed to be a simple bus ride to Saigon has turned into the ultimate life lesson in relationships for me. I would love to be able to send him a message apologizing for all of this, but my heart tells me it's still not time to contact him. Maybe it's too late. Or maybe he never wants to hear from me again. However I hope one day he finds it in himself to forgive me for what I did, and if he never does, I completely understand. I hope that I can take these new lessons and make myself the person that becomes the go-to for advice on holding onto a relationship, not the person used as an example for breakups. I never want to be the breakup example again.

He continues to be my greatest love and in the same breath my greatest heartbreak. I have never in my life felt so much love and so much pain for someone.

I also wish I would have been enough.

Becoming Miss Saigon

Ho Chi Minh City, Vietnam
May 25

I hit a turning point this morning. During my morning meditation I was told it was time. I tried to fight it, but then asked again. It was time to start releasing. Yesterday's epiphany was a significant lesson, and after all my reflections and analysis I have learned my lessons, and understand where my communication and actions will change in the future. But now it is time to move forward. I opened the gate and am allowing the release to begin. It won't be sudden, but it's a start.

It was so tough to come to that conclusion. I needed to talk to my mom. She gave me some solid words of encouragement. She told me that whether we end up together or not, maybe our paths had to diverge for a while. Maybe our timing wasn't right now. I won't know if it's truly right until I figure out everything else I want in my life first, and then try to put a relationship back in. But it won't be right until after I truly know who I am, what I want, and can say without hesitation that I love myself first.

My mood slowly started to get better as the day went on. I started wandering in a general direction towards a Buddhist Pagoda that I was hoping to find. If Hong Kong is the Asian London, Ho Chi Minh is the Asian Paris. It is unbelievably romantic, many buildings and streets give me the feeling of a hotter, less wealthy Paris. But they do a really good job with what they have. It is international, it is busy, the shopping is AMAZING, and there is so much to see and do.

I walked around for the day shopping and sightseeing. Shortly after lunch the skies opened up and the rain started to come down in sheets. My head was a mix between Bob Dylan's "Shelter from the Storm" and Forrest Gump talking about how the rain started in Vietnam and didn't stop. Pretty close.

The sun came out again as quickly as the rain started. I continued enjoying the city when I decided that I had enough of the bras that I have been wearing since the beginning of the trip. It was time for something new. I was ready for a proper strapless bra, and maybe something sexy. One of the things I miss most is my far too overpriced underwear drawer. When everything is completely stripped away I start to realize the things that make me feel more like me. I've reverted back to dresses and now sexy underwear.

The Vietnamese are very touchy people. I've learned this when women I don't even know want to hold my hand or my arm and guide me to a store or spa. I've realized this when I received more chest action than a typical western massage. Now I've learned this trying on bras.

I selected a couple of different bras and asked to try them on. All the sizing is in metric, and the only cup sizes they have are A and B, with an extra 2 cup sizes of padding built into every bra. There was no way I was going to find my standard 32C. I was led to an area of the wall where a curtain was pulled around a semi-circle, for ultimate privacy. The dress I was wearing couldn't have just the top pulled down, so the whole thing came off. Then in comes the saleswoman. She puts my bra on the same way a hairdresser would put on a robe. She turns me around, pulls the straps over my arms, buckles it in the back and spins me around. I had no time to even think about the invasion of privacy I just incurred. But it doesn't matter because once I am facing her she grabs a handful at a time, adjusts my boobs properly in the bra and then turned me around to the mirror for me to take a look at my new bustier, fully-padded chest. I bought two new bras and matching underwear.

Guns and Genocide

Phnom Penh, Cambodia
May 27

I had a great conversation with the taxi driver that picked me up from the airport and took me to my hotel yesterday. His name is Visal; he is 35, single and looking for the same things in life that the rest of us are. To find love, have a family, make a great earning, travel, wish the environment was better, and have a great life overall. We chatted about a lot of things on that short cab ride, so I thought I would ask him if he was available for hire the next day.

I had a list of things that I wanted to see, but was open to suggestions. We stopped at the Royal Palace then Visal asked me if I would be interested in shooting a gun. As a part of my open for anything attitude, I said yes. We drove to the military base and I decided to test my skills with two guns: an M16 and an AK47. I more than likely overpaid but I was okay with that. I told Visal that as long as it was cheaper than I would pay back home, I felt it was fair. I believe tourists should pay more than locals, as long as they aren't getting gouged. Tourism is around to help spur the economy and make the locals better off.

The afternoon was the heavy portion of the tour. We started out by going to the Killing Fields. In 1975 a political leader Pol Pot took over the government and started doing a "cleanse" the same way of Hitler during the Holocaust. Until 1979 his army killed over 2million citizens, including women, children and infants. He believed to "rid the grass you have to remove the root". The killing fields were the last point for the prisoners. Since bullets were expensive many of them were killed using the farm tools that the survivors would use the following days to work and harvest the fields.

As I walked through the place my heart couldn't help but feel heavy. Especially when coming across the "Killing Tree", which was used to beat and kill children and babies while their mothers watched. It made me want to cry.

We left the Killing Fields for the prison S-21. Since Pol Pot did not believe in education the former school was turned into a torture chamber, confessional and prison for his so called "traitors". Each victim room has a picture of the deceased the day they were found, along with the bed and shackles left exactly as they were.

I asked Visal if they teach this history in schools or if it something not talked about. He told me that they teach it, and they are starting to teach it to younger and younger students in hopes the education will prevent it from happening again in the future.

Visal told me his uncle was one of victims. His uncle was an accountant. He landed in Phnom Penh and within a week he was imprisoned and never heard from again.

I guess not all travel is sexy travel. But that's the reason I do it. I want to learn more about the world than I could ever imagine.

Ghosts of Relationships Past

After touring yesterday I sat down at the hostel and started writing my blog. I was invited to join an ex-pat Australian and the owner of the hostel for a drink. Within a short period of time I was surrounded by seven men, all from different countries. A couple of them said they liked me, I told them I was flattered, but I'm meeting my husband in a couple of days. Then I decided I had too many beers and went upstairs for an early bed time.

I am not interested in any flings or one-night encounters. I want a relationship. I want someone to hold me and tell me they love me. I am not interested in superficial connections. Plus I don't feel my heart is ready for new love yet. Which is funny, because I pray for love daily, and yet not willing to completely open myself up. The garage door is open to allow the current vehicle parked in the space to leave, but until it does I don't feel like I have any space to squeeze more in.

I woke up at my standard 5AM time, tried some focused meditations, but my mind was happy wandering into thoughtlessness. I couldn't even focus on the questions I wanted to ask. It kept drifting to nothingness, which foreshadowing is probably because it knew it was going to be running through overdrive today.

I wanted to go to Kratie today. It is known for having freshwater river dolphins. Yes, girls and dolphins.

I logged onto my Facebook quickly in the morning to send my mom a message that I was heading out and wouldn't be able to call her, that's when I saw a message from my unfinished love story. I wish it was more than what it was. I wanted it to be something heartwarming, maybe he forgave me, maybe he's sorry too, maybe he's ready to commit his life to me, maybe he's finally ready to say yes to all the suggestions. I wanted it to say he is determined to spend every day with me. Unfortunately, no. It felt like a nice note from someone working hard to distance himself from me.

Him: Had a disturbing dream this morning and know that it was something you would never have done to me but it was still heartbreaking. I would have rather it been something from our past, that would have been a lot better. I am glad to see that you are having fun. Be safe. And take care. Please don't take this message the wrong way. I wish all the best for you ex lover.

I was so overwhelmed to receive something from him that I had to respond right away. I wrote my response quickly, reread it to make sure it didn't sound too eager or overly emotional, and then sent it off.

Me: I'm so sorry to hear that. I would love to know more about it, if you ever wanted to share.
    I am having fun. It has been a great trip so far. I'm learning so much about the world and myself.
    I will always try to be safe. That's my first concern.
    Don't worry. I won't take this message the wrong way. I still care for you deeply. I know that you are trying to move on. I see that you are in a new relationship, and I hope she makes you incredibly happy. I had a dream about the two of you when I was in Halong Bay. I dreamed that she was falling in love with you and you felt indifferent towards her.

Sometimes I feel like maybe I could be completely over him, if it wasn't for my dreams. I keep dreaming about him. Always happy. Always in some future state. He visits me. I am overwhelmed with happiness that I am crying at the airport once I see him. We're sitting across a table in a restaurant and

133

I feel so much love for him. I'm pregnant with his baby. I see his family again and they tell me they are so happy to have me back. And every morning, *every morning*, I wake up with a little bit of hope that I then have to spend pulling myself back from, because I know he doesn't want the same things.

I broke his trust and that will never be repaired, and he does not want to come back to me. Yet sometimes I wonder why my dreams would lead me down this horrible path every single morning?

The tuk-tuk driver took me to Central Market to all the cab drivers standing around ready to make their long distance trips for some foreigners. Once we stopped I was surrounded by taxi drivers asking where I wanted to go.

"Kratie"

"$80", says one.

"Share?" I ask.

"No, one traveller only", says another when their glances all seemed to agree.

"Not $80, $60", I counter.

Two men each offer to do it for $60. I pick one, he grabs his car then we transfer my bag from the tuk-tuk to the car. A policeman standing around gets his cut from the driver before leaving the lot.

We start to drive and move from paved roads to unpaved and then what looks like a shortcut route along an even narrower road with trees lining the side. I immediately thought of the safety of the situation. My mind raced with thoughts that he could pull me over, take my stuff, and leave me on the side of the road. I thought I really should carry a knife. But realistically I wouldn't know how to use it, and if the situation was really bad I don't think I would get it out fast enough to be able to do any good. I kept telling myself that if he wanted anything it would be money.

I always carried three wallets, two with my own credit cards split up in them and a third dummy wallet with US$100, that I kept in an easy to reach pocket in my day bag. If something ever happened, I was mugged, or put in a worse situation I would throw the dummy wallet. If $100 was enough to save my life it was always worth carrying.

We arrived in Kratie safely, to the joy of my overactive brain. The driver asked me where I wanted to be dropped off and I told him anywhere. I didn't have a hotel booked yet. This is now a first for me. I have now shown up in a town and had to find a place to stay for that night.

I walked into a fairly decent looking homestay right on the river. I asked to see the room, and upon inspection I decided it was decent enough for a couple of nights.

I logged onto the internet when ghost #2 appeared. My third love. We bought a house together. We were together for three and a half years. My mom sent me a message telling me he is now engaged. I had to look. He dated the woman for about six months and they got engaged just before I left on my trip.

I laughed out loud and then my laughter turned to tears. I felt like my life was a joke. I just wanted one of these guys to decide on me. Pick me to be the one you want to spend the rest of your life with. I don't know if I should have but I sent him a note telling him I was really happy for him. A practice in my daily love exercise. Sending out empathetic joy.

I took a moment and really thought about it. I am happy for him. I would love to be with someone for six months and they know at that point that I am the one they want to spend the rest of their days with. They don't waste a moment more thinking about it. I'm not in another two-plus year relationship without commitment. I'm not with another "ring tease".

I felt so happy that he obviously found someone that gives him that full-body love. He found someone that he wants to share every day with. And really, I look back on our relationship and I am glad we didn't get married. We weren't the perfect match that I thought we were at the time. I knew that after meeting my unfinished love story. We had a love so powerful that I would be lucky to find someone that does that to me again.

I needed to change my mind up. I went for a walk and stopped at a place advertising Dolphin tours. As I chatted with the woman at the desk, and her 3 words of English, she kept saying "motorbike".

I responded "no, boat", and then used my arms to make a dolphin swimming motion.

"Motorbike", she responded.

I went back to the front of the building where I read the advertising poster and started to understand that "motorbike" meant I hire a driver to take me to the boat launch and then hire a boat driver.

I went back inside agreed to the motorbike, paid the fee then asked her what time do I come by tomorrow.

"Now, now", she says.

Well, I guess I'm going to see the dolphins now.

It was a long drive to the docks. I hired a boat for an hour, and as soon as we left the dock the dolphins started appearing. I could hear their blowholes as they surfaced. It was pretty cool.

The motorbike driver waited for my boat tour to finish. The entire ride back I couldn't stop thinking about both my unfinished love story's message and that the same day I found out my third love was engaged. I was angry. I kept trying to bring myself back to the present. "Anyone would trade places with you in a second", I told myself.

There was a new message from my unfinished love story when I got back to the hotel after dinner.

Him: There is no love for anyone at the moment and I don't think there will be for a while. I do wish some of my friends would leave me and my love life alone. Glad to hear you are doing well. Take care.

I didn't even know how to respond, so I didn't. Maybe some sleep will bring a brighter tomorrow.

Self Love

Kratie Cambodia
May 29

My dreams woke me up in the morning. At 1:30AM. He was in my head and I couldn't get back to sleep. I was still so angry with him. I needed to get it out. I wrote a letter to him that I was never going to send.

> Me: It was so nice to get an email from you yesterday. I felt so good that I was still in your thoughts. But here's the thing, as much as I miss our friendship, because I really do. I miss talking to you every day and sharing all my highs and lows with you. More than that I miss being loved by you. And the hopeless romantic in me is still hoping and praying and wishing that you will come back to me. I have spent the last two months reflecting on what I could have done differently, where I wronged you, and how I could be better for you. I'm hoping that you will reflect and see your wrongs too. I'm hoping you decide on me. That you want me to be the wife and the future mother of your children. That you decide money and work aren't the be-all-end-all that you thought it was and that you would rather wake up and go to sleep with me every morning and night the same way I have prayed for even before we broke up.
>
> But here it is. I still love you. My heart is still dedicated to you. I still go to sleep at night and dream of this future together that will never be. And I really do love getting notes from you. I do. But it kills me when it's not for the reasons I dream about. And as long as I still have love and hope for you I am not making myself available for love from someone who

could love me back. I want to find someone that will chose me, someone that will decide that time with me is the most important thing in the world and we spend every day and night together. And he decides he wants to spend the rest of his life with me and he doesn't waste another day making that decision. He picks me.

Maybe one day I will wake up and be lucky, like you, and no longer see a future with you. And when that day comes I will let you know, and we can try for our friendship again. But right now as much as it hurts to never hear from you, and it hurts a lot, it hurts so much, it hurts even more to get lovely notes from you that solidify that you will never be with me again.

If that ever changes, let me know. If you decide you do love me back and there is a possibility of a future with me, you can contact me then. Otherwise I'll let you know the day that you are no longer in my hopes and dreams. We can have casual chit-chat then.

The internet was down in the hotel and after tossing and turning for a couple of hours I thought maybe a walk along the river would help. I made my way down the stairs and the front desk person was fast asleep directly in front of the hotel entrance on a mattress that he had pulled out from somewhere. I didn't want to disturb him by walking past.

I walked inside the hotel trying to find any Wi-Fi signal, but nothing was coming through. I then saw one of the routers along the wall, unplugged it and plugged it back in. That did the trick. I then called my sister and my mom.

I reached out to a lot of friends yesterday. I was suffering from feelings of rejection. I couldn't understand how I could have been in all these long-term relationships and still no one has picked me. I was the weak kid sitting on the sidelines waiting to be on someone's team, and watching everyone go ahead of me. Some people were getting their second chance and I was still waiting for my first.

A lot of people gave me their opinion, but if it wasn't too kind, it was too hurtful: "It's not you, it's them", "someone will pick you", "it just wasn't your time yet", then "you've never really been available", "you sell yourself short", "you're always looking for the wrong things". None of it made me feel any better.

The entire night passed and by 5AM I laid in bed trying to shake the thoughts from my head. That's when I thought of one of my favourite movies, (500) Days of Summer. In it the female ends up engaged to someone other than the main character. He couldn't understand why she wouldn't want a relationship with him and then be engaged so soon to someone else. She tells him that with her fiancé she just knew "what I was never sure of with you". That was me. That's why I haven't been picked yet. There is something still about me that my previous relationships are still unsure of with me. And it's probably the same thing I am unsure of with myself.

Maya Angelou said, "I do not trust people who do not love themselves and yet tell me 'I love you'. There is an African saying which is: Be careful when a naked person offers you a shirt". I can't be asking for love when I do not love myself completely. That was the main reason I was coming on this trip, and I forgot that.

I have a lot of things I love about myself. However I hold a certain facade of confidence, trustworthiness and authenticity. These are traits that I wanted so badly when I was younger and I believed in faking it until I made it. I had this alternative "Business Kim" persona. But over time "Business Kim" never melded into "Actual Kim" and the disparity grew as opposed to coming together. I never converted my "faking it" to the real me. I know this because of the comment my unfinished love story made about our first date. He said it felt like a business interview. He was just so glad he passed to round two.

I handle all my personal stressful situations like a business meeting because it was easier to remove the human aspect than to look deep inside myself for the answers. Then those traits that I so desperately wanted to have never did become pure in the tough times of the relationship. I never exposed the core of my being to someone probably because I didn't know what my core was myself.

I lost the focus of my personal journey and seeking self-love. I reverted back to my unfinished love story because in the past I always sought a relationship to finish my puzzle. For a while I could feel complete, but then they all ended in the same way. I am the common denominator.

I need to complete me first, love me first, and then love will pour in. Love is attracted to love. If I love myself, whatever love is actually looking for me will find me.

I thought about what self-love would mean to me, and I put together a list: confident, authentic, secure, happy, self-priority, understand my self-worth, and acceptance.

I asked myself what my favourite part of a relationship is. It was those moments when I am with the person and I think I never want this moment to end. That became my mantra for today.

I wasn't in a hurry to leave Kratie for Siem Reap, so I thought I would just spend a chill day here and decided to rent a motorbike. I've never driven one before, but how hard could it be?

I was given a two minute crash course, and then I was off to explore the villages surrounding Kratie. I took off in the direction towards the dolphins and decided to keep on going. Until I ran out of gas. The speedometer wasn't working, so I assumed the fuel tank gauge wasn't either. Nope, the bike actually was empty. I pulled over to a small store and in motioning actions I explained that I was out of gas. How far of a walk was it to the nearest petrol station? About 5 minutes. I was able to get the bike started and moved about 50m at a time, until it was fully out after the fifth time, and thankfully, only pushing distance to the petrol station. The gas came out of a hand cranked funnel system, and the price for about 1/4 tank was around US$2.50. I gave the mother and son $5, took a bottle of water and told them they could keep the rest. They were overjoyed.

At various times throughout my ride my mind kept wandering to the past or playing out multiple future outcomes, and I kept bringing myself back by repeating my mantra "I am so lucky to be here. I hope this moment never ends". It worked. I started really enjoying the day, and I was feeling love for myself.

Here's to hoping that my self love will start to come. Then when I am truly ready the love I am meant to have in my life will find me. I never want these days to end.

Get In The Van

Siem Reap, Cambodia
May 30

It's Friday night. I'm sitting at a pub on Pub Street called Molly Malone's drinking a beer and eating lasagna. I was drawn here because this pub has the same name as one of my favourite pubs in Calgary. I can hear a local band nearby playing some excellent Black Keys. This might be a pretty good night. For an hour or two I am back home.

The couple I rented the motorbike from yesterday helped me organize a share taxi to Siem Reap. I paid double the price to guarantee me the front seat, closest to the air conditioning, with no one sitting on my lap.

Once I sat down in the taxi, I thought "this isn't too bad". I was made to believe that it would be packed with people. There was enough space for everyone, plus a little extra, that is until we started doing the milk run. I would love to have a better understanding how the taxi is actually booked. I don't know if it is that someone knows someone and "I'll give you the taxi guys number", or if there is more formality than that. As we left Kratie there was a man sitting behind me yelling at the driver, and then the driver would stop at these random places, honk the horn and someone would come running out of a building, give him some cash and we would be off again. There were a couple of times where we would actually pull over the side of the road, chat with the person standing there and in one case we just picked them up too. By the end of it, it really was people sitting on top of people. A van made to fit ten passengers had fifteen, including a young couple, a monk, a woman, her mother and a baby, another woman with a young son (both sitting on strangers laps), and a few single men and women. Beside me, a child's plastic chair was set up for another person to sit between me and the driver.

Inside the van there was an aftermarket DVD player installed in the front playing a mix between a Cambodian comedy show and local dance music. I tried to read my book but the beat of the music was just too good not to enjoy.

As promised when I arrived at Siem Reap I had a tuk-tuk driver waiting for me. My driver, John, spoke excellent English and we negotiated a price for the entire weekend. Our first stop was to Angkor Wat for sunset. I walked around the grounds with a self-proclaimed tour guide taking in the beauty and the history of the place. It took my breath away.

Being Fully Immersed

Siem Reap, Cambodia
May 31

After dinner last night I went walking towards the night market. I wanted to pick up a jacket or some type of outer cover for my shoulders. Many of the temples ask that shoulders are covered, and almost all my dresses don't have sleeves. As I made my way to the market I was approached by a small child, no older than 10, carrying a baby. He was barefoot and said that he didn't want money; he wanted milk for the baby. The baby was hungry. I wanted to cry right there. I offered just to pay for the milk and he could go and buy it, but he insisted that he couldn't buy it; he needed someone to buy it for him. That should have been my first clue. He grabbed my hand and pulled me into a store. I started getting nervous about the situation, so I stayed at the front of the store and started looking at the milk. The child then pulled my hand and said, the baby actually needed formula, and put a $25 tin in my hands. I told him that was too much, but my heart was breaking for the situation so I said I would buy it. The child then told me I had to buy two. The baby would cry if he didn't get two. I said the baby wouldn't know the difference. One was plenty. Then the child said to just give him $20 and he would find another tourist to buy the rest. My gut confirmed it. I was being suckered. I now wasn't going to buy anything, and went to leave. The child grabbed my arm, "you promised. You buy, you buy". I told him not to touch me. I tried to bypass in the other direction. I am so thankful I wear my bag in the front of my body, but it didn't stop him from grabbing the back of my dress and pulling me back. I turned around quickly and raised my voice, "don't touch me. I am done. I am not buying anything". I went to walk out of the store. The child made a desperate last attempt to get my attention and pinched my ass. I could have slapped the kid! I turned around quickly and yelled "Don't you dare touch me again"! That sent the kid running off in the other direction to find his next victim.

I was so worked up that I headed directly back to the hotel. I double checked my bag to make sure I wasn't somehow pick-pocketed. Luckily nothing had been taken. I decided this would be a great time to practice a quiet nighttime meditation to calm my brain before going to bed. I slept the entire night without a single dream waking me up in the middle of the night. It was absolute bliss.

In the morning my tuk-tuk driver was taking me to Angkor Thom and the surrounding temples. I noticed many people speaking with guides at Angkor Thom and I wanted one too. I asked around and was told to talk to the police officer to see if one was available, despite several guides sitting around for no reason. The police officer placed a phone call and told me to wait. I had use the toilet at this point and the officer offered to take me on his motorbike, side-saddle; I was wearing a dress after all.

We returned to Angkor Thom to his waiting friend. I tipped the officer then the guide and I headed off to explore and learn. I felt like a sponge gaining information. I was so happy to have hired him. If I was going to do something I may as well jump in with both feet as opposed to testing the waters. I would hate to say that I visited Angkor Wat and Angkor Thom and not understood what I actually saw and experienced.

After lunch we headed to the temple that was the scene for Tomb Raider. I never saw the movie and had no idea what I was looking at. I immediately felt the difference between walking through a temple with a guide and without one.

In the evening my driver took me to the floating market. The drive out there was fairly standard until I started to take real notice of the scenery. We weren't even ten minutes outside of the city when the impoverished conditions started breaking my heart. It looked the same as the drive from Kratie. Maybe it was seeing it again, or maybe it was because it was directly outside of Siem Reap, but I couldn't handle it anymore. There was piled up garbage on the side of the road, some of the houses had walls made out of tarp, they were all one or two room shacks, and it just kept repeating. And for the first time since I've been on this trip I cried for reasons other than myself. I couldn't help it. I couldn't understand how this could still exist in the world. I've seen it on TV, but to see it in person was heart-breaking.

When we arrived at the floating marketing I took a moment to have a full on cry. I pulled myself together quickly. These people live like this day after day; the last thing they need is to see a tourist crying about their situation.

I was given my own boat with an excellent English speaker, Visa, and his two boat mates. Visa taught me about his village of 3,000 people. He told me he thinks he is 27 but doesn't know for sure because the government didn't allow people in the floating village to gain birth certificates. This prevents him from getting an ID and therefore being able to get a real job outside of the village.

He was so jaded about life. He couldn't go to school because his family needed him to work. Although he speaks English excellently, and with a slight Australian accent, he said he learned all of it from watching TV and tourists, but he's completely illiterate. His father died a few years ago from a land mine while working in the fields. When he doesn't work he volunteers at the orphanage or the community food store.

Many of the orphans are the result of families that died from the typhoon three years ago, or given up by their families. However, many families would rather drop their child off in the middle of Siem Reap to prevent him or her from discovering their family in the future. Orphans stay at the orphanage until 15, at which point they are just released, and hopefully they can find a job and a home. At this point I cried again. I couldn't imagine being 15 with no family or support and being told "good luck" as I was kicked out the door. This is the reason many girls are victims of human trafficking.

I wanted to help, so they took me to the floating community food store. I bought two sacks of rice: one for the orphanage and one for the school. We dropped them off at each location. Each building was incredibly basic, with the orphanage sharing a room for schooling and sleeping. The orphanage separates the girls from their studies to teach them textiles so that they could possibly work in a clothing factory. All the cooking, washing and drinking water is lake water.

Visa told me his biggest frustration was the groups of tourists that come by, taking photos, saying how "beautiful" the village is and then leave without helping out any of the people that live there.

We picked up a few beers from the floating market and set our boat out to the middle of the lake. We enjoy our drinks while we watch the sunset. As the night ended, and the conversation turned somber and philosophical, Visa asked me what I dream for most. I said probably the same as everyone. I want love, I want a purpose in my life, and I want to feel like I am contributing to something bigger than myself. I asked him what he dreams for. He wished for a day where no one is hungry, everyone is clothed and sheltered and everyone is educated. It was Maslow's hierarchy of needs. My desire for love puts me in the mid to top levels and Visa was still wishing for the basics.

I am lucky, incredibly lucky, with my life. I will never in my lifetime have to hope that today the roof over my head and the clothing on my back will still be there in the morning. I will never have to worry that I won't have any food on the table. I will never have to wish that my children will have access to medicine and education. Since being on this trip I thought that the world is a truly amazing place, and now I mean that in both the most positive and negative connotations of the word.

A Little Piece of Home

Bangkok, Thailand
June 2

Last night my driver, John, took me to one of the oddest experiences. We headed to one of the few English karaoke bars. As we walked in there were about 30 girls sitting in the lobby. We were given a room; two women were brought in to manage the machine. We were then brought the 30 girls. Each girl had a numbered pin and we were allowed to choose one to be a "hostess" to ensure our drinks were always full while we sang.

It was rough getting out of bed for sunrise at Angkor Wat. We made it to the temple while the sun wasn't up yet but the sky was starting to glow. We arrived too late for the prime reflecting pool spot, but I knew where the next best spot was to see all five towers at once. I laid out my sarong as a mat, sat and waited for the sun to rise. I missed my morning meditation, and thought what better place than the grounds of Angkor Wat before the sunrise to ensure I didn't miss a day in my practice. I closed my eyes and meditated. My head was still cloudy from the drinks the night before, but my mind felt a wave of peace. I sat and felt the sky start to grow brighter on the other side of my closed eyes.

When the morning had passed, John dropped me off at the airport. Next stop, Bangkok. The flight was only an hour. I passed through customs, collected my bag and waited for my former Calgary friend to arrive and pick up. Ange moved to Bangkok in January and we were excited to see each other. I spotted her from across 4 lanes of traffic. I waved frantically. I crossed over to her and she started crying before we could get back to the sidewalk. I hugged her and told her I missed her. We both started crying. She told me that she was homesick and it was so good to see someone she knows again. I told her it felt the same for me.

Ange's company provides her with a driver. We sat in the back and chatted about travel, work, and relationships. We talked about men, things I want to see while I'm here, and waxing. We picked up a couple bottles of wine from the store nearby and walked back to her place. The wine was good, the conversation was better and we stayed in. We enjoyed the hot Bangkok night on her patio and talked more about self-love, meditation, and taking chances.

Then I told Ange that sometimes I really feel my unfinished love story missing me. Tonight it was coming on strong.

Twist and Shout

I felt something wake me up just before 5AM. I quickly checked my Facebook. A message from my unfinished love story, the first one in a week, sent only 20 minutes before.

Him: I must say, I sure do miss my old life.

I knew I felt him. I replied back, just as simply.

Me: I do too.

Typically when I wake up in the morning in a new city I spend a few minutes working out a plan of what I want to see. I load up Google Maps and head right out. Today I decided to take a slower approach. I'm going to be in Bangkok until the end of the week, so there really wasn't a need to be in a rush. Despite the list of things that I have to do (laundry, book flights, and mail a package home) and the things I have to buy (more memory cards), I decided it could wait. It was nice to take the morning slow and enjoy Bangkok in a place more comfortable than a hotel room.

Ange's place has two patios. I set myself up in a comfy chair, meditated and wrote my blog entry. I did some laundry and tried to decide which clothes I would be sending back home. I walked around in my pajamas a bit longer then called my mom. We were able to have a longer conversation than normal.

I intended on seeing a temple but as I started walking towards the BTS station I just didn't feel up to doing anything touristy. I passed a spa and decided enough was enough, I need to get waxed. Ange and I are going to be hitting the beaches next week. I didn't want to feel anything less than sexy in my bikini.

I walked into spa and the young woman showed me a picture of the three types of bikini waxes that were offered and I chose the one at the bottom. I hate getting waxed, but I love the results. It's a good thing I had a book loaded on my iPad. I was able to get through almost two chapters with the amount of wild that needed to be removed. But the highlight of the waxing experience was shortly after the aesthetician finished placing a large strip of wax over the top and was about to pull, when the bed started shaking. She stopped. Thank god she stopped. The shutters on the windows rattled. I looked at her.

"Earthquake"?

She said more of a tremor. Enough shaking that it may have been a rough pull on the wax, but small enough that when I told Ange and her friend about it in the evening they didn't even feel it.

Feeling like a new woman I decided just to walk and explore a bit of downtown. I decided to go pick up some snacks and something non-alcoholic to drink, besides water. While I was out I saw the flower vendor, and picked Ange up some pretty flowers. Who doesn't love coming home and seeing flowers on the table?

When Ange came home we got ready to meet the rest of her friends for dinner. The restaurant they choose was excellent, and there was a Beatles tribute band playing all night. I love The Beatles. I drank wine, laughed and chatted with the ladies, and sang all The Beatles songs the band played. I was definitely in my happy place.

Such Great Heights

Time moves at a funny speed while I've been on my trip. My days and weeks feel like they are long and limitless. I often forget where I was last week and will sometimes feel like a week has passed when it's really been three days. I think I've been consistently meditating every morning for about three weeks now. Although I have been meditating in parks or other quiet moments earlier in my trip, those count towards the skill development, but not to my consistency count. I feel consistently calmer. Answers to the questions I ask come clearly. There has only been one time when I doubted the answer that I was given, and the universe told me not to ask the question if I wasn't open to getting the honest answer. I also believe that the consistent mediation has made me much more easy-going and honest with myself and what I want in my life.

I wanted to do some sightseeing today. I was actually really pleased that Ange had made some solid recommendations on what I should see and how to get there. After doing two months of planning my days and sights it's refreshing to have someone else take care of me.

I wanted to see Wat Arun the most. It is a stunning temple with intricate porcelain tile work decoration. It also offers great views from the top if you're willing to do the steep climb, and don't suffer from vertigo. What goes up must come down. The levels to the top get steeper and more difficult to climb as you go, which from what I've learned in my travels is a common theme in temples. Three levels: the first one to hell, the second to earth and the last to heaven. It is supposed to be an easy path to hell and a difficult one to get to heaven, but if you're willing to put in the effort it will always pay off.

On the other side of the river I was stopped by a man who said he was with the tourist board. He made some notes on my tourist map, explained to me the proper tuk-tuks to hire then negotiated with a driver for my next destination. The driver on the other hand had a different interpretation and dropped me off at a random temple. I'm easy going, so I thought I would walk around and explore. That's when I met a local tourist. We started talking, he wrote on my map several useful Thai phrases then he recommended a great shopping district. He offered to negotiate a price for a tuk-tuk and then sent me on my way. The second driver also had another plan. He dropped me off at an overpriced gemstone store, and now I didn't know where I was.

I was meeting Ange's driver at 4PM and it was already 3. I jumped in a cab and showed him a picture of a temple that I knew was close enough to the pier. He didn't understand any English and we went back and forth between pictures and hand motions for me to explain the boat temple. My charades skills are going to be awesome by the end of this trip. And for the first time today I was dropped off exactly where I thought I was going. It was such a relief!

In the evening Ange and I had tickets to a Lady Boy show in the Asiatique district. At one point there was a random scene where they stripped this actor down to nothing and then danced around him. The audience didn't know how to react to it. Then I started laughing. My self-love is paying off. I just embraced it. I didn't try to hide or muffle, and eventually I heard more people laughing with me. I loved every moment of it.

Ange and I had a quick dinner at a little restaurant outside of a 7-11 for authentic Thai cuisine. We then quickly left before the country-wide midnight curfew to Sky Bar, from Hangover 2. Amazing views and overpriced drinks. There's time for more adventures tomorrow.

One Night in Bangkok

Bangkok, Thailand
June 5

Ange and I discussed a lot of things last night, including trying to predict the future. I have always been a future-focused person. I would think about possibilities of where I would be months from now, most of them never actually coming to fruition. A year ago I would have never in my wildest dreams imagined I would be here: sitting on a patio in Bangkok, having travelled to six countries in just over two months, and continuing on for another four. This time last year I was on another perfect vacation with the man I loved believing that I was going to get engaged and by today I would either be married or getting married before the end of this year. There was no way of knowing that the series of events in my life would put me here. I wouldn't give up this trip for the world, but I also wouldn't have chosen this path last year.

Ange gave me the use of her driver to visit a city called Ayutthaya. When we arrived Teak drove me to his favourite ruins in town. After wandering the ruins, Teak took me to a temple, where we both said a prayer and were about to leave the grounds when I saw a fortune teller. I wanted to have my fortune read again to see how accurate it would be to the palm reader I had in Hong Kong. Unfortunately she spoke only Thai and Teak did his best to interpret for me.

She told me that this was the year that I was going to meet my future husband. She said it was going to happen soon sometime between July and August. She said that he is travelling and he will travel to meet me. She said that he had white skin like me, he is very attractive, but has a bit of a belly, which made me laugh. But he is a very good man, she said. She told me to be careful with my travels because there

154

is going to be some misfortune near the end. When I asked her about the love that was to come, if it was someone I know or someone new, she said it was someone new. I felt a tinge of disappointment. I was hoping my unfinished love story would return. I asked her about work and my writing and she said that I will do well in my job but the writing will never pay off. Money will come and go, but the writing won't become lucrative. Then I asked her about moving from Canada and she said I could but I will miss home too much and if I did it might affect my love life.

When we got back into the car I was lost in thought. Teak asked me if I was thinking about my boyfriend. I said I was. I was sad that he wasn't going to be the one. Then Teak said that he is, that he will be a new man. So it may not be a new man in my life, but a previous man that has changed. I then realized it doesn't matter. If I try to play out who the love that will meet me is, a new love or a changed love, the result will be the same. It's someone that loves me and wants to marry me. He is coming. Only time will tell who my heart is calling out to. That makes me incredibly happy.

Back in Bangkok Ange and I were to meeting up with a couple of her friends. We went for Mexican and got generally silly. I laughed about the number of 7-11s in Bangkok, so we decided to play the 7-11 drinking game. Every time we passed one, we would take a drink. We had Teak drop us off to a district called Soi Cowboy. The entire avenue is known for its risqué attitude, lady boy bars and full-on nudity. We walked up and down the strip and weren't feeling overly inspired, then we decided to head into one of the bars. There were dancers all over the stage, hoping someone would bid on them. We watched them for a bit as the rounds of girls rotated all over again. It was quite the interesting night.

Perfect Conversations

Chiang Mai, Thailand
June 6

Ange and I were going to leave Bangkok, the City of Angels, to spend the weekend in Chiang Mai. Before picking up Ange from her office on the way to the airport I went out for lunch at a little restaurant that spoke only Thai. Those are always some of my favourite experiences. With iPad in hand, and a downloaded phrasebook, I point to something someone else is eating and say "I'll have that", "please" and "thank you". This time I ended up getting a noodle soup dish with beef liver and chicken balls. Not exactly what I was expecting but that's all part of the adventure.

The flight to Chiang Mai was just over an hour. One of Ange's friends told us to stay on a street called Nimmanhaemin Road, known for trendy cafés, restaurants and bars. We ask our taxi driver to drop us off there and we will find a hotel. He insisted that the road was so big, there were over 20 hotels on that street. We said anywhere in the middle is fine. He pulled up to a very large hotel that looked quite pricey. We told the driver that we didn't want to stop and to take us to another hotel. But he was done with indecisive girls. He parked and started pulling our bags out of the car. He refused to take us anywhere else. I'm fairly sure the driver was swearing to us in Thai. Ange and I decided since we were at the hotel, let's check it out. The lobby was beautiful. The hotel was very clean. And the prices were quite reasonable and included breakfast. Done.

Ange and I walked down the street and found a really pretty outdoor restaurant. We ordered a bottle of wine and a few dishes and started talking about relationships. She wanted to know more about my breakup, and how I still feel about him, and whether I want him back or not. I'm now at a point, for the most part, that I can talk about all of it without crying.

156

However, I still tear up and feel my heart breaking when I tell the story of the last time I saw him.

Our last night together; all our furniture was already out of the house. We set up a blanket on the floor, watched a movie on my laptop, ate oven-baked appetizers and opened a bottle of champagne in the saddest celebration of our relationship, remembering to still write on the cork and keep it in our collection. We both didn't know if we would ever see each other again, but we held onto that moment and decided to just be in love. In the morning he kissed me, grabbed his bag and made his way for the door, and another week, the same as every Sunday to be away, this time it would be the last time I would ever see him in person. As he left the house he said to me "You will never know how much I loved you". He turned to the door, his eyes already welling with tears and never turned around again.

I became overwhelmed with emotion when Ange asked me my favourite part of him and I told her it was the way he would smile at me and it would fill my entire body with that warm full-body love. Everything else I'm working hard to distance myself from. I can talk about the things that I would need to have change in order for us to work again. I told Ange, probably the same way I'm having this conversation with her, hopefully he's having the same one about me. I know I need to work on self-love more. I had far too much self-doubt and despite the fact that we would try, it may have felt to him that it was never enough. I gave back what I had, but I required more to be given to me. If love is like a vessel, only when it is full can the spillage be given to someone else. Otherwise anything I was given would be given back, and eventually there is nothing left over for me, and I can no longer give what I don't have.

I also know that I am ready. Really ready to have a husband and a family. I would need someone who is ready with me. I would need someone to be there with me. I would need someone to choose us as the priorities. When work becomes overwhelming he is willing to say, it's time for me to be with my family. He would be willing to tell his friends that he can't party every weekend because he has a wife and baby to be with.

Then I told Ange it doesn't matter who it is that I am meant to be with. My heart does want him, but it would now be a conscious choice. If he ever came back I would be able to lay out exactly what I need, and hopefully he would do the same for me. But if he never returns, which is a likely possibility, I can outline those same desires for someone else. Despite who it is, someone changed or someone new, I have still devoted this time to filling up my vessel with self-love that the person I end up with receives more love than they could have ever imagined.

As we sat there, drinking our wine, I told Ange that I was so happy to be here. I was so happy that I met her at this point in my trip. I am starting to view everything from the outside looking in, and I can really clarify what it is I am looking for. I know why I am on this trip. When I eventually get back, my life will be a series of deliberate choices and not a matter of circumstance. We left the restaurant on a perfect note, just as the police were coming in and shutting everything down for the midnight curfew.

Taking Care of Elephants

Chiang Mai, Thailand
June 7

Since leaving Australia I've been travelling entirely by myself for the last seven weeks or so. I'm used to doing my own thing, planning my own days and being fully selfish. I'm allowed to be. I have no one else that I need to be accountable too. It's been great having company again, even though it has its advantages and disadvantages. I love having someone to talk to during dinner. I love laughing over drinks with someone. I find it difficult to have flexibility. Ange has been great to just go ahead and pick a hotel on a whim, but discussing hotels and flight times with someone else is something I haven't had to do since being on this trip. The discussion about where to go to dinner is something I am getting used to again. However, sometimes those discussions work in my favour. Ange really wanted to go to an elephant sanctuary while we were in Chiang Mai, and even though that was not something on my radar, I told her I would go with her. I know that I could always say I'm not interested, if I truly wasn't. I could still go ahead and do my thing, but I have been enjoying the company, and one day devoted to something different opens me up to new possibilities.

Most of the elephant sanctuaries have to be booked in advance by at least two days. I sent a couple of emails, but never heard back. When we arrived at our hotel we decided to place a call to one. They said they could fit us in no problem.

We were picked up and taken to the elephant park. I felt a bit of mixed feelings for the elephants. They were chained and the trainers used bull hooks with them to keep them disciplined, but I didn't feel that the elephants were abused. The guide was also very upfront about all the reasons the chains and hooks are used. Many of these animals come from abusive and mistreated situations and to protect each one, and the surrounding crops, they said they chain the elephants to ensure their safety.

We started the morning out by changing into the mahout (trainer) uniform and feeding the elephant's bananas and sugar cane. We were taught how to get on, steer and ride the elephant bareback. Once on I shimmied all the way to the nape of the neck, very close to the head and then my feet placed behind the elephant's ear to steer either left or right. We were taught to kick both ears if we wanted our elephant to go.

The end of the tour came to a close in a pond where it looked like the highlight of the elephant's day. Jumping in the water and playing. We then were each given a bucket and brush to scrub our elephant down from all the dust and dirt and ensure they were nice and clean

Ange and I made it back to town and decided to go for some foot massages before heading down to this area called Walking Street. It was a massive market for many handicrafts. We left the market just in time. As we made it to a restaurant for a quick drink and snack the rains started to come down. They came so fiercely that the streets become slightly flooded. But then they stop just as fast as they started, and we were able to walk back to our hotel relatively dry.

Learning from Steps Back

It has been about a week since I've had any dreams that I remember. Last night they decided to come with force. I had two dreams. The first dream was my biggest fear. I dreamed my ex got another girl pregnant and he decided to get engaged to her. My heart was broken. I wanted to cry. The dream that followed it was wonderful; it removed the pain of the previous dream, and still left me wanting to cry. We were together. It wasn't like other dreams I've had where I felt like it could be something from the future. This one was just pure passion and love with elements of surrealism that made me know it was pure dream, and I loved it all the same.

When I wake up from those truly wonderful dreams, as much as I love the feeling I am filled with, I hate feeling like I need to talk myself down from that joy. It would be completely different if those dreams were of "someone", but it's always him. It's his face, his voice, his eyes and the way he looks at me.

I become so conflicted because if I hold onto the lingering feelings of love and passion, I end up remembering every aspect of him that makes me feel that way. Otherwise I talk myself down, tell myself to cut that attachment because every day I hold onto the idea of him is another day of feeding a hope that may never be. Sometimes I feel like I am taking two steps forward and one step back. However I know I am making some progress. I no longer overthink my days and hold onto that previous, endless hope of having him come back to me. I truly don't believe that I am wasting all my moments here by putting my head somewhere else. But some days, like today, I just really wanted to be with him. Badly. To the point where I want to cry. I decided to crack and I sent him a message.

Me: I hope you're having a great time in Montreal. I had two dreams with you in it last night. One was terrible and heartbreaking and I hope it doesn't happen. The other was amazingly wonderful. Take care of yourself.

By the way, your posts before leaving Calgary and arriving in Montreal sounded really happy. Your post about speaking French made me laugh.

Ange and I originally discussed going to one of the temples, Wat Umong, for a guided meditation taught by a monk. I am an early riser, so after finishing yesterday's blog in the hotel lobby and chatting with my mom for a bit, I made my way back to our hotel room. Ange was still feeling quite tired and considered not going to the temple with me, which was entirely fine, but it made me realize that I am now at a point where I prefer to be alone. But selectively alone. Here I was with Ange and I would have been very happy doing my own thing. However as I said those words in my head my second dream popped in my head and I thought I would give up my days alone for some time with him. I obviously haven't achieved the full level of the joy of solitude that I need.

Ange changed her mind and I suddenly felt like I was in a frenzy to get myself packed, checked out of the hotel and ready to visit the monks. For whatever reason if it was just me I would have moved at my own pace. Now I felt frazzled to be accountable to someone else. My calm and relaxed demeanor of recent was flipped back to my overanxious, stressed attitude from the past. I didn't like it. And Ange could feel it.

We grabbed a taxi and made a quick stop to the morning market to pick up some fruit as an offering to the monks. We were then brought to Wat Umong, which was a stunningly beautiful temple, grounds, and educational centre. It took us a little while to find where the meditation room was, mostly because it was located in the forested area and we completely walked right past it.

We made it to the room just in time for the meditation to begin. The monk spoke excellent English and told us to concentrate on our breathing. Afterwards we were told to concentrate on losing the attachment of our body, connecting with nature and becoming the air. This is the first time in any of my meditations that I really focused on being something other than myself. As I closed my eyes and really concentrated I started to feel it. I was the air. I was the wind. I was blowing past and kissing the leaves of the trees. I could be still and heavy and my stillness would weigh down on people in the heat, but be a relief to people in the cold. I could be a gentle breeze to a forceful wind. I could move boats and kites and entire sand dunes. I felt it all. I felt bigger than anything I've ever been before and still felt needed and loved and connected.

The monk had us break the sitting meditation and practice walking meditation. He taught us the slow pace to walk at, concentrating on the deliberate lifting and placement of each foot. He said eventually when that was mastered we could pick up our pace, but the idea was to be completely clear of all thought while walking.

He then released us from our lesson and I continued to sit and meditate as I normally do concentrating on the unconditional love I am creating for myself. I give myself words of encouragement, wrapping my arms around myself in a giant hug, and telling myself that I love every aspect about me. Self-love has been my focus for the entire month of June and I have been really feeling a change in my attitude and internal conversations.

We walked around the grounds to determine where we needed to go to drop off our food offerings. There were multiple inspirational sayings and Buddhist teachings nailed to the trees. Then I saw one that really spoke to me: If you can't have what you like, then you must like what you have. Maybe that was the answer to my conflicted feelings around my dreams. If I can't have him, I need to be happy with just the thought and the feelings that the dreams provide me. Yes, thinking about love makes me think of him, but it's the first part of the sentence that counts. Thinking about love.

Ange and I then decided to split ways. This was perfect with me. I really do love travelling by myself. I left her to go to the women's prison for a massage. The prison offers their inmates a rehabilitation vocational skills program. The money each woman receives from her services goes directly to her upon release from the prison. Had I not known it was a prison it would have looked like any other café and massage parlour I've been to in Thailand, except cheaper.

The rest of the afternoon was spent wandering the streets of the Old Quarter, stopping into a couple of cafés and shopping at some of the stalls of the Sunday Walking Market. Yet, despite keeping myself calm and doing the things that I really enjoy doing my mind was stuck. I couldn't shake him from my thoughts all day. There were a couple of times that I actually came close to crying I was missing him so bad. I couldn't understand why. How could I feel like I was making such progress and then today feel like I am so pulled back? Maybe it is a test.

A test, not in feeling like I am making progress in releasing him, but maybe a test in my self love. Accepting the fact that it's okay for me to be emotional. It's okay to have a bad day. I am still doing well. I am still making progress and I shouldn't be hard on myself if I have one day, or a couple or even, for no reason, a full week. I love myself for having the capacity to love someone so much that I could love and miss them for months after no longer having them in my life. I love myself for having a sad day, because tomorrow will be a better day, and I know that both my sad and joyful emotions are what makes me me, and I'm a pretty fantastic person. I can just give myself a giant hug and tell myself that all my emotional days are what make me perfectly unique.

I received a response from my unfinished love story.

Him: The amazing one is what I'd like you to remember. It is very nice here, but... Not as good as it could be. Very friendly people for a single traveller and everyone would rather speak English. I'm still trying my French though. Hope you're doing well.

Maybe. Maybe, Baby.

Krabi, Thailand
Tuesday, June 10, 2014

I arrived at Koh Phi Phi yesterday afternoon. In my new relaxed attitude I didn't bother booking a hotel before arriving, but instead got off my ferry and approached a man holding a sign for a resort I was interested in. It was a little out of the town site, and we had to take an additional long boat to get there, but it was so worth it. Instead of a standard room, I stayed in a stunning treehouse. There were floor to ceiling windows where I could see the ocean in between the trees. I grabbed my book, laid in the hammock, loved the moment and posted a photo to Facebook, captioned "I wish you were here".

I was actually really excited to chat with my sister this morning. I feel like she is going through the same thing as I am, or as the Thais say, same same but different. We're both dealing with our own personal challenges, especially when it comes to self-love and applying remaining love to others. I let her know that today I pray for two conflicting answers: please bring me the love that I pray for and if not, please bring me solace to get over my heartbreak. I'm in a tough position, the answers sit with him, but I have to move forward based on the information I have already received. We exchanged a couple of brief emails the last couple of days, I liked and commented on some of his Facebook posts, but never received anything back telling me that he sees us any differently than he has previously told me. Those few exchanges and the constant watching of his Facebook pushed me back into dangerous territory. My love for him was no longer being suppressed. I felt my love for him coming back. Not that it had ever left, but at least it was being managed, caged, and slowly moved into submission. But the recent contact was enough to move it back to a powerful state. I need to stop. I am creating my own heartbreak.

Candace told me that I just need to focus on the positive. I need to have happy days. I told her I was lucky. No matter what, today was going to be an awesome day. I was on an island. I was planning a boat trip and nothing else could break this excitement.

Our boat headed to Maya Beach, where the filming of The Beach was done. It was stunning with pure white, soft sands and crisp blue water. We stayed for a bit then we moved to the other side of the island. We drove around the inner areas and eventually stopped at a place that offered the clearest, crispiest water I have ever seen. After lunch we headed to Monkey Island, which is just a section of the same overall island that is inhabited with monkeys. We stayed deep in the water while watching them on the beach.

Back on land I decided to walk into town to watch the sunset from the island viewpoint. As I walked into town I became immediately excited. This was the main reason I didn't like staying at all-inclusives. No variety. The town offered so many unique restaurants, bars and stores. I made the exhausting trek up to the top of the mountain for the viewpoint and choose a place called "Hippie Bar" for dinner. I sat along the coast edge, ordered a white wine and a seafood platter. As I sat there, listening to Tracy Chapman sing in the background, I had a moment. It was so slight that I could have missed it if I blinked. I was happy. Truly happy. I was in love with myself. Truly in love with every aspect of myself. And, finally, I was going to be okay. I believed if he came back to me or not, I would be fine. At that realization my constant cloud of melancholy came back to me, but I felt something new for a slight, slight instant. It was the start.

Foundational Clarity

Phuket, Thailand
June 11

To get from Koh Phi Phi to Koh Phagen I have to take a boat from my hotel to town to catch a two-hour ferry to Phuket, a one hour bus ride from the jetty to the airport, a one hour flight to Koh Samui, a cab to the jetty then a 45 minute ferry ride to Koh Phagen. All for the full moon party tomorrow night.

I've been working really hard to not comment or like every post that my ex puts up on Facebook. It's been incredibly difficult. Sometimes I feel like he is posting directly for me. He tags himself at the bar where we met. His status says that his story is still "unfinished". He posts that his vacation is solo, and he wants to share the experience with everyone. Then when I succumbed the first time and said that I would love to see some selfies, he started posting selfies the next day. I used my energy just to close my iPad and not take notice of them. But yesterday, after having a few too many glasses of wine, I really lost control. He went on a bit of a posting frenzy, posting pictures and status updates. I held my composure. That is until he changed his profile picture to one of him wearing the shirt he wore from the day we met. He looked amazing. I could see he was online.

"Hi", I wrote.
Immediately I received "hi" back.

Me: You look like you're having a lot of fun. You look really, really good, by the way

Him: Thank you, I feel really, really good. Looks like you're having a good time as well. And that's nice to see.

Me: You know it's not the same

Him: It's what you wanted

Me: I needed this trip. I didn't know that I did. It's what I needed and not what I wanted. I was lacking in areas that I didn't realize until I was out here.
There is so much I want to say.

I did my best to keep my exchanges to a minimum. We're complete opposites in communication style. I obviously over-communicate and he says the bare minimum, if he says anything at all. And for a while I felt like I was really reaching him. I felt like he was digging deep to let me in. His responses were becoming more than one-liners.

He says that he was madly in love with me. He says that good things come to those with patience, and I, obviously, didn't have enough patience. He says just enough to scratch the surface but I need to hear what's deep inside. I don't want to assume. I ask him to tell me more about his thoughts.

Then things went the way they always do. His pain took over and he started to shut down. Did I miss something? Did I say too much? Then I did what I always do, I compensate for the silence by over-stating what does not even need to be said. I waited what felt like forever for a response, and eventually received a one-liner that kept me up all night. I asked him if we could try again, "what do you really have to lose"?

Him: The same thing I lost the last time. Everything..."

All I kept thinking was how much I miss him. How I still love him, so, so much. My head was spinning. I was on the other side of the world, and every day, for months, the thoughts and memories of him have been my only constant.

In a decidedly dying attempt I apologized to him. I asked him if this trip makes me a calmer, more patient and accepting person, isn't that a wonderful thing for us, as a couple? I told him about some of the realizations I've made about the must have things I need in my life: I needed to move away from Calgary, I needed to be in a relationship that no longer has distance, and I need to be with someone every night. I am ready to be a wife and a mother and need someone who is just as ready to be a husband and a father. I thought if I listed out the things I needed in my life he would either see that this trip has made a positive impact in my life or he would say outright that he really can't be those things to me, and I could shut the door forever on the story of us. I waited for a reply.

I lost sleep over the whole thing. I kept waking up hoping there would be something new from him. Maybe I was still missing something when I tried to look at it from his point of view. Maybe there is still something that I am not apologizing for. Maybe it was just one giant mistake to reach out at all.

It felt like suddenly it was sunrise and time to wake up. I could have chosen to sleep in a bit longer, but my morning meditations are now a significant part of my day and provide me with clarity. I definitely needed some clarity. As I sat my mind brought me back to June's focus of self-love.

Three months ago I would have berated myself the entire day, maybe longer, for reaching out. I would have analyzed and re-analyzed the entire exchange until the words completely lost meaning. I would have guilted myself and carried self-doubt about the reasons I am on this trip. Then my clarity came. First it told me to be kind to myself. There was nothing I said that was anything other than honest and from the depths of my heart. Honesty is never a bad thing. It told me that the reasons I am on this trip is to become a better, calmer, more patient person. I am definitely more of each of those than I was before I left, and I should be proud of myself for my progress.

The other reason I am on this trip was to really figure out the things I want in my life. In order to do that I needed to remove everything and then put back the pieces I wanted to keep. Although I knew before I left that I wanted to keep him, some of the other changes that I now want in my life may not be things he wants in his.

Then my self love really shone through and told me I am a fantastic person, I am honest with myself, I am honest with him, and if he ever sees it from my point of view, if he ever wants to, then he will understand that I needed to do this. I needed to be here. I needed to go through this growth otherwise I would have never been satisfied with the love he gave me or the life we were creating for ourselves. I needed to ensure my inner foundation was solid before I could build up a life for myself, for someone else and for the future family I dream of having.

I spent the rest of the day focusing on my long journey to the other side of the Thailand and being really happy with myself and where I am. For the first time I felt like I will be okay to wait for love to find me. When it does I will be in a perfect place to meet it.

He responded 12 hours later telling me he wishes he was stronger to visit our dog while I was gone. He can't handle goodbyes.

Full Moon Party

Koh Phagen, Thailand
June 12

It took a long time to get to Koh Phagen from Koh Phi Phi yesterday. Then once I arrived I was worried that I was in over my head. There were lots of young people, all super pumped, and talking all about how they are going to get so drunk and party so hard, some of them still recovering from partying solid for the last few nights. There was no way that I could keep up like that now, or maybe it's a new challenge. How late can I last while still being functional tomorrow?

The hotel provided a buffet dinner to all their guests, probably in their best interest to prevent as much sickness as possible. I finished eating and took a walk down the beach. The party was just getting started. I didn't want to start drinking just yet; I wanted to save that for a bit later in the night. I'm a fairly easy drunk and can rarely push myself past midnight. I needed to pace.

As I walked I was stopped by a group of young Aussies. They invited me to sit down and they offered to buy me a bucket, but I wasn't quite ready for that yet, so I offered to buy myself a beer. We sat and chatted. I think they were disappointed that I was much older than the mid-20s that they picked me for. They also couldn't believe that I could travel by myself. For anyone that has never gone on a trip solo, I highly recommend it. There are so many internal conversations that I never took the time to have with myself. Also just travelling solo I meet so many people and am sometimes put in some odd situations that otherwise I would have never had the opportunity. The conversation with the Aussies took a bad turn when I dumped out the last part of my beer because it was too warm. They were appalled. Oh well.

After a break back at my hotel room for a shot of Red Bull and a beer on my patio, I left for the party again. By this time it was starting to really pick up. People were dancing everywhere, some were feeling daring enough to try the fire rope and empty buckets were starting to pile on the tables. I was watching one of the fire ropes when I ran into three Mexican amigos that I had originally met on the boat ride to Haad Riin. We started chatting and they invited me to join them as they wandered the beach. It was fun to have some company.

The beach is like wandering through multiple nightclubs. Every few feet there is a new DJ and a slightly different vibe. It was now time to try my first bucket.

I polished it off and felt the courage go through me. I went down the water slide. I did the fire limbo. Although in my head I aced it, the pictures unfortunately show a different story. I was painted with the glowing paint. I was going to jump the fire rope, but watching so many people get burned by it turned me off. I thought I could do quite well at it, I just didn't trust the other drunks.

I made it until about 1:30 in the morning and then I was done. I walked back to my hotel and realized that I no longer had my room key. I paid to have the front desk open my door and change the lock. Small price to pay for a much needed fun night.

Seaside Recovery

Koh Samui, Thailand
June 13

It was a slow-moving start to the day. By the time I crawled out of bed, took a much needed shower, including scouring off a layer of skin to remove the "YOLO" stamps that were all over my arm, I had missed breakfast. Minus a slight headache I was actually in fairly decent condition. Especially after seeing some of the other party goers throughout the day, many of them more than likely either had not even gone to bed, or they slept on the beach. Once I was packed I went to the hotel reception, checked out, picked up a ferry ticket for Koh Samui and was shuttled to the port. The ferry was packed. Realistically there probably should have been a person and weight limit, but who's really counting? Once all the seats were taken, people were sitting and lying on the floor of the two decks. The look on everyone's face just said "get me off this island".

The ferry ride eventually arrived at port, and there was a scramble of people looking for taxis, shared vans or other transport. Ange had arranged a cute bungalow hotel for us. I hired a motorbike taxi and we took off.

As I waited for Ange to arrive I booked my next destination to Bali via Kuala Lumpur. I arrive in Bali on Tuesday for a couple of weeks of relaxation, maybe some snorkeling or diving and a volcano trek. I've heard beautiful, romantic things about Bali, and it will be the perfect way to end my month of Self-Love.

Losing What I Had

There are so many things I want to write about today, and so much else that I don't. My head has been filled with thoughts about my trip, my personal progress, my friends and family, but mostly, and always, about him. Ange met me at the resort last night. We had dinner and chatted over wine, picking up right where we left off last weekend. The conversations lately have been focused around self-love and trying to build a foundation of love for ourselves before allowing the other pieces of our life to be added.

My focus on self-love has been almost two weeks now and I already feel a significant difference in my attitude and my feelings for myself. I feel really happy about who I am as an individual. I feel like I can accomplish a lot in my life. I feel I am capable of making deliberate choices in my life and designing the life I really want.

But as Ange and I talked last night she asked me if it was that I never had self-love or did I lose it? I had to think about that question. I believe I did have it at one point. I would walk around with and air of confidence that I believe was me. I was secure in what I wanted in my life and what that looked like. So if I had it, when did I lose it? Was it something that just happened suddenly or was it a gradual loss? I had enough self-love when I first started dating my unfinished love story. Was I filled enough? Probably not. But I had enough. So then when did I notice that I was out?

There are points in the last couple years that I can see as moments where my self-doubt started to take over. I received a couple of criticisms about my work that personally affected me. I started to doubt my sales skills when I couldn't bring the deals to the contract signing stage. I started to doubt that I was enough for my love story. There were so many little points, but they all started to add up. I never worked at containing those doubts and feeding my positivity. Eventually I found myself with nothing left, and it was nobody's fault but my own.

But if I can recognize the elements that caused me to lose it, I can recognize in the future when I am falling back into that pattern again, if ever. I don't want to be at a point in my life where I feel like I have to rebuild my confidence and love for myself. It will now be part of my daily meditations, because when I am full I also have more to give others.

I woke up this morning and I missed him. Really missed him. More than anything else I missed having my best friend. My hope of us has ebbed and flowed over the last month because I didn't want to hold onto a strong hope if I was the only one that still wishing we could be together again. Although sometimes the hope was suppressed, it never left. Today, for whatever reason, the hope of my unfinished love story came back really strong.

I no longer ask in my meditations if we will be together again. I received my answer weeks ago and now only time will tell. My heart is, and always has been, dedicated to him. I'm in no rush. I will wait for him as long as it will take.

Leaving Thailand

Koh Samui, Thailand
June 15

I always feel a bit nostalgic every time I leave another country. It's a bitter-sweet moment for me. Another country finished, a lot of memories, and excitement for the next journey. Thailand is a beautiful country with wonderful people and it provided me with a lot of great memories. Every evening out was eventful and filled with fun, new people. It was great to help break up some of the homesickness by meeting with Ange. She and I had some insightful conversations, and having the chance to speak to someone about the thought processes and growth I have been going through since being on this trip has really left me feeling like I am at a turning point in my own development.

For my last night in Thailand, Ange and I headed out to the town of Chewegan. We took a truck taxi there, which are quite easy to catch. The flatbed of the truck is fitted with seats and a bell to ring once you want the driver to stop. Ange and I didn't quite make it to the town centre, when we hit the bell to stop the truck. We saw a store with some really pretty dresses outside. Shopping now became the priority over eating. Ange tried on several dresses and outfits and picked herself up a brand new wardrobe. I on the other hand had to be really selective with trying items on. I didn't want to fall in love with a bunch of clothes and have to send another package back home so soon. That being said, I still fell in love with a super cute romper that I had to have.

We went for dinner at a decent fish restaurant and by the time we were finished it was too early to head back to the hotel, so we went to another pub for a bottle of wine. At this point we were talking a lot about my hopes and wishes for my unfinished love story. I told her that I wasn't being completely honest with him. I had asked him to come meet me on my journey for something non-committal in hopes that he would be comfortable not feeling any pressure about us, but in actuality if he did come I wouldn't be able to look at it any other way than wanting to be with him the entire time. She said that I needed to tell him that. She was right. If he came I would never let him go. He needs to know that and make a decision based on that, not based on flakey propositions. If he decides then that he doesn't want to come, then it would be the right decision for both of us. He deserved to know what my heart was telling me and what was pure and honestly true.

Ange and I decided to head out a bit more and check out another bar that we heard about, Ark Bar on the beach. They serve a selection of Shisha, so we thought why not. We had such a fun night, and a perfect way to end my time in Thailand. But the moment I got back to the hotel I sent my unfinished love story my message. The sooner the better. I told him that if he showed up in Greece I would never let him go. I would make him spend every moment with me. I said I want all of him or none of him. I still love him and for the last 3 months it has been him always in my thoughts every day.

He responded to it almost immediately: I will respond later. Sweet dreams.

I woke up in the morning with anxiety waiting for his response. My anxiety got so overwhelming the only thing I could think of doing was to meditate and calm myself down. I can't believe only three months ago I would have driven myself to crazy in a situation like this. Now my meditations help to calm me down and clear up everything.

The answer that came back to me said "dream really big". It showed me an engagement ring. I saw Australia. Could my last honest, loving email have changed the trajectory of our life?

Ange and I spent another day by the pool, this time my head filled with ideas of all the things that I can dream for. By mid-afternoon it was time to go. We were both sad to leave each other, but I'm off to my next destination and another adventure.

Trying on the Layover

Kuala Lumpur, Malaysia
June 16

There were no direct flights to get to Bali from Koh Samui so I have to fly through Kuala Lumpur. If I had to layover anyway, I thought I may as well check it out.

I arrived late last night, and I am getting far too relaxed in my travel plans. Three months ago, I would have already planned how I would get from the airport to my hotel and based on either time or cost, choose the option that fitted me the best. When I arrived last night I was surprised that I really didn't have a plan. I surprised myself! That in itself is a statement to end all statements.

However the morning is where things got really interesting. A couple of weeks back I was meditating on my unfinished love story. I asked two questions. The first one being will he ever come back? The answer was simply "with certainty". With certainty. What an interesting choice of words. That's when I really started believing in the power of meditation. With certainty is not a combination of words that I would ever choose, but they were simply powerfully concise. Okay, meditations, let's assume it's correct. When will I hear from him again? June 15th. My 15th or his 15th? His.

Now whether it was outside forces, or me creating my own reality, at this point it doesn't matter to me. He and I exchanged a couple of emails throughout the week. But I was suddenly feeling like we were at a turning point. The email I sent on my last night in Thailand telling him I would never let him go. Sure enough when I woke up in the morning I finally received the long awaited response from that night. His response: "you're the only one that I ever wanted to be with for the rest of my life and I cannot get over that". I responded right away: "I don't want to get over that. I pick you". Then I saw him online.

I spilled. I couldn't stop. Three quick statements in succession. I told him about the amount of self-reflection that I have been doing. I couldn't be engaged to him before, my stress and anxiety was too high, but I am getting better now. My meditations help me to see and enjoy the journey and not the destination. Each time I would see that he was typing I was hitting send, and his typing would stop. Break my heart. Every time I sent a new statement he would have to read it and perhaps change or revise what he wanted to say based on whatever new information I gave him. Then I stopped. I waited. And finally, *finally*, he wrote back. He didn't think about us in terms of helping me fulfill my needs. He was sorry. That statement alone was enough to end all statements. It was a really big turning point, for both of us. I felt like he was suddenly open to the possibility of us again. I asked him what he really wants.

Him: In what sense? I am glad you are doing what you are doing. You need this, I was lucky to have done it when I did. However, when we see each other again I'll have to get to know this new you and we will see if it was meant to be. As for now, I have changed my outlook from what it was and that is a good thing. Maybe a date in Greece, but we'll see. What do you really want?

Me: Anything you want. It's really an open-ended question.

I didn't even know how much I needed it until I was here. The whole self-discovery process. The redefining my goals and re-prioritizing the things in my life. I'm not dramatically different, but there is a slight change.

I have been thinking of arriving in Greece on Aug 1, but I can be flexible with the date. I have a tour group in Cairo on the 21st.

I want a lot of things. I want to feel like the most authentic version of myself. I felt that in Australia. I want a career that I really enjoy. Corporate sales is not that. Too much stress. I don't even care about the money anymore. I want to be a wife and a mother. I want to live my days and enjoy each one. And I want a lot of good sex, daily.

Him: I get it. I like remembering how you seduced me.

And without saying the words, I felt his love for me again. He didn't need to say it. Not yet. I have nothing but time. He is much more conscientious with his words than I am, and that's okay. Then I proposed a FaceTime date. I told him I missed his face and the sound of his voice. He agreed to the first time I offered. Be still my heart. I only have to wait two nights.

With my one day here I had the plan to get my hair done, do a little bit of shopping, including picking up some essentials and a few non-essential items. I somehow hit three malls, plus a knockoff street market where I picked up three items, all men's gifts. My favourite item was a watch that I knew my unfinished love story would love. A gift to give him when I do see him again in person.

The entire day however, he was in my thoughts, and in the best way I could imagine. My stomach had fluttering butterflies. It was like I was preparing for a first date all over again. I am so anxious and excited. Just be calm.

Turn of Events

Life works in mysterious ways. In the morning I was off to catch a flight from KL to Bali. I've heard beautiful things about Bali, and despite many of them being how romantic and loving the place is, I thought it would be a very appropriate place for me to celebrate my regained self-love.

I arrived at the airport early and went to check in to my flight. However there were signs all over the airport that the counter for Malaysian Airlines doesn't open until 60-minutes before flight departure, which I thought to be quite odd. The airport was quite massive but the departure board didn't have any counter listed for the Bali flight. So I went to grab a coffee and as I sat surfing Facebook I saw that he was online. We were planning on having a Skype date tomorrow, but I was so excited I asked him if he was interested in chatting now. He agreed.

The moment our call connected my face lit up. I couldn't stop smiling. I was so excited to see him again. I told him he looked really good. We talked for 45-minutes or so. We chatted about new things with ourselves, how each of us sees things differently than we did before. He filled me in on some of the new things going on with his work. He then said he still needed some time apart from everyone to clear his head. I get it. I've had months to clear my head. When the conversation ended I let him know that I still missed him, and thought about him all the time. Then I hung up before I started crying.

I left directly in search of where to drop off my bag for the flight. The departures board had still not been updated, so I was getting a bit anxious about my flight. I had to ask around to several people, when I finally found the correct counter. As I checked in, the woman let me know that my flight was closed, and I wouldn't be able to get on. No way! Not happening. I told her that I still had an hour, and I will be getting on the flight. She finally issued me a boarding pass and I ran. I ran through security, onto the monorail and then finally to my gate as it was halfway boarded. Big sigh of relief. Hopefully my bag arrives to Bali with me.

It was a 2.5hour flight, and a massive plane. From the departure there was a short line-up to pay for the visa-on-arrival, but from there it was a 60-minute wait to actually be issued the visa. At least they offered free Wi-Fi.

As I stood in line there was another young traveller in front of me. He was also travelling alone. We started chatting about our trips. He was just entering day one for an unknown length of time. We chatted about Indonesia and his home in the UK. As we passed through customs, he asked how I was getting to my hotel, if I would be interested in splitting a cab, since we were staying fairly close to each other. Why not? When the cab wouldn't allow us to make two stops, he then asked if I would be interested in joining him for dinner. Company for dinner sounded really nice. So I agreed. Then suddenly I realized that I kind of said yes to a date.

I arrived at my hotel and had just enough time to change my outfit. What do I wear? I didn't want him to think that I was interested in anything other than dinner conversation. I don't want to look eager or overly feminine, so I decided on the new romper that I bought in Thailand. Shorts would be a perfect compromise.

When I arrived at the restaurant he was there waiting. We sat down at a table on the patio and started chatting. Eddie let me know that he was currently going through a breakup with his wife and the only thing he could think of was to get away and travel. I breathed a huge sigh of relief as I told him my story too. I let him know that I was so glad that there were no expectations for the evening, and he thought it was really nice that we could be each other's therapists over dinner. As he talked about his wife, I told him about my own personal journey with self-love. I said that maybe his wife was going through the same thing. She was empty. He kept providing her with more, but it wasn't enough, not because it wasn't enough love, but for her it really wasn't. She fell out of love with herself. There was never going to be enough love that he could give her until she took the time to fill herself up again. I loved the candid conversation that Eddie and I were having.

After we finished dinner, and a couple of drinks each, I decided I was having a really good time. I wasn't ready to say goodbye to the company just yet. Let's go to another bar. I then suggested since we are completely unavailable, let's be exactly the opposite, let's tell people we are on our honeymoon. Maybe we'll get a free drink or two out of it. The night continued on, Eddie and I just laughing and chatting. The servers at the bar said that we looked like we were so in love. There's something to be said about pretending. When we want something bad enough we actually make it real. I actually wanted to believe I was on my honeymoon. That the man I was with loved me enough to marry me.

We left that bar and headed to another. The night kept getting later and the drinks kept us feeling good. At the third bar we were dancing and having fun. I don't know how it happened, but then we kissed. Passionately. Authentically. I felt dizzy. It was the same passion that I remember being kissed the first time by my unfinished love story. It had been months since I have felt that intensity fire through my body.

"I need to go back to my hotel", I told Eddie, "come with me". We stopped at a convenience store and picked up water, Pringles and condoms, and jumped into a cab.

We arrived at my hotel and passed by the inner courtyard where there was a small swimming pool. I dared Eddie, "go skinny-dipping". He took off his clothes and jumped right in, just as the hotel security was passing by to check things out. Eddie hid his naked body in the shadows of the pool.

"Uh, we're going skinny-dipping", I said. My drunk mind couldn't even come up with a lie or another story.

"Okay, I'll bring you towels", the security officer said as he left.

Eddie was laughing in the pool, "don't leave me hanging", he said.

I smiled. I stripped down and jumped in. He kissed me again. I didn't know what was happening. I don't think he knew either. I was so involved in the moment, and this man, and his gorgeous British accent. He made me feel everything that I was wanting from my unfinished love story.

We wrapped ourselves in the towels, grabbed our clothes and headed up to my room.

Know when to hold
'em and fold 'em

Kuta, Indonesia
June 18

I woke up around mid-morning still in a half-drunk haze. Oh, shit, what did I do? I looked over to Eddie who was still asleep. I rolled out of bed and covered myself with one of the sheets on the floor. I made my way to the washroom, washed my face and brushed my teeth. I took a shower and came back into the room. He was still there. He opened his eyes. "There's an extra toothbrush in the washroom if you want to brush your teeth". It was the only thing I could think of saying. "There's also a breakfast downstairs, if we can get down before it's done. I'm only booked for one night. I have to let them know that I won't be checking out today", I finish saying.

"Do I have time for a shower?" Eddie asks. Thank God he is as nervous as I am. My brain is trying to figure out the events of the night. I barely remember coming up to the room. There is an unopened can of Pringles on one of the night side tables. I offer him the last of the bottle of water after I take a long drink.

I wait for Eddie to get out of the shower. I try to write yesterday's blog. What do I write? I notice the time then breathe a big sigh. Thank God, again, I spoke with my unfinished love story yesterday. I would have missed our call if I was supposed to make it this morning. If he would have called me there would have been another man in my bed. How would I ever explain any of it? Just when I finally started to get him to open up with me I had to go ahead and screw everything up.

Eddie got dressed in yesterday's clothes and we went down to the lobby for breakfast. The breakfast was terrible, but all I needed right now was a good cup of coffee. "Do you want to go for a walk?" Eddie asks. He already knows I would be lying if I said that I had other plans. Maybe I could redeem my promiscuity if I get to know him a little bit. Then when I realize he's a simple person, no personality, no conversational skills I won't feel bad to ditch him.

We decide to walk around the neighbourhood to see what was around town. Before leaving the hotel I negotiated and paid for another night in cash. I can always change hotels the following day or pay for more nights here if the neighbourhood is good. I have no idea what is even in the area.

As Eddie and I walked I asked him if he was getting hungry. He was. I was trying to do my own thing, run off my own agenda. I told him that I needed some time to write my daily blog. I am already hours late from my daily post. Eddie, in a relaxed way, said I needed to take care of myself first. He can entertain himself.

We stop into a little café and between a few typed sentences we continue to chat about life, relationships and travel. He told me more about him and his marriage, and I started to feel my own message that I had heard so many times before start to resonate. He told me all about how he tried, really tried, to hold onto his wife's love. He didn't want to give up. He loved her, and still does, but at some point he had to decide it was too exhausting. Then it started to click with me. For months I have tried, really tried, to hold onto my unfinished love story. Before we were done I was trying. Once I ended things I had been trying. Ever since being on this trip I have been trying. I would only need to hear from him that he still loves me, that he wants to be with me, maybe he still needs time or reflection, but his heart still loves me. That's it. Simple. Yet, here I am, still waiting, still exhausting myself and energy, giving him everything I have while I wait for a return response.

I told Eddie all about the conversation I had with my unfinished love story yesterday morning. How I was so excited and thrilled, and I felt that my ex was distracted. He looked like he was surfing online while I was focused on him. I tried to give my ex the benefit of the doubt that he was really tired, maybe had other things in his head, but then Eddie asked if I felt loved during the conversation. I didn't really know. I should know. I should feel at least loved. I should be told it. And if he couldn't find the words to say, he could at least write them. But the only messages I received since our conversation were about camping and how he misses our dog, but doesn't have it in him to pick her up. Maybe I never will be fully loved by my ex again. I have been trying so hard and no amount of energy I put in will bring my ex to that place. He has to come to that place himself. All I'm doing at this point is continuing to exhaust myself.

Eddie and I finished lunch and took a walk along the beach. We talked about our careers and I let him know that I'm at an interesting point in my life where I feel like I have the capacity to design whatever life I really, truly want. I told him that I was thinking about simplifying my life. He told me that I am so smart I need to be challenged. I need someone that is going to support me while I do adventurous things and push myself to my limit. He said not everyone has the potential that I have, and although he hasn't known me that long, somehow he knows. It was so easy chatting with him. Maybe it was because there were no expectations. Maybe it was nice to have two completely unavailable people available just for each other. But the conversation flowed, and it was honest. There was no need for me to hide my history, or prevent myself from talking about my ex. And Eddie the same. Every time he talked about his ex, I felt like there was a moment where I could listen, truly listen, to how I was probably sounding saying the same words to someone else.

Eddie and I continued to walk along the beach and towards his hotel. He hadn't been there since he dropped off his bag last night. He had just enough time to get changed for our date. He asked if I would be interested in sitting by his hotel pool for part of the afternoon. I didn't have my bikini; I didn't want to go back to my hotel. We walked into a surf shop and I bought one. We headed to his hotel and rested by the pool.

Somehow the afternoon turned to the evening and we left to watch the sunset on the beach before going for dinner. I told him I was really glad I had met him. I truly believe people enter our lives at very appropriate times. The messages they have for us somehow stick. There will be several people that I will remember; many others will fade into my memories. But those brief conversations that we have with certain people can help put everything into a new light, make it brighter, and we can really appreciate what it is.

I don't know where I will be if my unfinished love story does eventually say he wants to be with me. The most I've heard back is maybe a date in Greece? I want something definitive. I am waiting. I have been waiting to hear him tell me he loves me. Even three words would be enough right now. Yet none of this was this urgent three days ago. But I will wait. I will cross the bridges as I come to them. I guess timing is everything.

Eddie and I continued on throughout the night, having more drinks, more laughs and having more fun than we did the night before. More than anything we decide it was so nice to sleep next to someone, and he asked me if I would come back to his place. He doesn't want me to leave.

Something in the Bali Air

Kuta, Indonesia
June 19

I have never in my life been to any place like Bali. Those that have been know what I'm talking about. Those that want to go want to know. All others I hope that they desire it at some point.

It's a beautiful place. I don't know if it's the most beautiful place I've ever seen, but beauty is far more than looks. It's like meeting the love of your life. They could be attractive, maybe not the hottest person you've ever met, but they are kind, and generous, and they make you feel really good about yourself. That is Bali. An infatuation that feels real, and true, and everlasting. It is meeting someone that you know could turn your entire life around and at the same time keep it exactly the same. Bali is that all over love you feel for yourself and everyone around you.

Over the last couple of days I have had some of the calmest days I have ever had. I have enjoyed the most beautiful scenery and stunning sunsets. Had some great conversations with a variety of people. Yet I have taken fewer pictures than anywhere else I have ever been. The days escape me, in the best possible way imaginable. The days just are.

I was already considering switching my hotel in the morning. Over breakfast Eddie and I discussed me getting a room in his hotel. I wasn't ready to do that just yet. He might still get bored of me. I looked on Booking.com; there was a hotel right next door that still had availability. We could still be together and separate when the time comes. No matter what I had to check out of my current hotel. I caught a cab and arrived at my hotel with only about 30 minutes before check out. I quickly packed all my items, laughed about the unopened can of Pringles still on the night table, and caught another cab to

191

the hotel that was right beside Eddie's. I walked in, negotiated a room, and upon being shown one decided it was enough. I got a cheaper price if I decided against breakfast. Eddie said his hotel came with two breakfast vouchers. By the time I was moved into my new room I was already late meeting Eddie. I told him I would be back within 90 minutes and it was already 2 hours. I had no way of contacting him. I immediately walked over to his hotel and knocked on his door. My last knock on the door started my doubt. Maybe he already left. He answered the door. "I was waiting for you", he said, "I fell asleep".

It was already time for lunch. We walked around and found a Mexican restaurant and sat on the patio to do some people watching. I originally wanted to go surfing but by the time lunch was finished the wind had picked up and it was going to be too difficult for my beginner surf skills, so we decided to hit the mall across the street.

There was a mini arcade on the top floor, so I challenged Eddie to a couple games. As a Canadian I had to challenge him to air hockey. I won the first game, he won the second, and so I let him win the third. We then played Dance, Dance Revolution against some of the small children that were hanging around outside. They beat us easily and as their reward we gave the kids the rest of our game credits. They were thrilled and ran off to decide which games they wanted to play next.

Eddie and I slowly made our way back towards the beach, where the winds had started to settle down. Our conversation somehow never stopped. Without agenda Eddie suggests we just sit in the sun and chill. I laid out my sarong. I read, he slept, and we relaxed until the sun started to come down.

There are many places to find a drink on the beach. The entire beach is lined with men with coolers, umbrellas and chairs selling beer, water, or other drinks on the beach. Ange told me to be on the lookout for "Tommy's Bar", which despite asking around we couldn't find, so we choose a random spot to sit and have a couple of beers.

After the sun set we enjoyed dinner at a little seafood restaurant, walked around and stopped at any pub that caught our interest on the way back to his hotel. We chatted with a retired Australian couple. Then Eddie and I had our first fight. It was either drunkenness or self sabotage or a combination of the two, but we argued. I was angry. I walked out, he followed me, but at a distance. He wanted to make sure that no matter how mad we were at each other I was going to make it back to my hotel safe. When my unfinished love story and I would have a drunken fight I often found myself abandoned by him.

I ducked into the first McDonald's I saw and ordered a McNugget meal. Eddie didn't see me disappear, but was relieved when I came back out with a smile on my face and a mouthful of french fries. He was mad, but so happy that whatever reason I was mad about was now gone. I couldn't be happier that he stayed. He laughed as my mood made a 180-degree turn and we went back to his hotel.

Our conversation has had no pause. Since the moment we met back in the queue two days ago we have been non-stop. How does this even happen? He doesn't have an answer either.

Eddie reads this entry as soon as it's posted and asks, "Am I Bali"?

This is My Story

Kuta, Indonesia
June 20

The day finally came. That day my angel on the train, Anjulie, told me about. The day where I saw that glimmer of a possibility of getting over my ex. Where I would truly know that I would be okay. I could see that there could be a future with someone else and my heart could finally be ready to release my unfinished love story. I saw that glimpse yesterday.

I promised my ex that when I saw that day I would let him know. I sent him a message last night before Eddie and I went to dinner. I made Eddie wait for me while I wrote, read, edited and made the message to my unfinished love story a priority. I wanted it to be perfect. I needed to know if my unfinished love story still loves me, if he sees me in his future, and would he be willing to commit to our future with me?

I told him I saw a glimpse of the alternative and I could truly get over him. I could be happy with someone else.

I told him that part of the reason we were currently broken up was that I didn't fully let him in on the thoughts in my head. I didn't inform him the potential consequences of his actions, or really inactions. I know he is a far more cognitive person than I am, and it takes him a long time to go through his thoughts and then to either finally say what he needs to say or do what he needs to do.

I told him that I still love him and I can still see myself forever with him, but that possibility is fading. I needed him to either say he loves me back, he really wants to be with me, or he just doesn't. Our day has finally arrived. I would wait for him, or I could really move on, but I needed an answer from him. Is he willing to make it work with me or not? The choice was up to him.

I knew he was going camping this weekend. I hadn't heard anything from him in the last two days. I told him to clear his head, and ask his heart what he wants. I then wished him hope, happiness, security in his decision and honesty with himself and with me. I sent it on his Thursday morning.

I woke up in the morning with Eddie beside me. "What do you want to do today?" he asks me. I open my iPad and play Rhianna's "Stay". He loves this song as much as I do and we spend the entire day singing single lines to each other, the other person joining in the impromptu duets.

I tell him I would love to spend the entire day in bed being held, but if we had to do something I really want to go surfing, so he agreed to come with me and watch.

There is no lack of surfing on the beach. There are plenty of men standing around their selection of surfboards ready to offer a quick lesson and be a private cheerleader in the water when you finally get up on the board. I can now get up a majority of the time, and am starting to learn how to turn on the board so I can ride the wave a little longer. I negotiated a board and a small lesson, Eddie decided to stay on the beach.

Before I jumped in the water Eddie asks me where my camera is. "It's in my bag", I tell him, "I trust you". He stood on the beach and took my picture as I jumped up on the board, rode the wave, and paddled back out the ocean. I encouraged Eddie to also give it a try. He did quite well and was so excited when he could actually ride the wave into the shoreline. Surfing very quickly became exhausting.

Afterwards we found a little hole-in-the-wall restaurant with plastic tables and chairs sitting on the beach. As we ate we talked a lot about a lot. He told me somehow when I told him that I trusted him to go in my bag it meant so much to him. It was one of those small things I thought nothing about. Then I realized I do trust him and we just met. I apologized that I didn't get the ultimate picture of him on the board, his camera was out of memory and I went to go grab mine, at the very wrong moment.

We then talked about how it has been difficult, up until now to find the "shady", locally-flavoured stores and restaurants. We decided to make it our mission to walk down some of the dark alleyways and see if we could find more. As soon as we put out that request to the universe, we walked and found ourselves directly into what we were looking for. I found a little spa, where I decided on a much needed manicure and pedicure. Eddie had a massage. Afterwards we went for a shake at a local diner.

We parted ways for the first time since I checked into my hotel, which I still hadn't slept in, and agreed to meet soon for dinner.

We met just before sunset. We found the much anticipated "Tommy's Bar" that Ange had told me about. We sat on plastic chairs on the beach, drank a few beers and watched the sunset while Tommy played his guitar and serenaded the beach. Eddie and I talked about romance and money, and he said this was far more of his thing than my previous life of champagne in 5-star all-inclusives. I agreed. I grew accustomed, and exhausted of my pretentious lifestyle. I love camping and chilling out, and really I need more of that in my life. I need balance.

Eddie and I walked down the same locally cultured alleyway from lunch and found a food court. There were plenty of stalls that had a variety of food items. We ordered from a stall, were sat at a table in the open space and eventually brought our meal.

I really enjoy his company. We chat about so many things, and there is never a lack of things to talk about. Eddie has opened my eyes to a new way of viewing my relationship with my ex, and really deciding that I shouldn't feel like I am settling.

Here I am chatting with a 31-year old that was trying for a baby with his wife a few months ago, and he worked so hard to keep her in his life. I am working so hard to convince a 39-year old that it's time to get married and have a baby, and he still hasn't decided, or at least told me, if he still loves me back.

Eddie helps me to slow down and realize when I am overthinking. I told him again that I am really glad I met him. That no matter what, he will always affect me in a really positive and special way. Timing is everything and people will always enter into our lives when we are ready for the lessons that we need to be taught.

A woman offers to take Eddie and my picture as part of our on-going honeymoon. I offer her my camera, and Eddie and I sit close. When I get the camera back I look at the photo. "You look really happy", I tell him.

"So do you", he replies.

My heart melts in a way I never thought possible, and I immediately wonder if I'm ever going to hear back from my unfinished love story.

Surfing and Sunset

Kuta, Indonesia
June 21

I have been losing track of my time and days in Bali. Before arriving here I was so stuck on my routine: wake up, meditate, if I didn't write during dinner I would finish up in the morning, and then head out for the day. Since arriving my mornings seem to flow from waking up, having breakfast with Eddie, the two of us walk around town, we enjoy a couple of sunset beers, dinner then head back to one of our hotels and lay in bed and talk until we both fall asleep. My days feel like I do so much in them but then I realize they are all starting to get away from me.

Eddie and I go for breakfast. One of his friends arrived into Bali late last night and another one would be arriving later today. Eddie wanted to show James around and asked if I would tag along. Absolutely, as long as at some point I can also hit the beach and go surfing. Absolutely.

James joined us as we were finishing breakfast. I felt incredibly awkward. Of course he knows that Eddie's here because him and his wife broke up, and now Eddie's been hanging out with a "crazy Canadian bird". But James was cool. While the two friends catch up, I check out of my hotel. Eddie and I decided last night that we haven't spent a night apart yet, so there is no sense in paying for two hotel rooms. "Four nights is long enough. It's time to move in together".

The three of us decided to all walk towards the beach. We had a quick bite to eat at one of the BBQ beachside stalls and then walked over to Tommy's Bar. The boys decided to sit down with Tommy and enjoy a beer with him, while I rented a surf board and hit the waves.

The surfing wasn't as great as it was the day before, but it was still great practice. I rented a smaller board than the last time. It was harder to get up on, but I was able to steer and cut better than the long foam board. Surfing could definitely be my sport.

Eventually the waves were getting far and fewer between and when I looked around, I hadn't noticed that the undercurrent had carried me out a far ways from where I started. I spent a long time swimming back towards the area of the beach that Tommy's Bar was located, and by the time I made it there I was completely exhausted.

By the time I made it back to Eddie and James they were joking around and people watching. Eddie said he was glad I returned because he had no idea how he was going to explain to my mom that I disappeared in the Bali ocean. James couldn't stop me from laughing. He was leading on some of the beach vendors and then would completely dismiss them because it wasn't "exactly" what he was looking for.

The beach vendors all wear hats with their names written on the top, and there was one woman that was selling sarongs by Tommy's Bar. The name she had listed on her hat was "Big Boob". Singular. She spent the entire time we were there sleeping on her chair with her sarongs in her hand. When she woke up an hour or so later, she walked over to the three of us and tried to sell us sarongs. We said we weren't interested, but we asked her how business was today. Apparently it was a really slow day. She hadn't sold any sarongs because she didn't see any tourists. There are just "no tourists", she says. James leans over and whispers loud enough for us all to hear, "no one to see when your eyes are completely closed".

A few nights ago I told Eddie about all the things I had on my list that I had to do while I was in Indonesia. Finding love was not one of them. I was continuing on. I was determined to continue on. I still needed to go to Ubud for the rice fields and yoga, and I was going to climb a volcano. Okay, says Eddie, I want to come with you. He'll check out of the hotel tomorrow. He paid for another 2 nights, but some things are more important than money. It's just money, he says. There is only one reason that I would tell him no, and I still haven't heard a single thing from my last email. Let's go on an adventure, I tell Eddie. Eddie and I buy a couple of tickets for tomorrow's Ubud shuttle.

Eddie and I met up again with James and we headed to Tommy's Bar again for sunset. We sat on the beach, in our plastic chairs, drinking beer. It was Eddie and my last night in Kuta. Eddie held onto my hand and we watched the sun go down. It was like every night since I arrived. Simply romantic.

Once it was dark the three of us made our way towards a small avenue for some dinner and an early night. James headed up to the airport to pick up their other friend, Maya, while Eddie and I stopped off at a convenience store, picked up a couple of beers and sat around the hotel pool and chatted about life back home and music. Eddie says to me that there is a stereophonics song that will always remind him of me: Dakota. He plays it to me. I fall instantly in love with it. We stay up chatting by the pool until we are both too tired.

Eddie is so nice; he makes me laugh and helps me to forget about the things that are spinning through my head all the time. He helps me become patient. There are no expectations for anything more than enjoying each other's company and really good conversations. Maybe one day I will be ready for something different than the idea I've had in my head for so long or maybe not. Time will tell. As it is right now, I'm not looking for anything different than what I am currently doing. All of this is okay with me. I am just in this moment.

Uncertain Loyalties

Ubud, Indonesia
June 22

I woke up in the morning so confused. Confused and heartbroken. I called my mom. I haven't spoken to her in a couple of days. I told her I didn't know what was going on. I would consider myself to be a very loyal person. Maybe too loyal. Loyal to a fault. I told her that I was enjoying Eddie's company, but I still hadn't heard anything from my ex. Eddie and I were now continuing on to a new location and if I would have heard anything from my ex I would tell Eddie it ends here. We have an expiration date; does it matter if it's today or a week from now? I felt like I was holding my breath for a response from my ex. Anything. It was my Sunday. It had been days since I sent him that last message; the one where I asked him to tell me that he loves me. He wants to be with me. Mom's advice was just to have fun. Don't overthink it. Enjoy this moment. If my ex is interested, he knows where to find me and how to reach me, but maybe it sends a pretty clear message if I have to wait days to hear "I love you too. I want to be with you. I will do everything in the world to make that happen".

Just do what I've been doing. Some pretty solid advice. For now.

Ubud was a two-hour drive away. It is a lush, green, jungle with monkeys walking everywhere. The shuttle Eddie and I booked picked us up and had people already jammed inside. All the travellers spoke about where they were going, what they were doing and where they were coming from. At this point I thought it was time to stop telling people that Eddie and I were on our honeymoon. Our actual story, we met five days ago in the visa queue, was so much more amazing. We haven't been apart since. Before I knew it we had arrived in Ubud.

Just as I was walking out of our hotel in Kuta I made a split second decision and booked a place for Eddie and me to stay at in Ubud. I was looking at something a bit more than my typical budget, but not by a lot. I thought Ubud deserved a splurge based on the pictures I have seen of the place. Especially with this new found romance. I could never have expected what I received when I booked.

Once Eddie and I were dropped off in Ubud we grabbed a "taxi", or really some guy that said he was a taxi, but using his own van. He took us a little ways out of the town to this long driveway. As we pulled up to the reception desk it blew me away. The hotel was a series of bungalows and infinity pools placed up along the mountain side overlooking the jungle. It was simply gorgeous.

The staff dropped our bags off at the bungalow and Eddie and I walked around the grounds enjoying the different tiers and pools that the resort had to offer. We caught the shuttle into town and enjoyed dinner with some local culture.

Ubud is much more of what I was wanting from Bali. A little bit smaller with a variety of chic stores and restaurants. After some walking around the town, and me buying a small overpriced anklet, we stopped to have dinner at this cute café that overlooked the rice paddies. We spent the entire evening each lost in our own thoughts. When I returned to the table after going to the washroom I saw Eddie entrenched in his phone. "What is so important right now?" I teased. Eddie turned his phone around. It was a picture of me. I was gone a moment and he was thinking about me.

So where should my loyalties really be placed? I have the worst love triangle in the world. One man I could be in love with and I'm thinking about someone who needs days to tell me he loves me. Please, just bring me the right answer.

The Difference a Day Makes

Ubud, Indonesia
June 23

I woke up in the morning from a dream. I dreamed that my ex was getting married to another girl. It jolted me awake and I couldn't get back to sleep. So I decided to get some writing done. It was my Monday morning, and it was my ex's Sunday night.

As I opened my iPad I saw that I finally received the response from the email I had sent him on Thursday. It was short. It made me sad to read it. I waited days for any response and what I received felt worse than getting no response. To add insult to injury it felt like it was sent as a last minute reminder before his weekend was done. He waited until my weekend was done. His message said this was not his final response. He did love me and he could love the new me. He will go on a date with me when I am back, but am I over him?

The breath I have been holding onto finally was released. I told him about the dream that woke me up. I replied back to him that all this time I just wanted him to grab me and hold on. He needs to pick me. But the longer it takes him to decide that the more unlikely I will be there when he is ready. I tell him that he gave me the full-body love feeling that I never had before, and I doubt I would ever have again.

As I write my morning entry he replies again. He has been holding onto me. He never wanted to lose me. I did something to his heart and that is never going away. I hold onto his words, but I don't know if that is enough. He says he will have more for me soon but I don't know if I believe there will be.

Eddie and I have been together for almost a week now. Whether either of us are in a place to be ready for something more than this moment is not my focus. I am really enjoying the days, the laughter and the company. I really enjoy feeling like someone wants to be with me and will do anything possible to enjoy my company, and that's all I'm really happy to have. I am finally starting to learn to not overthink the days or the future, and just allow things to be for the moment.

Before leaving the resort I do get another message from my unfinished love story. Was it his more? He tells me to have a good dream of us. Maybe looking at some photos will help.

I don't even know how to reply anymore. I am upset it took him four days to respond with a few lines. I am upset with myself that had I received his response yesterday it could have been enough for me to have said to Eddie not to join me. I am sad that the only action my ex is willing to commit to is maybe a date when I am back. My overactive head doesn't know if that means he still wants to be with me now or if he wants to wait until I am home and see where everything shakes out? I stop thinking about it. Enjoy the moment I am in right now. Decide when, and if, my unfinished love story does tell me the more he wants to say.

Eddie and I decide to walk over to Monkey Forest. Monkey Forest is a sacred site dedicated to a few Hindu temples, and saved as a park for the monkeys to live in. Despite a few monkeys around the town they rarely leave the forested area. As Eddie and I walked around we had monkeys all over us, climbing on our arms and heads. I had a great time, but there is something a little fearful and unpredictable about monkeys. I don't like them near me.

We left the park and walked over to an organic café with a great selection of juices. The day was hot and we needed a break. We finished our smoothies and decided to stick around for a light lunch. My mind was stuck on my unfinished love story. Eddie then asked if it would be okay if we stopped being physical in the bedroom.

"I just want to see if this is something more than sex", he says.

I felt disappointment throughout my body, but yes, I agreed. Let's see what this really is.

We went out again for dinner and chatted the night away. I still didn't know what to think about my unfinished love story or even my now new non-physical romantic fling. Eddie and I made another plan to go to one of the other islands together and see where things go from there. At some point I know his company will have to end. I am supposed to be in India on July 6th, and that will be a good thing. It will give me back the self-reflection time to clear my head and look at everything. But until that day, which is still a ways away, I'm not going to worry or stress about it.

I'm here right now. Eddie is here with me. My ex has always known how to reach me, and what he would have to say, and when I finally feel like he is starting to get there I have someone else capturing my heart.

What a difference a day makes.

Yoga in Ubud

Ubud, Indonesia
June 24

I woke up in the morning and saw there was another message from my ex on Facebook. It wasn't the "more" response that I was told to wait for. Instead it was terrible news.

> Him: My storage unit got broken into. Everything is gone. The camera you bought me. All my personal stuff. I'm just lost

> Me: It's just stuff. You have your health, you can rebuy items.

I wanted to be there for him. I felt truly terrible for him.

Eddie could see that I was visibly upset in the morning and he asked me about it. I don't feel there is any need to lie or hide any part of my life around him. He already knows about my history, and he understands that I am not completely jumping into us with both feet right now, but he does appreciate that for the next two weeks we can just be each other's significant others and see how we feel about each other when we do have to eventually walk away.

I told Eddie what my ex had said, and he asked me why would my ex would feel it was necessary to fill me in on those details? I knew, but I don't know if I really knew. I want to believe that I know. Then in Eddie's simplicity he said, "it's because you are tied around his finger". Eddie tells me I waited days for my ex to tell me that he still loves me, and when his life is falling apart he wants me somehow provide him with comfort?

I blankly stared at Eddie when he said that. He has no reason to make me upset, or to try to shut the book forever on my ex. Eddie just is, and his opinion offers the same. I know that I am not completely over my past yet. I have been hanging onto my unfinished love story for months, when everyone was telling me to move on. I haven't been dishonest with Eddie about any of the events or my exchanges with my ex. But maybe he was right. My ex knows that I will respond to him. I will provide him with comfort, even after months of asking for his love, and not receiving it. I'm not unhappy to provide that comfort, but I do need to be aware at what point being there for someone who couldn't be there for me before affects the good things in my life.

"I feel like life is putting my through a test that has been hard to handle", my ex says.

I am so angry as soon as he writes that. I know what the test is. It's the exchange we had a couple of weeks ago. When I asked him if we can work on us, what does he have to lose? He responded "the same thing I did last time. Everything". Life came back and told him that now he has LITERALLY nothing to lose. Now what are the most important things in your life?

It takes me a while to find the right words. I tell him that Buddhists believe we should release all attachment. Our materials, our bodies and our connections to others can all disappear. Without saying more I tell him that I am in a happy place. Then as a petty stab in the event he hasn't taken the moment to see the bigger picture I tell him "you make a lot of money. You can buy almost everything back".

The tables have turned. Now he is the one holding his breath for any responses from me. Almost immediately, "I worked so hard for that stuff".

I want to scream "I worked so hard for us"! I think to myself you're so concerned about losing your stuff, and you took no action when you were losing me. I decide instead to leave it. I have nothing to say.

Eddie and I decided to check out of our hotel on the hill and find something within the interior of the town.

Eddie wanted to show me an alternative way of vacationing with someone. On my own I have no problems staying in budget accommodations, but with someone else this is a new experience.

We jumped into the free shuttle to take us into the town site, and started chatting with the driver if there was anywhere he would recommend for us to try out now. He had a friend that owned a place. Of course he did. We asked him if we could be dropped off there instead of the Central Palace stop, since we were the only ones in the vehicle. Not a problem.

We were dropped off down this tiny little alley and told to walk down another little alley, where we came to a row of different homestays. We walked into one, and they said they did have space and he showed us a room. We checked in and then walked the town. The only thing that I absolutely had to do today was to go to a yoga class. It had been so long since I was able to practice in a proper class and I missed it so much.

The entire morning and afternoon was spent wandering and sitting in little cafés. We stopped at a cheap little place for lunch and sat along the sidewalk edge to do some people watching. At one point a tourist woman stood on the street, holding out a plastic bottle while she made her son take a pee in it. Then shortly after that a local old man came up to Eddie, rubbed his shoulders, asking him if he wanted a massage. Despite asking Eddie several, several times, Eddie still insisted that he was good for a massage. I could have peed myself I was laughing so hard.

By mid-afternoon Eddie needed a nap and I finally found the peace inside myself to reply with the love and support my unfinished love story needed during this time.

"I know it's so tough right now, but maybe there is a bright side to all of this. Maybe you're not really lost, but now you have the opportunity to be really found. This massive setback gives you a chance to look at your life and really figure out what is really, truly important".

I left Eddie at the hotel and I headed by myself to yoga. I was under the impression that there were yoga studios all over Ubud, but the locals kept telling me just to go to Yoga Barn. I walked down the street and caught a taxi. I arrived at the studio just as the class was getting started.

The instructor played his coconut guitar and in a mix between song and speech he informed the class on the format of the session. It was supposed to be an intermediate Vinyasa class, however it was an intense class that included stalls, holds and inversions. At one point, when the class was working on doing the splits, the instructor talked about it being a position of surrender. That it was not to be forced and to allow the body and the mind to relax and be in the position. The instructor said that we should surrender more in our lives and stop trying to force so much. It really spoke to me. I do have a lot of good things happening in my life right now and if I surrender to the good and stop trying to force other elements I could continue to have a lot of happiness. Yet despite understanding that I need to let go, I still couldn't stop thinking about, and wanting to be there for my unfinished love story.

Welcome to Paradise

I'm not sure if I would have decided to come to Gili T on my own, but I am so glad I am here. When Eddie and I met with his friend, James, earlier in the week he spoke about going to the Gili islands. It was something I originally considered before arriving in Indonesia, I don't know if I would have made it, but here I am. Paradise.

As I was eating breakfast, and catching some Wi-Fi, I read three messages my ex sent me. Two were sent in his early morning, another 11 hours later. He was angry. My last couple blog posts started mentioning Eddie. I also revealed some of my doubts that I didn't know if my unfinished love story was even interested in loving me anymore. He said he would rather Skype over sending messages. His last message turned all to business. He needed information for his insurance company.

I responded with back with anger. After our last Skype date I told him I would love to do it again, but I never heard anything from him again. I sent my long message saying I needed to know if he still loved me. I felt like when he eventually responded it was a last minute thought.

I barely had time to send what I wrote. The shuttle Eddie and I booked to get us to the jetty in Padang Bai was early. The two times that I've caught the shuttle since being in Bali they have both been early. We arrived at the jetty and waited for our speed boat to the Gili T.

The Gili islands are made up of 3 small islands. Gili T is the biggest, but it would still take only a couple of hours to ride around the perimeter of the island on push bike. There are two smaller, quieter islands, but most people stay on Gili T for the restaurant selection and nightlife while still experiencing the natural beauty that is the Gili's. There are no dogs, no motorbikes, and no cars on the Gilis. You get around either by walking, push bike or horse and cart. The side streets aren't lined with lights, and depending on the accommodations, such as ours, there is no hot water. As basic as it is, it is unbelievably romantic.

Once Eddie and I arrived at the island we barely had enough time to catch our breath and take it all in. We hadn't booked any accommodations, but were immediately greeted by a young man who showed us a picture of the bungalows that he was trying to rent out. Upon inspection it looked good enough, so we said we would take it for at least one night and then see from there.

We dropped off our bags and walked almost the entire length of the Main Street. Restaurants, hotels, pools, sunbathers, dive shops, and convenience stores line the entire length of the street. Every now and then we would have to dodge out of the way as a horse and buggy would come barrelling down the road. It felt unbelievably surreal.

Eddie and I met up with James and Maya just before sunset and took two horse and buggies to the Sunset Bar. By this point I was really starting to feel like Eddie and I were turning into a real couple. Maya wanted to hear all the details about how Eddie and I met and how we were enjoying our time together. She kept saying how romantic is all was. Eddie insisted it felt like we were right off a movie. It was hard to understand how two people, who just met a week ago, could be as in-sync as we were.

We lounged on a raised platform while we ate and drank with perfect views of the most perfect sunset. We laughed at the worst performing fire dancer. I only wanted to be right where I was. In this moment.

Snorkelling Open Water

I went to yoga early this morning. It was easy to wake up. A majority of Indonesia is Muslim and the call to prayer was played around 5AM, which could be heard all over the island.

It was nice to go to a slower class. Since meeting Eddie I have been off on my normal routine that I've created since being away. It's not a bad thing, just something that I needed to be aware of and remind myself.

For me the biggest thing was that I hadn't been doing my daily morning meditations. My head was getting muddy. I wasn't clearing my thoughts daily anymore. I wasn't working on releasing the thoughts that were not creating positivity in my life. I was losing my concentration that I am here to learn how to calm down and to focus on the many, many really good things in my life right now.

While I was receiving messages of support from so many people, excited to read my postings mentioning Eddie, they were also concerned that I was still putting in so much effort into my unfinished love story.

When Eddie and I got back from the sunset bar last night I checked my messages again. My ex was no longer going to be reading anymore of my blogs, or looking at anymore of my pictures. I didn't even know that he ever was. I asked him several times if he read them, and he never responded. It's not that I would have ever changed my writing or postings if he was or wasn't, but knowing that he was reading them would have let me feel that he was supporting me. I wanted him to read them. It would have been a symbol of love that I desired from him for so many months.

He said he was not in the space for all this hurt.

I responded back, "completely understand", because I did. I had been hurting for so long. "I do not regret anything I write or post. This is my story. I don't regret the amount of effort I put into us. I feel bad that it took you too long to return that effort". I couldn't figure out if I gave up right at the finish line or if Eddie was brought into my life to show me that I had already put in too much effort.

When I got back to the room from yoga, Eddie said it looked like I just finished a very intense conversation. I said I did. With myself. I told Eddie that I realize now that I must mediate daily to keep myself in check from now on. My head is busy enough and at least when I work at cleaning it out daily I'm in a better place.

After a shower and washing my yoga wear I sat down to get my writing done, when Eddie asked me if I was interested in having us join James and Maya on a snorkelling boat. He said we can miss it if I would rather write. He knows writing is important to me, I told him it could wait. I wanted to head out the water.

We met his friends and unfortunately just missed the group boat. We thought we could charter a small one for cheap enough. After negotiating with a couple of vendors we were able to get a glass-bottom boat with all the snorkelling equipment. We grabbed a few snacks and jumped into the boat.

The ride was bumpy and sprayed water all over the place. Our boat driver stopped just before the second island, Gili Meno. There was plenty of coral and lots of fish to see. The sea swells were intense and it was easy to be carried away by the current. At one point I looked up and couldn't even see the boat. A wave passed over and I finally saw it, meters away. It was going to be a long swim back. After swimming for several minutes back towards the boat I had to pause because I was laughing too hard. I said to Eddie that we probably had to pay extra to have the boat stay close.

When the four of us were back in the boat we drove over to the next location, Turtle Point. We swam around for a bit, but it wasn't until the very end that we were able to see the silhouette of a turtle swimming away from us.

Our third stop was Gili Air, where we docked and had lunch at a little café. The souvenir peddlers were all over our table showing us bracelets, necklaces, one man trying to sell us a bow and arrow set. James in his classic teasing fashion would quickly scan the entire selection of bracelets and say he was interested in buying a purple one, but since they didn't have purple he has to pass. We would laugh as the woman would try to convince him that no one wears purple and maybe a shark tooth one would be better for him. After several minutes of us all laughing, James eventually bought a couple of bracelets.

As we finished our lunch we all decided that the swimming in the open water was exhausting and we were all pretty much done with snorkelling for the day. When we made it back to Gili T, the day was still early so Eddie and I had a sleep on the beach, met up with his friends for dinner and drinks and had a great night "out out", heading to a couple of bars and dancing the night away.

Eddie

We all partied too hard last night. As the night progressed we were all feeling fun, flirty and loose. At some point we were sitting on a patio drinking and James was passed out at the table. The failure of drinking too early in the day. Eddie walked James back to his hotel while Maya and I drunkenly talked about my two different relationships. I told Maya that Eddie and I stopped being physical to see if our relationship had the potential to be more. Maya asked what I thought the potential with Eddie was so far. She asked, "do you think you love him? You look at him like you do". I told her there is definitely something more there than a standard vacation fling. When he looks at me he looks so deep into my eyes that I feel a connection far deeper with him than what's on the surface. Maya asked if he has said anything to me, and I said it was far too soon. "You know when you know", she said.

"That may be true", I replied, "but it's also easy to fall in love in Bali when there is no daily responsibilities. It's the daily routines that really determine how strong a love can be."

By this point Eddie returned from the long round trip of ensuring his friend made it back to his bed safely. Eddie took a seat beside me, grabbed my hand. If both of us didn't have our situations maybe we would have completely released ourselves into whatever "this" is. However, it might be because of our unavailable situations to begin with that we were able to connect at all. We had another drink each and decided to walk back to our hotels.

James, Maya, Eddie and I all agreed in the morning that a day of poolside lounging was the perfect plan. The pool had Wi-Fi, which allowed me to update my blog. Eddie made a point of reading every one of my blog postings the moment

I would post it. He loved reading them. My heart would fill with warmth when I would look over at him and see he was staring intensely at the screen of his phone; the open page was my words.

I then checked my Facebook to see if there were any more messages from my ex, but instead of seeing his picture on my frequent contact list he was completely missing. He deleted me as his friend. We met back in 2007. He added me after we met casually at a bar. He said the moment he saw me something in him said that I was the one he was going to marry.

For years he would send me a message here or there, never having the courage to ask me out on a date. I somehow kept him around, despite having a long-term relationship after our meeting. When things were falling apart with my third love, he sent me a message asking about one of my cryptic status postings. For some reason I felt compelled to be so honest with this perfect stranger. He sent me another message when I made a mention that I was single, "same story, just a year later" I said to him. Then, eventually, when I posted that I was ready to start dating again, he finally found the courage and said "pick me", and I did. That was our official start. Suddenly all our history was gone. More history than just our years of dating.

I told Eddie that my ex finally deleted me. "Kimmy, maybe that's a good thing. Your heart can now completely be open to someone that *will* never let you go". Eddie then tells me since meeting me all the things he thought he wanted with his soon-to-be ex-wife he no longer does.

Eddie does show me a new possibility. He has helped me see things differently, simply. I am honest with Eddie about the thoughts that cloud my head. He listens and then tells me to slow down. I just wish it was that simple to turn off all my thoughts of my ex.

I sometimes think that I am similar to Carrie, from Sex and the City, I have my Big and Eddie is now Aiden. Everyone wanted Carrie to stay with Aiden. He was really, really good to her.

As the sun was setting Eddie and I left the pool and found a restaurant that had lay down service by the ocean. We ordered pizza, he held me close and we listened to the waves crash against the beach. I tell him no matter what we will always be really good friends.

Like everything else in my life right now, I don't have to make any decisions today. I am having fun. The moment I am in now I could have never imagined it a month ago. I still have my own personal adventure to continue and I will be back to travelling alone soon enough. For now I love the company that I am keeping. I feel like there is so much potential with this open door. I am scared beyond belief. But life is about taking chances and risks. I may have all the answers when I am done, but for now I get to enjoy the days with someone who has really turned my entire story around.

Time for Goodbyes

I read an article many months back that said never date a traveller. She will be fun and exciting, but will always break your heart. Travelling is her goal, and eventually she will have to leave.

I woke up early in the morning to try to get back into a bit of a routine. I dressed in my yoga wear and headed down to the beach early. I wanted to get back into my morning meditations and start clearing my busy head again. I sat down on a platform, facing the sea, and went right back into it. My head started to feel calmer immediately. I asked about the things and people in my life, and I heard back that I should just have fun and no decisions need to be made right now. When I opened my eyes the sun was rising over the horizon. It made a perfect yellow line across the sea. I just thought about how beautiful all of this is. It was time for yoga.

Once yoga was finished I headed back to my room. I chatted with my mom for a bit and let her go as soon as our breakfast had arrived. Eddie suggested we rent push bikes for the day and ride around the island. It sounded like a great idea.

We headed to the closest place that rented bikes and picked up a couple for the day. We then headed out at a slow, relaxed pace. We definitely didn't want to go too fast, it could cause a horse and buggy traffic accident.

We rode around the island, making a couple stops here and there to take a look at the sea, to relax in the shade, and then finally grab some lunch at a restaurant that had platforms above the sea.

Eddie and I started chatting about what my schedule was going to look like for the next week. I had a flight booked to Singapore. I picked Indonesia as a destination because I wanted to climb a volcano. That was a non-negotiable. As we were backtracking dates we then came to the realization that our days were numbered. We knew going in that we were going to have an expiry date, it was just so surprising that it was all the sudden here. If I wanted to do my volcano hike, I would have to leave tomorrow, and that means tonight would be our last night together.

I cried. How could this be? I definitely was going to miss the company; it was so nice to have someone so close to me again. But I truly felt I was going to miss him. How could I feel this connected to someone after a week and a half? It was time to face reality. For both of us. For him I was the distraction that he needed to get him through his own pain. For me he was the voice of reason and encouragement that I needed to move me to the next chapter in the love for myself. We sat listening to the sea while he held me, and I let all my tears out. It was finally time to let him go.

We finished the rest of our ride around the island and met up with Maya and James on the beach and chilled out in a lounger. We all agreed to meet for dinner that night, and have a fun send-off for me. We went to this amazing kebab place, ate and drank most of the night away. When Maya asked if Eddie and I would ever see each other again I found it tough to hold back the tears. I didn't know. Tonight was not about being sad though. Focus on fun. We found so many things to laugh about throughout dinner. Then it was time to end the night and this amazing chapter in my life.

I told Eddie we will always be friends and he will always have a super special place in my heart. I can't believe that he was brought into my life to begin with, but the universe conspires to bring us what we need when we need it. In such a short amount of time I could have really fallen in love with Eddie. Then as quickly as it started, this intense, fun and amazing relationship is now over. I wouldn't change a moment of it for the world.

Head Above the Clouds

I woke up, silently packed my bag and left the room without saying goodbye. I wrote Eddie a love letter on the back of a hotel receipt and I slipped it into one of his books before leaving. If I never see him again I want him to know how much he meant to me. I could already feel the tears forming. I needed to get out of there before I really started to cry.

I caught the boat to Lombok to start my Mount Rinjani adventure. Like most other Indonesian bookings, there is no set check-in plan and I have to go with a lot of faith that someone will actually be there to take me on my tour. Thankfully when I got off the boat there was a man there calling out for "Mr. Kim". Close enough.

I was partnered up with a 25-year old Brazilian man who had spent 9-months living in India and was now taking the next three months to travel SE Asia. We were loaded into a horse carriage and taken to a homestay for a quick breakfast prepared for us. After four days on the Gili's it took me back a bit to see motor scooters and cars again.

We then jumped into a van for the drive to base camp of Mount Rinjani. Mount Rinjani is the second tallest volcano in Indonesia and is considered to be in the top 10 of most stunning in the country. Realistically, it doesn't matter. The whole country is stunning and I don't think I could have gone wrong choosing any volcano to hike.

I chose the 1 Night/2 Day Mt. Rinjani tour which takes me to the rim of the volcano, spend the night and back down the next day. For an extra night I could have hiked down to the hot springs with an optional mountain summit. But with limited time I was fine with just viewing the volcano rim.

At base camp, the organizer said our group had already left and we would meet them at the 2nd post for lunch but we had to move. So we started hiking. The hike was not easy. There were lots of slopes and steady uphill climb. I stayed close to our guide, who was hiking in flip flops and because of Ramadan he was also fasting. The guide chose a dance song on repeat from his cell phone and we hiked staying steady with the beat. The Brazilian struggled, stopping several times to catch his breath, and complain about how exhausting the climb was. I told him to stop looking up and just concentrate on putting one foot in front of the other.

After two and half hours we made it 3.5km to the second outpost. We ate a meager lunch, and a short rest before continuing on now with the larger group.

The terrain turned from tropical to arid and dry. The ascent was tough and my head was spinning with thoughts of the last couple of weeks. I worked to try to stop it and only focus on the moment; enjoy where I was right now. I counted my steps and every time I got to 8 I would stop and take a slight pause and then carry on. I no longer wanted to stop. I was afraid that my muscles would seize and I would have nothing left to push through. I looked around and saw that I had climbed above the clouds. I was so close. I pushed my body harder and further, trekking over dirt and dust which eventually moved into rock and hard surface. When I saw tents a wave of relief flowed over me. I made it to the top.

I saw a lot of people standing around and joined them. The view took my breath away. A volcano surrounded by a lake surrounded by mountain. Absolutely breathtaking and worth every step of the way up. 7.5km. 2555m.

I sat on the edge of the cliff side and watched the sun set over top of the clouds. There are no words.

Surprises at the Bottom

West Lombok, Indonesia
June 30

It sounds a lot sexier to say that I slept on the top of a mountain than it actually was. The sleep was hard on my little foam mat, and the Brazilian, who shared my tent, kept moving over to my side.

I woke up as my tent started to glow. Sunrise was coming up, and what better place to see it from the top of the world?

I walked over to one of the viewpoints, but because of the position of the mountain peak the sun rose behind the mountain. I walked to another, quieter, area and started to get in a morning meditation when I was interrupted by one of the porters for breakfast. I ate fast; my downward team was already heading out, while my current team was making their way towards the hot springs.

The trek down I spent chatted with a 29-year old Belgium woman who had been living in Australia for the last couple of years, and was making her way back to Belgium. I realized that as a busy-head myself I attract other busy-headed people, and it actually leaves me feeling quite exhausted talking with them. I had no idea that is what I do to other people. She was telling me stories about her career, love life and her feeling that she is still lost, but now has to go back to Europe to prove to her parents that her travels were well worth it. I gave her my advice, and maybe I've grown so much over the last few months, but I felt like my advice was coming from a place that was much older than our two-year age difference. She dismissed all my suggestions, and I realized that I need to stop asking people for advice if I'm not going to take it either.

I made it down to base camp and had a much deserved beer while I waited for the shuttle to take me back to Senggigi.

As we drove I had this feeling that I received a message of love. Maybe my ex had something more to say.

We stopped briefly to switch vehicles. I checked my email. There was only man that messaged me, a Facebook message.

Eddie: I missed you so much this morning.

I smiled. I missed him too.

I was lost in thought during the final drive to my hotel. I went to check in and the receptionist said my friend already checked-in for me. I was taken to my room, and there stood Eddie, nervously smiling. "I said I would travel the world for the right girl, so I took a boat."

I laughed.

"I wasn't happy with the way we said goodbye. It wasn't good enough", he said. "I hope it's okay that I'm here". Yes, of course!

I answered, "Only if you would rather delay the goodbye instead of trying to create a better one."

All my life I have been looking for someone that would hold me tight and not let go. Someone that if I tried to leave would tell me simply, "no. I will follow you because I don't want to lose you". I don't care that it was only a boat ride. He was here. My heart melted in that moment. I was so excited to have this unexpected company for dinner, and for my last two nights in Indonesia.

Back to the Start

Kuta, Indonesia
July 1

Eddie and I decided Senggigi was too dead for us to enjoy so we bought a boat ticket back to Bali. We thought it would only take us a few hours to get back. How wrong we were.

I woke up back in my groove at my natural 6AM time and decided to make the most out of the day. I called my mom then decided to do a morning meditation. Like any skill missing my practice takes me back a few steps so I wasn't able to stay for the 20 minutes straight like I used to, but I know getting back to a consistent morning routine will get me there. I finished my writing and then woke Eddie up to grab some breakfast.

I was feeling homesick in the morning. Maybe the 3-month hump has finally hit me. I really wanted a "real" cup of coffee and not the powder stuff they serve here. I was tired of banana pancake and craved a proper omelette with bacon and toast. Thankfully Eddie was feeling to same. We found a seaside restaurant and watched the waves crash on the beach while I ate a proper vegetarian omelette. Unfortunately I had to go without the bacon; I had a hard time bringing myself to asking a Muslim for bacon on Ramadan.

The boat ride back to Bali was the milk run. By the time we made it back to Kuta, grabbed a very late lunch and found a hotel, we had just enough time to head over to Tommy's Bar for our sunset ritual.

There was a group of Aussies already sitting at Tommy's Bar. We chatted with them then I told them it was Canada Day. I poorly sang my national anthem at the top of my lungs for their enjoyment.

Eddie and I chatted over beers about each of our head space being elsewhere today. Long commutes will tend to do that. After sunset we met up with Maya and James for dinner, drinks and watching fire dancing. Maya suggested we celebrate Eddie and my romance by going to an overpriced champagne bar where we split a bottle of sparkling wine. We laughed the entire night.

Don't Ask Me Why

Kuta, Indonesia
July 2

Every now and then I dream of a little boy. This time he was older than I have ever seen him. I was potty training him. It was a mess. There was poop everywhere, and I was covered, yet my husband thought he had never in his life seen me looking sexier. The dream woke me up, along with a song in my head: "Don't Ask Me Why" by Billy Joel. I don't know the last time I heard that song.

Eddie was still sleeping when I woke up. I quietly left the room and sat on the patio for a morning meditation. My head held onto blank thoughts and then said my next couple stops, India and Dubai, were going to be "transformative". I was so intrigued by that word.

It was still early so I took a walk to grab coffees for me and Eddie. I returned, wrote, and waited for Eddie to wake up. I told Eddie about my dream and he said he would definitely find the mother of his child looking sexy in every moment, even that one. I then found the Billy Joel song on YouTube and played it for him. It was probably the first time in years I had heard the song. It had lines in it that reminded me of two men that were occupying my heart. But it was the chorus that touched me. It is not up to us to decide who, when or where we will meet someone that captures our heart. Accept the gift from the universe of the person that was brought to us. Give gratitude for their presence. Allow people to choose to be in our lives.

It was my last day in Indonesia. There were only two things I had to do: buy new shoes and get one last chance on the surfboard. Eddie and I skipped the free breakfast and went for a much needed big breakfast. I held back the tears while we ate, knowing this might be our last time together. When we finished we walked, holding hands, down the street. Eddie quietly sang lines from "Stay", and without needing to say more, I sang with him.

I popped into the first Havianas store and bought myself some new shoes. My current one had been worn every day since my first day in Australia and they finally broke. Those shoes had walked more of the world than most people, and it was a bitter sweet moment to let them go.

The morning had already passed us by, so we grabbed a quick, light lunch and hit the beach. Our last time visiting Tommy. Eddie sat and had a beer while I took out one of the shorter boards and rode a couple of waves.

Once I was done we sat for a bit longer on the beach while I agreed to have a woman paint my toenails until it was time for the sea turtle release. There is a turtle conservation habitat on the beach and every day there is a sea turtle release. Eddie and I waited patiently while the kids were given their turtles first, then we were given ours. I was beaming! Everyone with a turtle lined up and gently tipped our containers for the turtles to crawl along the beach until they reached the ocean.

Eddie allowed me to pick a restaurant for our last dinner together. I chose an interesting Mexican place. Then we met up with a large group of friends that had arrived last night for a blowout final night. As the drinks and shots poured freely Eddie could see that I was finished. He left his friends and walked with me back to our hotel. We then had a last moment as we sat on the balcony chatting about what an amazing ride it has been for both of us. He played me Stereophonics "Dakota", this time both of us quietly singing the words. This was not going to be our goodbye, but it was the perfect end to the first half of my trip. Three months left to go. I will miss everyone I met over the last two weeks.

Solo in Singapore

Indonesia provided me more than I could ever imagine. For the first time in months I felt like I was loved again. I truly missed that feeling. More than I would have ever expected. I spent months reaching out to my unfinished love story and I felt like all I was getting was handfuls of sand. Every time I received a bit I would hold onto it so tight, but the tighter I would hold onto the sand it would spill through my clenched fist and I would be left with nothing again. The months in solitude slowly provided me with a clear head. I always knew what I wanted in my life, but now I felt like I could articulate those needs and wants more clearly. I was also learning to become really okay with losing my plan and accepting the mystery and surprises that life wanted to give me. I hated being open to the plot twists that the universe loves to give. Now I was finding happiness in the unexpected.

Two weeks. 16 days. The words, the time, the intensity, all of it seems so surreal. I spent two weeks in Indonesia. I was with one person almost every hour during that time, from the moment that we met in the queue. All I wanted from my ex was more time. As I sat with Eddie over drinks last night I was brought to tears because I came to the realization that I spent more consecutive time with someone I just met than I did in the two years I was together with my ex. I could feel it in my heart that I needed more time with someone, and the time I spent with Eddie made me know that really was what I needed. I need conversation and touch and long stares into someone's eyes. I want to feel like I am touching their soul and they are embracing mine.

228

Eddie taught me a lot over that short period of time. We were each other's therapy in our individual heartbreak. But the thing I will take away most from him is the way he would talk about his (ex) wife. Despite the fact that she left him for her own journey he still loved her so much. The way he would talk about her, use her nickname, and deep in his heart wish her nothing more than the best things so she could find herself again. It made my heart skip a beat. He believed they would never get back together because she is stubborn in her decisions, but my heart prayed for the tragic love story that was his. I would love to have someone talk about me the way he talks about her. Someone that, if we couldn't be together, he would still feel nothing but pure, intense love for me.

Before finally leaving Eddie he reminded me of my initial focus and task of why I was on this trip.

Remembering to slow down and not trying to rush and plan my life. Two weeks. It took me only two weeks to forget three months of work. The feeling of being loved again made me revert back into my former "plan and schedule" Kim. Slow down, Eddie said last night. Then it hit me. What is my rush, especially right now? My head moves faster than the minutes of a clock. If I planned it all out, if I was determined on the single outcome that I had in my head the moment I landed in Bali I would have never had the conversations and learned as much as I did over these two weeks. I feel like since arriving I somehow walked down a path and am now staring at the house I built from the outside. My chair has been slightly moved and I am now beginning to paint that same bowl of fruit from a different viewpoint.

And as much as I loved my time with Eddie, and would never give up one moment for the world, I am so happy to be taking this plane to Singapore on my own. Back to the joy of solitude. I spent the entire flight listening to Billy Joel's "Don't Ask Me Why" and Stereophonics "Dakota" on non-stop repeat hoping that when the words of the songs started to lose meaning I will find the answers to something. Maybe the answer is just to be solo again. Reset my head. Back to self-awareness and time for reflection.

I am fully prepared for whatever comes next. Surprise or not.

Sowing Happiness and Patience

Singapore, Singapore
July 5

As I was being dropped off at my hotel in Singapore on my first night my cab driver tells me one of those things that any solo female traveller never wants to hear: "So, you're staying in a red-light district. There are brothels all around you. If you hear any sounds or your neighbours are being noisy, just go to sleep. Don't leave your room. Try to avoid going out at night". Great. I booked another hotel for my following two nights.

I had another dream wake me up in the morning. This time it was my deceased grandfather. I was walking my dog and he stopped me and asked me to join him for a drink at an outdoor bar. He wanted me to talk things out over a drink with my unfinished love story. Not only did it wake me up, but it made me feel sad and regretful for some of my actions. I hadn't heard anything from my ex since he deleted me from Facebook a week and a half ago. I meditated on what it meant, and all I heard in my head was "I'm sorry" over and over. That morning I sent my unfinished love story a simple email saying "I'm sorry I hurt you". I didn't want to ramble, like I typically do in my messages to him. I thought the simplicity would either be enough or it won't. I felt good for reaching out.

I officially hit the 3-month homesickness hump that I was warned about. The one where homesickness really starts hitting and it feels like a better idea just to go home. All day yesterday and today I was filled with anxiety, fear and sadness. I thought a lot about Eddie, but I thought about my unfinished love story even more. It saddened me to be stuck in rotating painful thoughts especially after feeling I had worked so hard to get to a good place. I didn't know why my head and my heart couldn't just release. I finally told myself to stop, just stop it. I am done chasing and finding answers about love. Clear my head. Allow love to find me. I will be enough for someone to come to me. Thankfully I leave for my Indian tour tomorrow, that will help keep me right here right now, but I'm not too sure for how long. Time will tell.

I was taking a cab back to my hotel after visiting the zoo when the driver told me that I looked sad. We talked openly about my split heart then he said no matter what I wish for as an outcome I will never get it if I am sad while waiting for the answer. Sadness breeds more sadness and if I was happy I would receive more happiness. What an amazing line to be brought into my life at this moment. We reap what we sow. If I focus on heartbreak that is exactly what I will get.

I realized I lost the patience that I was working so hard to gain. I was spinning myself out thinking too much about my undetermined future. Eddie and I chatted about when we would see each other again. We had brief conversations about me flying home via London and staying with him for a few months. Is that what I want? What would I do for work? Am I willing to immigrate to the UK? However two weeks ago I wanted my life to be with my unfinished love story, moving to Australia and the two of us getting married and starting a family. How could I flip so dramatically?

I still had more I wanted to say to my unfinished love story, so I sent him another message in the afternoon. "I don't want to add confusion to your life, but here it is: if you are in a situation where you literally have nothing left to lose and you still choose me, I am in a situation where I would give it all away to be with you. If you asked me, I would end my trip tomorrow. I would book the first ticket home. I know if we just had the time to talk, to be in front of each other, we would know for sure". My heart felt that was the right thing to say. Now it was time to let go.

I said to myself that I am exactly where I need to be. I can wait again. I can wait for my answers, for love, for people, for all of it. None of it is anywhere as important as where I am right now, and that is my journey, but only in the here and now.

I grabbed a couple of beers from the 7/11 and took them back to my room to enjoy while I did some writing and decided my biggest contemplation right now should be whether I should pack my backpack today or first thing tomorrow.

Indian Arrivals

New Delhi, India
July 6

I woke up received a response from my unfinished love story from the second email I sent. He said he was really hurt and he looked through all our photos to make himself feel better, but all it did was cause him more pain and he decided to take another painful step of deleting me. He said he would talk as long as I don't lead him on. Maybe one day he will meet the new Kim.

My heart was just so overjoyed to hear something from him I barely read the words. I wanted to talk to him now. I sent him a message asking if we could chat before my flight to India.

I went from sadness to overwhelming excitement in only a few hours. I needed to slow down. Meditate. What do I do now? What do I say? My meditation said wait until after India.

Wait until after India?!? Are you kidding me? I potentially have love waiting for me right now. I was too excited. I needed to contact him. The only reason my meditation would want me wait is because I still have too many people giving me outside judgment. If I don't tell anyone about me and my unfinished love story trying to make things work then I won't have to filter outside opinions. This is my story. Today I finally get a happy ending. I sent him another message.

> Me: I'm not going to tell anyone about our exchanges. I don't need outside commentary muddling up my thoughts. I know what I want and how I feel about you. I hope we can work it all out. You are always in my thoughts and my dreams. I truly miss you.

I enjoyed the rest of the morning with my heart and coffee cup full, packing and listening to Ben Howard.

For a while now I have missed many things that I take for granted back home, such as new music, movies and TV shows. I was thrilled to board the flight and see that there was a large selection of new Western movies available.

When we landed my anxiety started to get heavy. I was anxious about arriving in India. So many people told me many fear-mongering stories and I was finding it difficult to rationalize what I should believe and what I should dismiss. I walked off the plane, through customs and then to the pre-paid taxi counter. The cashier wrote me out a chit for my destination and then on a separate piece of paper wrote his cell phone number and made sure I put it in my pocket away from the taxi chit. He told me that he doesn't expect me to need it, but if I run into any trouble to call him immediately.

I walked out of the airport and found a group of men by the very specific black and yellow taxis I was to find. I told them where I was going and one of the men said that he knew the place and asked me to get into his car. He opened the back door for me and I tossed my bag onto the seat as a cloud of dust rose where my bag landed. I sat down, and felt a sting of fear as the floor mat moved and I imagined there was a giant hole from the floor to the street. The entire cab was missing pieces, had wires hanging around and electrical tape holding it all together.

We left the airport and within a few minutes of leaving the terminal the cab driver pulled over. My fear kicked in again. I thought "this is where I die". The cabbie walked over to the passenger side of the outside car, where I was sitting. He bent down and pulled out a rusty nail from the tire. He got back in and I asked him if we had to turn around. He said it was fine, and we were off again, with a flat tire.

As we entered the city I understood the ridiculous Indian traffic. Vehicles were everywhere. There were no such things as traffic lines. There was one person fixing their vehicle, top up, two people underneath, right in the middle of the street. Cars were backing out. Others were moving forward. There were no rules whether a car should only move forward. They could move forward, reverse, and do whatever it takes to get generally where needed. Eventually, after stopping and asking people on the street for directions we made it to the hotel. Addresses are arbitrarily assigned and numbers don't move in any order.

I dropped off my bag and ordered a large meal of butter chicken, rice and naan bread. I felt disgusting for eating so much, but it was so good. I was so full, but forced myself to go for a short walk to the market to check things out. Walking through the streets of Delhi isn't much different than any other Asian city, minus the garbage. There is so much trash on the streets. At one point walking towards the market I saw a dead dog lying in the street. It made my stomach churn.

I walked through the market for about an hour and made it back to the hotel for the meet and greet of the group that I would be hanging out with for the next two weeks. I think India is going to be an eye-opening experience for me.

Day in Delhi

I couldn't sleep. I was hoping to receive another message from my unfinished love story, and sure enough just before 1AM he gave me a short reply. I responded back that I want to be fully committed to him, that I want to work through everything; I also needed to know if he loves me or if he is completely done with us. He responded that he was so hurt by my other relationship and he is willing to talk and get to understand me but right now I should just enjoy my trip and we can see what happens when I get back, then he signed off sweet dreams.

It was 5AM and I replied back. I told him that I loved him, I want to fall in love with him all over again and he is the only man I want to spend the rest of my life with. As if he was waiting for my response I received one right back. He apologized for not being there for me. He told me that I was his everything. He was sorry for not sending me messages when I was first gone, he wanted me to take my trip for me and he didn't want to confuse my growth with communications about how much he loves me. He was opening up so much and he said more than I have heard from him in months. I wanted to write back right away, but more than that I wanted to see his gorgeous face, look at his smile, hear his sexy voice and hopefully make him laugh. I asked if we can Skype. Yes, he says.

I called him from the stairwell of the hotel. We chatted for almost an hour. It was honest, pure and loving. He told me he was sorry for the pictures of him and the other girl. He said his friends were trying to hurt me. I told him it worked. I told him I'm sorry that I left but since being here I realized that it is something that I really needed. I am learning to be a better person and I can't wait to see him again to show him how much I've grown. He told me he joined a dating site three days ago, but he didn't think he was actually ready. I told him I understand and I support him with whatever he needs to do, because I will always be there for him. I told him that since being here I realize Calgary is not the place that I want to settle, and hopefully he is open to moving somewhere else. He said he was scared to have his heart hurt by me again. I said I never want to hurt him again and I will give him my full honesty for everything. He told me he missed me so much and he can't wait until I am home. He wants to take things slow and we could go on dates when I am home. Then we agreed to talk again tomorrow. My heart could have exploded. I was in love and I was really, really happy. For the first time in a long time I didn't feel confused.

After a traditional Indian breakfast of curry and bread our group was taken to a street boy's home. Children run away from their families for a variety of reasons, including physical and sexual abuse, forced labour, bad home environment or extreme poverty. NGOs, like the one we were visiting, send volunteers to walk the streets, train stations and other gathering places to bring the children in before they are blinded by begging ring leaders or get into drugs such as glue huffing.

We were shown the two-room facility where the children eat, sleep and are taught then we were introduced to them. The girls are kept in a separate home, but the boys were all eager to play. I played clapping games and arm wrestling and then showed them pictures off my iPad of snow, my house in the winter, and the many animals I saw at the Singapore zoo. They were all astounded.

We toured the oldest mosque in Delhi and then walked through the winding streets. Raghu, our guide, showed us the different street food and street vendors. The first thing I saw was a man rolling tobacco, nuts, mint and lime paste into a leaf. I bought one, popped the entire leaf in my mouth and chewed. It tasted like black liquorice and made my tongue feel numb. Then when Raghu pointed out the samosas I had to have one. They were spicy, and the potato was so creamy. It was definitely the best samosa I've ever had.

Our group was then taken to a Sikh temple and we were taught a bit about the religion. The back of the temple had a kitchen, where anyone, without any discrimination to wealth, gender, or religion, can come and eat for free. I was touched by their hospitality that I offered to help roll out the naan bread.

A couple of ladies and I separated from the group and visited India gate. After getting a tired of the unwanted male attention and numerous asks for pictures, we decided to take the metro back to the hotel.

For the first time on my trip my head was stuck on my unfinished love story and this time I knew he was thinking about how much he loved me too. I knew what I needed to do next. I tried to FaceTime Eddie, but the connection kept breaking in and out. Finally I sent him a message. I had to tell him today.

Me: Eddie, I appreciate everything we had over the last couple weeks, but when I got to Singapore I sent my ex a message. We chatted this morning. I don't know what we are just yet, but I need to take the next couple of weeks in India to figure it all out. I still love him and I need to focus on that. I am so sorry.

Eddie: Kimmy, you're a great girl. I hope it all works out. I mean what I said that I would travel anywhere in the world for the right girl. Let me know in a couple of weeks if you want me to come meet you. You really captured my heart.

I breathed deeply. I didn't want to cry. I have my original love to focus on.

I emailed my unfinished love story immediately. I needed him to know that I was chatting with Eddie, but that is now over. I told him I would like to keep Eddie as a friend on

Facebook since he helped me through my difficult heartbreak, but if my unfinished love story felt better about me not having him as a friend, I would do whatever to make him feel comfortable. I was not going to do anything to jeopardize our newly sparked love.

The Road to the Pink City

Jaipur, India
July 8

We were Delhi early to head to Jaipur today. Before loading into the bus I called my unfinished love story on Skype again. We chatted about my time in India. He talked about the events he was going to at the Calgary Stampede. I told him about my upcoming destinations and he said he would see about meeting me. We agreed for the time being we wouldn't tell anyone we were chatting to ensure we didn't have to deal with outside opinions. We chatted until I had minutes left to meet up with the group. We agreed to chat again tomorrow. I had a permanent smile on my face.

Although Jaipur is only 285km away from Delhi it took us over 6 hours to get there. The roads in India are often closed or in such bad shape that vehicles groove new paths beside the main roads. Jaipur is also called "The Pink City" because all the buildings are coloured terracotta.

We checked into our hotel, and were given flower garlands as a welcome gift. The hotel then said their Wi-Fi was down and my heart stopped. I finally have been speaking regularly with my love and I didn't want to miss a day. I borrowed my guide's cell phone and sent a quick message to my renewed love letting him know that I would have to miss our Skype date. I prayed that he got the message and that he would understand.

Our guide arranged a sunset tour of the city via rickshaws and we all piled into them, 2-by-2. We cycled through the inner, old city, feeling like a mini parade. People were waving and smiling at us. We went for dinner and were entertained by a couple of young boys performing a marionette show and singing a Bollywood-inspired version of Bruno Mars "Just the Way You Are" on the bongo drum.

When arrived back at the hotel we joked about crashing an anniversary party going on. Our guide encouraged us so we decided to go for it. As soon as we walked in we were greeted by a young woman and man, brought chairs, offered food, and then taken up on stage to be introduced as their "special guests". We were then taught some Bollywood moves and I danced until exhaustion. It's embarrassing in our local culture we would never be that open to anyone that crashed an event, and these people welcomed us with open arms and graciousness. Things to remember in my own life.

Heat Exhaustion and Home Cooking

Jaipur, India
July 9

The heat and cranked up air-conditioning started to get to me today. Since arriving in India I wake up in the middle of the night with my throat feeling incredibly dry and tight. I feel like coughing, but it isn't relieved until I drink enough water. I upped my daily water intake to 4L per day, but I may have to increase that even more. By mid-morning I felt like I was being affected by heat stroke.

We visited the Amber Fort in the morning. I was enjoying the beauty of the fort when heat exhaustion started to hit me. The heat radiating from the stone and marble of the palace, combined with the humidity, was becoming too much for me. I separated myself from the group when I felt an intense headache, a heavy pit in my stomach and general body exhaustion. I drank another litre of water and started feeling good enough to eat something over lunch.

I still didn't have internet in the morning and felt terrible to miss my Skype date. Over lunch I tethered my iPad to my guide's cell phone. A couple messages from him. He was waiting for my call, but assumed I still couldn't get internet. He was still talking with the girl that was in the photos I saw when I was in Vietnam. He let her know that we were talking again and he couldn't communicate with her anymore. I had just enough time to send him a quick message. I told him I was sorry I wasn't able to make our date and I didn't know when I was going to be able to call him again. Maybe the day we leave Agra on Saturday? But more than anything I wanted him to know that I love him, I trust him and I can't wait to kiss his lips again.

I skipped out of the additional sightseeing to rest at the hotel. I woke up after an hour and one of the men in my group and world-traveller, Sean, agreed to join me in the search for some high speed Wi-Fi. We negotiated with a tuk-tuk driver to take us to a café that our guide recommended. When we arrived we both felt like we had reached heaven: a beautiful café with air-conditioning. I ordered a masala tea with a chocolate cake and ice cream. It's been a while since I've had chocolate and my taste buds were in heaven. I sent my love a long message first. I wanted to address his concerns about why I wasn't going to tell anyone that I was talking with him just yet. I didn't want to say anything to anyone not because I made him out to be bad, I truly didn't believe that, but because I cried so much over him. People would be concerned that I would get my heart broken again, and I would probably have the same concern if this situation was one of my friends. I told him not to worry though, he has always been the one for me and I am not worried about having my heart broken, because I know him and I are meant to be. Before ending the email, since we were being so honest with each other I wanted to know why it took him so long to respond to the message I sent him in Indonesia where I said that I needed to know if he still loved me.

I sat eating my chocolate cake, updating my blog and uploading photos. It was early in the morning for my love, but I received a short message from him. I quickly asked him if he could Skype right now. He said he could. We didn't have a lot of time to chat, but every time I see his face I completely light up. Everything does it for me: the sound of his voice, the way his deep brown eyes would light up, the little wrinkles around his eyes, and his random little tuff of grey hair. Sean said he had never seen a girl in such a giggly, happy mood as I was when I was chatting with my revived love.

After finding out that our guide is from Jaipur, we convinced him to take us to his house for a home-cooked dinner. He agreed. On our way to his house I popped into a shop and bought a sari. Raghu walked us to his house and introduced us to his mother. She said she was impressed that I was wearing a sari but joked that my sari was see-through since I didn't have the matching petticoat for underneath. However she was kind enough to show the ladies the different ways to properly tie it on, clasp it and ensure it stayed put for an entire day.

We looked at family photos, asked questions about arranged marriages, and listened to the stories about how their current house has been in the family for six generations. We watched as Raghu's mother oversaw the cooking and serving of her male helpers. We gorged ourselves on many fantastic dishes and went home after a unique night.

Small Town Break

Tordigarh, India
July 10

During the 90-minute, 80km, dive to Tordigarh, just South of Jaipur I tethered my iPad to my guide's cell phone for essential internet, the only email I wanted to read and send, one to my unfinished love story. Seeing his name in my inbox immediately brings a smile to my face. My cheeks hurt the smile is so big; it reminded me of the way I would beam when we first started dating. His messages were long, they would tell me funny stories about his day, his plans for the weekend, they hinted at beach vacations, but they all ended with him telling me his missed me and how he's looking forward to our life together. I would have just enough bandwidth to send a matching response. I would tell him about my adventure, the things I was learning, how much I was missing him in return, my dreams of us holding hands and kissing again. I would always end with how much I loved him. My heart never stopped loving him. It was tough to describe, but despite it being months since the last time we saw each other in person I felt that I loved him more today than I ever have.

We made it to the converted farm house, now hotel by lunchtime. The days have been getting hotter and once we finished lunch we stayed inside the cool dining room. The air conditioner would work periodically, but the electricity would often cut out, and we would go back to hand held fans until the air conditioner would work again.

The ladies passed the time by having henna designs drawn on our hands and feet, while the bigger group played cards.

We took a walking tour of the town. We were just outside the property gates when the children started running up to our group, "One photo, one photo". They were asking for their photo to be taken. They were amazed to see themselves immediately after the button press. The children laugh and the adults do the Indian head bobble to indicate they approve.

I bought a couple packages of cookies from a local store. I offered a cookie to a little girl, who misunderstood and took the entire package. I wasn't going to argue. I then gave the other package to another excited young girl.

We returned to the hotel and rode camel carts over to the sand dunes for a sunset viewing. The people waved and blew us kisses as we passed through the town with our decorated camels.

We sat at the top of the sand dune, drank masala tea, which then changed to beer, as the night sky changed colours from pink to orange to dark blue. We rode our camel's back and drank and played cards until late in the night.

Sean and I were the last ones to go to sleep. We stayed up and chatted about each of our world-travel adventures. He asked questions about my revived love story and questioned me if I have been so stuck on my single outcome that I wasn't allowing something bigger and higher potential into my life. Maybe I have outgrown my unfinished love story. I was upset that he would challenge my heart, but then I began to doubt my enthusiasm.

The Road to Taj

Agra, India
July 11

One of the other things Sean and I discussed last night was that I meditate daily. He asked if he could join me. I naturally woke up at 5:45, knocked on his door, told him to bring a pillow, and we headed to the watch tower to meditate as the sun came up. In a country of over one-billion people, where horns honk day and night and there is barely enough room for personal space, we found a pocket of time where the only sound was the singing birds.

Sean's challenge from last night still bothered me. I asked in my meditation if I was limiting myself. I felt my answer in my heart: There will always be someone for me, but if the goal is to find a person that I love so much, and they love my back, I can see myself being challenged and supported, if I am committed to that person and they feel the same way is it worth the energy to keep looking? It felt like a perfect answer. I still have choice, and my choice is him.

On the bus I fell in and out of sleep. I was tired, dehydrated and I had a headache. This is the hottest place I have ever been. Every day is 45-degrees and it is ridiculously humid. By this time India should have received about 30% of their rains for the season, and I have been told that it hasn't rained in 14 days. The humidity hangs in the air and it is impossible to stand outside for more than 5 minutes before the sweat starts falling down my forehead and the small of my back.

I was in for a treat in the morning: two messages from my love story! His first one was his explanation about why he didn't respond to my desperate plea for love when I was in Indonesia. He was in a dark place, and my email came at a time when there was so much in his head. He was sorry he didn't at least acknowledge the message if he needed some time to sort through his head. He said he did try to stop loving me because he wanted me to enjoy my travels and to open myself up to all potential so if I came back I would not have a single doubt but since it's been three months and I am still here, he is so happy. His second email said that he was telling people that he works with that he is committed to me again, and the only person's opinion that he really cares about is his best friend's, which is me.

I loved reading his emails. He always sounded so happy and loving. My heart would fill with overwhelming warmth. I responded back about my meditation session in the morning. I told him I still hadn't told anyone we were communicating but only because I haven't talked to anyone else but him. I told him that I will never, ever let him go. I said that I am already a better person, a better future wife and future mother. I hoped that we would make it to Agra early enough in the evening that I would be able to call him before he went to work. Then I closed off the email letting him know that I loved him, that I always have and always will, and a few lines that described and reminded him about the hot sexy time we used to have.

We were already running about an hour behind schedule due entirely to the traffic and then as arrived in Agra the traffic became even worse. There was sludge on the side of the road, and our guide warned us to not use the tap water to brush our teeth. We pulled through the stop-and-start traffic until we finally hit a road that seemed like we were smooth sailing. Then we were pulled over by a traffic cop saying he needed to "check our permits". In other words, he saw a tourist bus and wanted his "fair share". After about 20-minutes a "fine" was negotiated and we were allowed to leave. We arrived at the Agra hotel 2 and a half hours later than expected. I was exhausted, hungry and heartbroken that it was too late to call my love story. He sent me a message saying that he would keep his computer on while he got ready in the morning in case I was able to call him. He said that he finally told his dad that he and I were together. This was big. I ate, sent him a good night email apologizing and explaining for the delay. I told him I hope his dad becomes okay with us and me. I said that I still have pictures of the two of us on my iPad that I still look at, and I carry his business card with me, that I pull out every now and then to kiss in hopes that my kiss will somehow be felt by him. I closed with a possible plan for the future. I still have some Canadian airline flight credit, maybe a trip for his birthday as soon as I get back?

It was time for bed. I was going to be waking up in a few hours for our sunrise Taj Mahal visit.

Commitment to Love or Playing with Fire

Agra, India
July 12

Commitment to Love

If there is one thing that India will teach me more than anything else it will be the men's commitment to the women that they love. Throughout all the palaces and forts that I have seen every king dedicated their love to the wife they loved the most with a gesture of love in a way that has withstood centuries. I know love today won't have that same grandness, but the idea that there are still men today that are willing to do something so amazing for their wife is something every woman has ever dreamed of.

Raghu gave us very strict orders the night before. Our bus was leaving for the Taj Mahal at 4:45 with or without us. Anyone not in the lobby at that time would have a note left for them at reception with directions on how to get to the Taj.

We jumped on the bus and after a few minutes of driving we stopped on the main road leading us to the East gate. We had two tuk-tuks idly waiting to drive us before the road was blocked to vehicle traffic. We ran the rest of the way to the opening of the East gate and were first in line. As we stood in line, more tourists started to pile in. Raghu whispered to our group the direction we had to go in. He said that we would have to run to ensure we had plenty of time to get our pictures taken before the rest of the tourists came through.

We passed through security and ran as fast as we could to the entrance of the Taj Mahal. Each one of us took turns standing on the first platform switching prepped cameras back and forth. Once the first photo was taken we ran again to the main platform and the "Princess Diana bench". We had no

251

more than 10 minutes before people caught up to us. Our brief window of the perfect Taj Mahal photo was over.

We were then lead to a Taj Mahal specific guide. The guide told us the story about how the Taj Mahal was created as a mausoleum for the Emperor's deceased wife. The Emperor met his wife when she was only 19 and he immediately fell in love with her. They stayed married for 19 years, and during that time she bore him 14 children. He insisted that she would travel with him always because he could not live without her and he knew she could never be without him. On the birth of her 14th child, the Emperor was away at war. Her delivery provided several complications and she suffered internal bleeding. The attendants asked the Queen what her final wish would be, and for her it was to see her husband, the love of her life, one last time. He returned from his battle and went to her. When he arrived he held her and they looked deep into each other's eyes. She told him she wanted the world to know how much they loved each other and if he could provide her with three wishes. The first was that he would never marry again. The second ask was that he would take care of their many children. The final ask was that he create something for her that would show the entire world how much she meant to him.

The Taj Mahal took 22 years to build. The marble and jewel work is so exquisite that it glimmers in the sun. The entire building is dedicated to her. Her tomb is in the centre, and he is placed off centre, so that his body would forever be beside her.

We finished with the Taj while it was still early in the day. We headed back to the hotel for some personal time before leaving for our next destination.

Before leaving for the Taj I received a couple of messages from my love story. He wanted me to continue to enjoy my trip and not to think about home too much yet. I needed to enjoy the moment that I was in and all the amazing things that I would be seeing. He did let me know he was thinking about maybe renting a house.

Before I left on my trip I told him when I get back I will be in a better place. I wasn't walking away from us; I was actually helping to speed up our timeline. We used to talk a lot about our future together. He wanted a house on the west side, and I would say only if we were engaged.

I replied only briefly in my morning fog that he should really consider a three-week vacation in the Greek Islands next month so I didn't have to wait another three months before finally seeing him again.

Playing with Fire

When we arrived back to the hotel after the Taj, I logged onto my computer hoping to see something new from my love story and when there wasn't I found myself wasting time on Facebook. Eddie just posted a photo of him and James wearing robes and having fun in a hotel room. In the background of the photo there were a couple of pink suitcases. I wanted to tease him about it so I sent a message: "Checking out girls rooms with James? Good on ya, boy". Eddie immediately came online.

> Eddie: My heart just sunk I know it would look like that. It's not like that. There were loads of us. It was a bit of a party. I was going to get hold of you today. I couldn't wait any longer. I simply can't stop thinking about you.

> Me: No. It's a good thing. Don't even worry about it. Don't think of me. You're doing everything you need to and should do. Live and have a great time. Take back the time and the moments that make you single. Enjoy that time. You deserve it.

> Eddie: I wanna be with you. There now you have it. That was so scary.

253

Me: Eddie, you are so wonderful. Have fun. Meet lots and lots of girls. Keep being you.

I was already getting in over my head. I should have never messaged him.

Eddie: Talk to me this is hard right now.

I wanted to, and I knew I shouldn't.

Me: Okay. Facetiming you right away. Let me pay my breakfast bill.

He told me that he's been holding tight, but he needs to change his flight. He doesn't want to go back home. He was hoping that things with my ex wouldn't work out and his next flight would be to wherever I was going to be. The conversation had to end right there. It was too much for me to hear, and he was afraid he was going to say more than I would be ready to hear.

I didn't know what to do. My head was spinning with thoughts of both of them. I made a new commitment to my former ex, my unfinished love story, my current love story. I told him that I am willing to be invested in us. I've wanted it for far too long. But the things that I really want, someone to be there for me, someone willing to do whatever it takes, to drop it all to meet me, to be with me, those promises were coming from someone else.

I called my girlfriend, Kim, to talk it out with me. She reminded me why I was here to begin with. "You were going on a self-discovery mission. Do you feel you really know what you want in your life? If you don't know then you are not to make any decision".

She said I needed to focus on the moment I am in right now. I needed to design my life the way I want it to look. The right man will ensure he is in it. I will never be happy if I go back to fitting my life into something that someone else has designed. She was absolutely right. I had said it before, and now I needed to commit myself to that truth. Stop chasing love. Love will find me. It will find me when I know exactly what I want and where I want to be. I need to be here right now because there is still a lesson to learn and I am fully distracted on a future outcome when I don't even know what I need in my present. India was going to be transformational for me, or so said a previous meditation, and I need to give focus to this time to allow this transformation to take place.

My doubts and fears were spinning in my head. There was only one person that I needed to talk to. Maybe there is something he could say that would put my head demons to rest. I sent my unfinished love story a message. I need to talk. I have had a lot of heavy thoughts in my head, I don't want to chase love anymore.

It was the middle of the night for him and he responded back with a photo of the two of us laughing together from our vacation together last year. I was in his thoughts while he slept but I really needed at that moment was to talk to him, see him, hear his voice, and have him comfort me. Our group was heading out on some additional tours. I gave him an hour-long window that I thought I would be back at the hotel and able to call him.

I didn't make it back to the hotel in time. Before the hour-long window was closed he sent me a desperate, love-filled email. He had to leave to take care of the last of his storage unit break-in. He was still in love with me. We are meant to be together and not even Romeo and Juliet will have a better love story than us. But my worrying head has him worrying. He loves me and right now he is mad that he can't be with me to show me. Am I worried that he is with other girls, because that is not the case. Right now he is being brought to tears with fear of being hurt again. If anyone is promising me anything I shouldn't listen, because they will never be able to follow through. He is fully invested in us. Signed "Luv" unfinished love story.

I just missed him by the time I got back to the hotel. I apologized for having a far too active mind. I really needed reassurance. The days are hot. I left him a Skype video message. I will try to call him in the morning.

My heart was torn. I need someone to hold me.

Trains and Temples

Half the group headed up to one of the rooms for beers, cards and dancing after dinner last night. My unfinished love story sent me a message during his afternoon. He was about to head out with some friends for one of the final nights of the Calgary Stampede. He let me know that in the event there are pictures of him with other girls his thoughts are always with me. He wished we had a chance to talk.

"Feeling a bit drunk here. I promised myself that I was no longer going to chase love, but allow love to find me. You're doing a good job. Like I said I had a tough emotional and head focused day and needed someone to talk it through. It's too bad we're so off on our times. We will find another time. There's always time. I do love you. I always have and always will. I wish desperately that I could feel your kisses again. I can't remember how they feel..." I left the hotel lobby and passed out.

We left our hotel at 7AM for our 8AM train. I received two messages from him before he headed out for his evening. He said he wished he could kiss me too. He is glad I am having a good time and he will do his best to show me how much he loves me while I am away. If only he could come home and bring me flowers, or even just send flowers to me, to show me that I am the everlasting beauty in his life. He is constantly thinking about our future. "I love you and that is something you need to remember babe". The second email was sent a few hours later: "Feeling pretty drunk but I wanted to let you know that I am totally taken. In my mind we're the same way we were before. The difference is, I'll quit my job and do what I have to for us. I will not come and travel but maybe meet you in Greece... maybe...Baby".

Upon arriving at the train station we were immediately surrounded by beggars, disabled people and others that were in need of medical attention, all asking for money. There was a person missing their entire lower half of their body, scooting around on their hands, there was another person that had severe elephantiasis on both their feet and was using a modified wheelbarrow to move about, there were plenty of mothers with babies and children all motioning for money, rubbing their thumb against their two fingers. It broke my heart to have to walk away without giving.

We were told by our guide to stay close, walk quickly and be aware of pickpockets. We walked quickly through the train station and only stopped when we reached a small room reserved for first-class passengers. We piled all our bags together and started the potentially long wait for the train.

The train ride was relatively quick. The train barely stopped when we jumped on the platform to meet our next bus for the 30-minute drive to our hotel in Orchha.

Every evening at 8PM a ceremony dedicated to Raja Ram, one of the Hindu gods in the form of a king, takes place. People chant to the King and have their offerings blessed by the priests. We observed the entire ceremony, asked tons of questions about Hinduism and the story of Lord Ram. I felt moved by all the chanting of the devotees. It was interesting to see the offerings being given by the devotees and previous ones being blessed and given back in no particular order. Each person to give something gets something in return.

The internet at the hotel was down the entire day and I let my thoughts and fears take over. I didn't want to do emails anymore. I needed to talk to someone. My special someone.

Cooking Class and Staying in a Palace

Bundelkhand, India
July 14

We had the opportunity to sleep-in. My head has been fuzzy. I am doing my best to maintain my focus on truly knowing what I want in my life. I feel like I know and then the comments and questions from outside provide confusion I don't need. More than anything I wish I could turn off all the commentary. For my morning meditation I went to my mantra back in Vietnam: maximum clarity for maximum pleasure. What do I want my life to look like?

I tried to clear my head with a walk into town. I had breakfast at the same restaurant I had dinner at last night. I ate my omelette, drank a decent coffee, and was walking back through town when I ran into Sean. He was waiting for the post office to open. I sat down to talk small talk. I wanted to completely turn off my brain.

As we walked back to our hotel I bought a monk some crackers in hopes good karma will come my way. Sean and I then stopped to visit a grouping of cenotaphs. Each cenotaph was constructed for a different king and contained his remains below. We walked to the top of one, and looked down to see a group of men bathing in the river. They were shouting and waving at us, inviting us to come down and join them. I waved back, and laughed as I blew them kisses.

I finished packing my bag and checked out of my room. In the afternoon there was an optional cooking class at a local woman's home. As I waited in the lobby I noticed the internet was finally running. It had been down since we arrived. There was a series of emails from my unfinished love story and a response to my Skype video message. He told me about his day and night. He said that he's told more friends that we are together and he is fully committed to me. He stopped at a pet store to look around. He apologized for all the emails but he wanted me to know that I am constantly on his mind.

In my head I didn't know what I doubted. He kept saying he loved me. That should be enough. We can't change our past. I can't make him ask me not to be on this trip. I would have gone anyway. I didn't know what I needed to hear from him. I was fearful that I would give him my entire heart and he wouldn't be ready to commit. I really want to be married to him. Why can't I just say that to him? That would make all the difference. Or at least come see me. Let me know how much I mean to him in his actions. I was afraid that he was full of empty promises. Why can't I just say that to him? Why do we have to be on a twelve and a half hour time difference? This is the worst time change to deal with. I don't want to say too much in case I scare him off. Maybe if he thinks I am fearful he'll want to back out. The less I say the safer we will be.

I responded back with a short email. I apologized that I couldn't send anything earlier. The internet had been down. I told him about the Hindu ceremony.

Back at the hotel, after the cooking class, I sent my unfinished love story another message. I might be able to call him at 7pm my time when we arrive at the next hotel.

The drive to the next hotel, a converted palace, was a relatively short 2 hours. We played a drinking game on the way there, and didn't even notice that the first of the Indian monsoon rains started coming down. The rains had stopped by the time we arrived at the hotel, but not before knocking out the power, and internet, for the night.

Too Hot for Kama Sutra

Alipura, India
July 15

The problem with drinking alcohol in the Indian heat is despite how much water I drink, which now is 7L per day, I wake up incredibly dehydrated and it takes the entire morning to drink enough water to feel back to normal.

I woke up and walked over to one of the palace roof terraces to listen to quiet of the world. I wanted to meditate and concentrate on what will bring me happiness. Unfortunately my hangover brain didn't want to do the same, so after a few minutes I decided to end the session.

The internet was back, but patchy at best. My unfinished love story sent me messages saying he waited for my call. He sent me another one saying that he was looking for the link of my travel blog, but he couldn't find it. I became angry at that. My link was available on my Facebook timeline to my Facebook friends. If he wanted to find it he would have to add me as a friend. I was angry that I couldn't Skype with him. I've wanted to talk to him for days. I need to hear him say the words that he loves me. I was frustrated with email. I waited for months to have my love back in my life and he is, but on the other side of the world. I want him here with me. I want to scream. I want to be held while I cry.

We left for the Kama Sutra temples around 10AM. It was still a two-hour drive to the temples and I was overheated and dehydrated. I went to sleep.

Every day it's been at least 45 degrees and the humidity has always been incredibly high. The days always feel like they are going to rain, but the skies stay blue. I fill my water bottle with powder electrolytes. I carry my umbrella to all the temples to maximize the shade. I go through tons of tissues from constantly wiping sweat from my face.

I walked around the temple enjoying the intricate details of the carvings that show women getting ready, writing letters to their lovers and dancing. There are carvings of couples writing letters to each other to coitus. There were funny ones of having an attendant watching through peeked-through hands, or the pinnacle of the men having their way with a horse. I was too exhausted to do anymore exploring. I wanted to get my thoughts out of my head.

I needed to talk to someone. Any one. I tried to Skype my unfinished love story. He wasn't available so I left him a video message.

Then I sent Eddie a message. I had been avoiding him since we chatted after the Taj.

> Me: I hope you're doing well. I wish the internet was better here. I've had a lot of thoughts the last few days. One of them I'm heavily considering not going back to Canada but maybe that's just the heat… it's ridiculously hot here. Take care.

Our group sat on the rooftop terrace as the skies became darker before enjoying our last dinner in the palace.

Predicting the Finish to My Unfinished Love Story or It's a Sabotage

Alipura, India
July 16

Predicting the Finish to My Unfinished Love Story

Since being in India I feel like something clicked in me. Maybe it's been the stories of undying love, maybe it's the coincidental accumulation of three months of travel and being away from home. Maybe because my months of prayers were finally answered I was able to really look at my life and evaluate if this is exactly how I would want it designed for myself. I don't know what it is, but there is definitely a change inside me. Part of it may be that my heart and head have been opened to so much experience and so many people that the knowledge I have about myself and the world has expanded my possibilities to more than I could have ever imagined. I feel like somewhere the trajectory of my story has completely changed.

I look forward to all of my unfinished love story's emails. He is always very sweet and says all the right things. I wish we were able to Skype more than we have been. The already patchy internet makes things worse when the power knocks out the internet. But the last time we did Skype he told me that he loved me. I was giddy. I waited months, even before I left on my trip, to hear him say those words to me. I had never in my life felt three words brought me so much emotion. I wanted for so long to hear that he still loved me.

As soon as I heard those words I was head over heels in love with him again. We were back to being madly in love and we weren't going to miss a beat. We hit a temporary pause in our relationship. I had the chance to explore and search for more purpose in my life. He realized that his life wasn't the same without me. There are no other options for him. I am the one he wants to be with.

My head had been spinning with so many thoughts over the last few days. I thought about the reasons I broke up with him. I questioned if things could be different if we got back together. Then I pictured in my head my perfect ending. I had thought about that ending so many times I wasn't open to any other variation than what it was supposed to look like in my head: he drops everything, meets me in Greece, we get engaged, our love is so good when we see each other again that I get pregnant, then when I come home three months later I get to announce to him the exciting news.

It's been a week and a half of us talking, it's been three months of him realizing that I am the one he wants to be with, I didn't understand why I haven't heard him address anything on a real commitment with me. I needed to lay everything out on the table for him.

After breakfast I was finally able to articulate the things I wanted in my life; the things that were bothering my head the last several days.

I went into the small office. My iPad wasn't connecting to the Wi-Fi so I couldn't Skype. I used Sean's laptop that was hardwired to send my unfinished love story the first message that was longer than five lines since my night of drinking after the Taj.

I told him that I was going to be taking a night train to Varanasi tonight. I started talking about my travel plans: need to book a flight to Turkey and a hotel in Dubai. I was also planning on being in Greece in a couple of weeks, and I will need to know if he is planning on meeting me out there. I then said I thought about all the things that I want in my life and I would have preferred to talk to him about them, but it might be unlikely for us to connect until Delhi or Dubai.

I listed off my wants. I want a baby. I am ready and want to start trying as soon as I am back home. I want to travel more like how I have been travelling, with local accommodations, climbing mountains and likely staying away from resorts. I want to simplify my life with a small house, nothing more than necessary. Finally I don't want to be a part of his best friend's life since he went out of his way to hurt me and my family. I finally told him I wanted to be supported in my creative effort. I then told him I will always love him.

He responded to me within 40 minutes. He doesn't have any vacations planned over the next while because the money isn't coming in the same way it did. He had an opportunity to take a job 700km North from Calgary, but money isn't the most important thing to him anymore, it already ruined his life once. When it comes to my own job I still have a lot of time to brainstorm, but I should do whatever makes me happy. He will know a bit more in a week or two if he can take any time off, but he does have some time booked off in September, and he was hoping to go to Costa Rica over New Years. In the meantime he is going to work on his mind and body. It has been so tough not talking to me. He is confused by my statements that I am done chasing love and that I want a baby within two years. He is unsure what my intentions are with those statements, it sounds like I have a lot of things going on in my head and he would love to hear more about them.

It's a Sabotage
I read his response then decided to take a break from the heat by going for an afternoon nap, but I just couldn't stop my brain from spinning. I had to write. I needed to get all these thoughts written down so I could clarify them. As I wrote I started crying and then I stopped. I said to myself that I wasn't being fair. If I told him that I was going to commit to him, I needed to tell him my concerns. I needed to give him the opportunity to either help me see it in a new perspective or give him the chance to re-evaluate the things in his life so that we both would be incredibly happy.

The reply I sent him was excessive. Like a boiling kettle I had held back so many of my thoughts they all came out like an explosion. I had so much I wanted to say, and I said it all at once. I stressed that money should never be the most important thing in life, and that's why I want a simple life when I get home. All our extra money will be spent on experiences. I don't want to be a wife and a mother, that's something that my heart is crying that I absolutely need. I stressed that I want to do more adventurous travelling. I explained that when I said I was done chasing love it is because I felt like I was chasing him for months with the number of messages and unsent letters I wrote to him. I wanted to kiss his lips. I needed his touch. I asked him to search deep inside himself and whatever he decides to make it happen and never turn back. I told him that I believe in him and I know that he is capable of so much in his life.

Despite me saying I wasn't going to be listening to outside commentary the people I was hearing plenty of comments that was making my fear feel more real, he is never going to commit. My entire life I struggled with relationships that say they are going to commit and never do. I believed that my unfinished love story was different, but at that moment all the irrational fear took over. Unless he was call me and tell me he was currently on a plane there was little that my fear was going to accept as a reasonable solution.

After an hour I checked to see if there was a response from him, which there wasn't; I sent the message in the middle of his night. However Eddie had responded to the message I sent him last night.

> Eddie: Hey smiler, how are you? How are things with you and your unfinished love story? I've heard England and California are nice places to live.

There was nothing I wanted to say to him. I was upset that I opened that can of worms yesterday. I can't be playing with those flames.

I tried to go for a nap, but just couldn't. My fear had taken over my mind. It narrated all the terrible outcomes that

I was supposed to expect. I let it loose like a dog that realized the gate was open. The lesson I was supposed to learn in Bali, slow down, don't rush, stop planning my life, was completely forgotten all over again. The panic switch was turned on and no one was going to be able to turn it off this time.

I allowed my thoughts to spin, run and rotate. I told myself that he wasn't emotionally invested in our relationship. Who signs off emails with 'Luv"? It's flakey.

He has told me that everyone knows we are communicating, he says he feels fully committed to me, yet since deleting me from Facebook, he hasn't taken it upon himself to add me back. He said he looked up my blog, but couldn't find the link. Of course not, you need to be a part of my life to see things I post.

I then thought about one of the reasons I broke up with him. I didn't feel I was a priority in his life. For me I felt it was work, then his friends, then me. He has told me that he's changed, but I'm not really sure if I see it. I don't feel I am any more of a priority.

I drove myself to anger. I went from writing him bare minimum lines of text to entire novels. I didn't even give him the chance to respond. It was 3:15AM for him and I had more to say.

I opened by saying my biggest fault is my ability to overthink to the point that I will create problems that aren't even there. My writing both brought out my overthinking but also brought a sense of clarity to my life. I liked writing about my day-to-day travels, but my emotional wave, and the corresponding growth is what I loved writing about the most. I said as I tried writing about "us" and found myself too far removed from the story. I needed him to just hear my busy head so it could finally stop. I wanted to work on us more than I ever have before. I told him it really bothered me that he hadn't added me back on Facebook, since he deleted he should add back. I wanted someone that was going to be active in my daily life and I said it would mean so much to me if he read my daily blogs. I know he read some of them, I don't know how many he read, if he liked them, or if he found any of them funny. My writing was my creative outlet and I wanted someone to support my creativity. I told him how much I disliked it when he would close his emails with "Luv". I said I was so giddy when I waited months to hear him say he loved me, but seeing it written in such a way made me feel his heart was still guarded and if I feel that I want to guard my heart in return. Then I said I want someone to choose me and never let me go. I want a man who is willing to go anywhere in the world for me. He not only says it but follows up with action. I want to be loved in the way I deserve to be loved and I wanted him to be a part of my romantic ending. I ended my email the way I ended all of them: "I love you. I always have. I always will."

I sent my new email and had Sean read both of them after I sent them. I wanted his opinion. I would have taken anyone's opinion. I didn't know if I had fallen off the deep end. Sean said it got my point across. It definitely did that. I asked what Sean thought about all my stories, about Eddie, and my unfinished love story. Sean said that I should give up on both, that he thinks there is still some dark horse that hasn't appeared in my story yet, and only when I give up with my love story will this new man appear. Then with resentment fueling my thoughts I told Sean I almost hoped my unfinished love story doesn't book a ticket to Greece, then I would know everyone was right, he was never going to commit to me.

I couldn't understand what was holding him back from putting himself back in the full involvement of my life. Maybe all the damage has been done. Maybe it will never, ever be the same despite what we both tell ourselves.

A stream of soft tears came to my face at this thought. I had been hearing it from others; I would tell them "I know, I get it". I could feel so much pain in my heart, despite the layers of bandages that I continued to put around it. It's like I could see this beautiful scene with him and I in this perfect setting, but every time I tried to get there the path was filled with obstacles and more pain. I continued to walk down this path that really has no happy ending; only a mirage of something that never will exist, despite what we tell ourselves today and in the past. Maybe we are two soul mates that are not meant to be together in this lifetime.

I felt ready. I was really, truly ready to release. But something had to be different. I had said this to myself again and again before, yet here I am today no further ahead than I was months ago. The only difference is that now I have more layers of bandages. Maybe instead of cutting the cord I just stop feeding the line. I stop trying. I instead release the effort of both trying to keep us together as well as the effort of trying to bring us to an end. My release becomes one of effort instead of to him. There was a certain soft harmony to that thought.

I packed my bag and our tour group took a three-hour bus ride to the train station to catch a sleeper train to Varanasi. I sent my unfinished love story a quick message saying I dreamed about him and his cuddles. I told him that I send him kisses until I get to see him again. The messages I sent him finally released all my nagging thoughts. I felt momentarily peaceful.

When we got to the train station the men's waiting lounge was filled, so the ladies stayed in the women's-only lounge. We had an hour plus a 30 minute delay to wait before our train. My guide would say Indian rail lines are very generous because you would sometimes get an extra two hour ride free for the price of a 10-hour ticket.

The train stopped and we had only a few minutes to arrange ourselves in the bunks. Since we weren't on sleeping together, Raghu was going to speak to other passengers to shuffle ourselves in order to get as many of our group together. I am one of the more "advanced" travellers so I was given one of the bunks further away from the larger group, but still cuddled up to my day bag and only an arm's reach away from both Sean and Pers.

Night Moves

Varanasi, India
July 17

I woke up when the train stopped at one of the stations. It took me a second to realize where I was. I was able to get as good of a sleep as one could expect after spending an entire night on a train surrounded by people.

I saw that Sean was already up and I quietly got out of my bunk, and headed for the train door. At each of the stations people will either pass through the train with fresh chai tea, or they will stand at the entrance of each of the train cars and will sell a small Dixie cup of chai for 5 rupees each (or 10, with the "tourist discount"). I picked up a couple of chai teas and played cards with Sean as we waited for the others to get up.

The locals that were in the other bunks around us had already collapsed the middle bunk on the side I was sleeping, to turn it into a couch area. The bottom bunk across from me slept another man from our group, Pers. We collapsed the middle bunk on top of him while he continued to sleep. We joked with him that his bag and shoes were missing, but none of it fazed him for at least ten minutes when he eventually opened his eyes to check. We laughed hysterically at how someone could not care.

We arrived in Varanasi just after noon. Everyone was hungry and aching for a shower. Our hotel was thankfully right across from the train station. After a long train ride I only wanted to nap, shower, eat, and get Wi-Fi for my perfect afternoon.

I logged on and had a concise response to my paragraphs of emails I sent my unfinished love story the day before. He was confused by my "new vision" but there is time to look at all of it when we have to cross each bridge. He completely understands the new ideas that I have because travelling brings new opportunities and ideas. He said money isn't everything but it still has to be made. He didn't know "Luv" and "Love" were different, but he wants me to know that he loves me. He gets the impression that I want someone to follow me and not grow as a couple. He closed that he hopes I have a great day.

I was feeling only slightly calmer than I was the day before. At 1:30AM his time I asked if I could Skype him at 5:30AM his time. I said I really miss his kisses and cuddles and I definitely didn't want to go six months without seeing him. I asked what his plans were for his September vacation and if he was thinking I would join him for his trip to Costa Rica over New Years.

I went upstairs to my room. I took a shower and as I got out I heard a ping on my messenger.

Eddie: Not long until Dubai, you must be getting excited

Me: I am. I didn't mind India but it's always nice to go someplace new. I still need to book my hotel and my flight to Turkey

Eddie: Wanna FaceTime?

Me: Just finished a 12-hour sleep train. Arrived in Varanasi to float to the Ganges. Yes.

I changed from my towel to a dress. I called Eddie. We hadn't spoken to each other since the day after the Taj. He told me how much he missed me, my voice, and my accent then he told me about the different things he's been doing that he thought I would enjoy with him. I told him that I was still working things out with my unfinished love story, that until it is completely done I really need to focus on that.

Eddie challenged my unfinished love story's words and the fact that he hasn't done anything to come get me. Eddie then told me he would meet me in Dubai.

I felt myself being pulled back into the infatuation and passion I felt for him in Bali. I loved the way he would say my name "Kimmy". Only he could say it that way and it would sound sexy. No one in my life has ever called me "Kimmy". I was feeling naughty. I shouldn't even be talking to him. He was at an outdoor bar. I was sitting by myself in my hotel room. I wanted to see someone look at me with those eyes that say "I need your body right now". I started touching myself and I let him watch.

Our group was meeting again at 5PM and I hadn't eaten at all. I told Eddie I had to let him go after almost two hours of talking. We ended our conversation that nothing was happening unless I was completely finished with my love story, and I didn't know where I was with that. I was desperately hoping that he would meet me in Greece. If he did that, only that, I was done. I needed an action from my unfinished love story and that was the only one I needed.

I finished my late lunch quickly and logged onto Skype hoping to finally, *finally,* connect with my unfinished love story for a live conversation. When he wasn't online I met up with the rest of the group to take tuk-tuks to the Main Ghat to catch our boat on the Ganges River. For many people this was going to be the highlight of the tour. For me, I remember reading about the Ganges when I was in school. I may have been in elementary, but I do remember hearing about how people would swim in the river at the same time dead people were in it. I thought it was one of the grossest places I could ever imagine. Being here now, it was completely opposite of what I ever thought it was as a child. The place was overwhelming with emotion and spirituality.

We boarded a boat to take us down the Ganges. As we approach Little Burning Ghat, we were asked to stop taking pictures out of respect for the families and cremation ceremony for their lost loved one. We sat in our boat, took in the moment, and left silently to ensure we didn't linger over the process. We then headed towards the main Burning Ghat. For each cremation, only men are allowed to attend the ceremony. It is believed that the soul will not move on if it feels attachment and the feeling that it will be missed by their loved ones still living. If anyone cries during the ceremony the soul will feel attached to this lifetime and won't be able to move on. Since women are more likely to cry, they are not allowed to attend.

As we came to Burning Ghat there were already 13 cremation ceremonies taking place simultaneously. Our guide said that if you sit and listen any bad thoughts are taken away. The Ganges is a symbol of life and it will renew your spirit in everything you do. I closed my eyes and meditated on the moment. I started to have odd physical sensations that I had not had before in any of my meditations in the past. I felt my tongue go numb and my mouth and throat get tight. I realized I had a blockage of my throat chakra. I didn't even know what it meant, but I knew the next day I would need to find a Reiki master to help clear me of this blockage.

We turned the boat around and headed back towards the Main Ghat to watch the daily night ceremony. Raghu handed us each a candle surrounded by flowers in an aluminum cup. Each one of those represented a wish that we could release to the gods and pray for them to grant. I lit my candle and made the same prayer I've made for months. Please let love find me; bring me love when I am ready. I watched as my prayer floated away.

The night ceremony was the perfect example of what India has been. It was loud, moving, spiritual, chaotic, and somehow through the mess of individual pieces was one of the most touching displays of art I have ever seen and heard. Bells rang in no required sequence. People clapped and chanted in repetition and off beat. There was no buildup or climax. It all just was.

When I got back to the hotel I logged onto Skype hoping my unfinished love story would be able to chat with me. It was the middle of his workday. I called my mom with panic in my heart. I told her everything. I didn't know if I should hold onto my unfinished love story or if I should cut my losses. She told me that if he wanted to see me he would be here with me, not home partying with his friends. She said if he was serious about loving me he would have booked a flight to see me long time ago. I cried. Any clarity I was hoping to get was completely blown out of the water. I cried and told her I had to go. I had a sunrise boat tour in the morning.

I checked my email before heading to bed. My unfinished love story sent me a message, he couldn't Skype, he was so sorry to miss me this morning, he went out late with a bunch of work buddies last night and it was a late morning. He misses his best friend (me) but there is so much more than he can explain. Having me as his best friend is just the base, and everywhere is where the love lies. He loves me and misses me.

I logged onto Skype. He wasn't there. I had to prove my mom and everyone wrong. He loves me. I sent his a desperate message: "Come see me. Book a flight tonight". I stayed up a little bit longer hoping for a response, and then I had to go to bed.

The Best of India

Varanasi, India
July 18

Over sunrise on the Ganges there are holy men giving blessings, head shaving ceremonies, and other rituals. Our group was planning on taking a sunrise boat tour to view all of it, however the prayers for rain were finally answered the morning we woke up. It started thunder showering in the middle of the night, and when we awoke at 4:30AM the rains were still coming down heavy. We decided as a group to go back to bed and see if the rains would stop a bit later.

I received a message from my unfinished love story.

Him: where would I go? How long are you there for?

Me: Athens. Aug 2 until August 21. Come not because I ask, but because you miss me. Because you couldn't see yourself spending another day away from me. But also do it because I come first in your life. Before work and friends. We should talk about it before you book too.

I sent him another message before going back to bed letting him know that the boat tour was cancelled and I would call him around 7:30 or 8ish his time.

I went back to bed and set my alarm for a couple hours later. When I woke up I opened Skype and waited for my unfinished love story to join me. After waiting ten minutes I sent him a message saying I woke up for our call. I then went for breakfast to wait for a response, and for the rest of the group to wake up.

Sean and I have always been the early risers of the group, and Sean was just receiving his breakfast when I arrived. We

275

talked about me still waiting to hear from my unfinished love story and how before going to bed last night I sent a "Hail Mary" pass telling him to book a flight to see me.

As I sat I received a message from my unfinished love story. He was out for dinner with one of his work colleagues, and was only on his phone. He thought my last few emails sounded demanding and he wanted to know if this was "my" relationship or "ours". I responded a few minutes later saying I would be online for another two hours.

Sean and I continued to chat over breakfast, the rains were settling down, but still had not stopped. We talked about how we were both disappointed to not make it to the Main Ghat this morning. We were both interested in sitting there and meditating in the space. With that much concentrated spiritual energy it could probably produce some powerful meditations. I told him that I was really interested in having a Reiki session and an astrology reading done too. We then discussed that if we left now we could probably get that all done and then meet the group at the Main Ghat later.

I was getting impatient waiting for my unfinished love story to be available for my long-awaited conversation. It was the exact time that I said I would be available until, so I sent a passive-aggressive message.

> Me: Sorry, I was wrong to assume you would have time for me today. I'm sure your colleague and you had some very important work-related things to discuss. I know that you love me and given the option you would choose me over everything else, if there wasn't other more important things to do and discuss.

My head and my heart were never going to feel calm until I was able to talk to him. I then made a couple of bold offers. I said I would wake up in the middle of the night. I told him that I will cancel any tours scheduled. I told him that he was the most important thing to me. I meant every word.

I didn't even know it that morning, but this was to become my favourite day in India. Sean and I grabbed our rain gear and hired a tuk-tuk to take us to the Main Ghat. We were wanted to sit on the stairs, meditate and take in the energy of the whole place.

As we rode along in our tuk-tuk, the driver pulled over. It had rained so much that the streets were flooded and he couldn't take us much further. We still wanted to make it to the Main Ghat and decided to walk the rest of the way.

The water quickly became deeper and it was up to our knees in a very short instant. Sean offered to have me ride on his shoulders, which out of hilarity I accepted. We became an instant sensation among the crowd of locals and the orange-dressed pilgrims. With Sean standing 6'5" and me on his shoulders we towered above everyone. He moved along, I held my umbrella as close to us as possible and the people were shouted, cheered and gave us the OK sign. Some in broken English were saying to me that I'm "like monkey" because of being so high up to avoid the water. This caused a few people to playfully splash us.

As we came closer to the river, the water in the streets started to subside, and we were able to make it close to the river bank. As we walked along a young man started a conversation and offered to walk with us to the main burning point. When we told him we weren't interested in a guide he insisted on no money, so we agreed. Although we had seen some of the burning ceremonies from the boat yesterday, it was interesting to see it so much closer. As we were about to leave the young man asked if we could please just visit his shop. We reluctantly agreed, but then decided that perhaps he could lead us to places we were actually interested in seeing: Reiki and Astrology.

The astrologer needed at least an hour to prepare our readings after we gave him our full names, birthdays, and time and place of birth. We headed to the much recommended Blue Lassi Shop and we treated our young guide to one. I was then taken back to the Astrologer for my reading while Sean went to a nearby Reiki place, and we would switch after an hour.

My astrology reading was terrible. The astrologer told me many things about personality. He said that I am an over-thinker to the point that I can create problems. I have felt a very strong urge for a marriage and family, particularly over the last few months, and that urge is going to grow more over the next 2-3. Which made me roll my eyes a bit, since he probably uses that line with all the women in my age group and he's able to get it right 80% of the time. He then told me that I have an entrepreneurial spirit and I should spend the next couple of years thinking more about a business idea, but the best time for me to start will be the end of 2016 and beginning of 2017. Finally he said I had a sense of adventure. I thought to myself no kidding, I'm visiting India. I was going to ask him about relationship but I didn't want to waste any more of my time.

I had our young guide stay with me to ensure I could find my way to the Reiki place. He had fallen asleep during my reading, so I woke him up and we headed back out.

The Reiki session I found much more enjoyable. Reiki is a form of energy clearing. The Hindus believe we are a combination of 7 different energies, or chakras. When the chakras are blocked or out of balance it can create anxiety, physical issues or heavy emotional baggage in our head and bodies. A Reiki master's job is to use their energy to clear these blockages and encourage a positive energy flow. Once I walked into the room the Reiki master said he could tell I was dealing with a lot of emotions regarding my relationship. He said that my dreams have not been a positive experience for me, and the blockage was causing me more anxiety than I needed. He could tell that there was a blockage in my throat, which was causing a block in my stomach. He started by putting his hands on my head, and I was immediately put into a state of Zen. I thought about meadows, white flowers and oceans. He then moved his hands down and I was suddenly brought to thoughts of previous relationships going as far back as a guy I dated briefly in university, Chuck. My constant giving and trying efforts, beyond what is reasonable, started with him. He was so good on paper, he had all the checkmarks I needed and somehow we just couldn't make it work. We tried, and I was brought to ugly tears so often. I became a version of myself that I couldn't stand. It took us way too long of being on again and off again before I eventually decided we were better off to never be, but that took too much energy to get there.

As the Reiki continued I started to feel more relaxed, and happier about myself. I finally found the answer that I was looking for. In particular I thought about the emotional baggage I am carrying around about my finished/unfinished love story. Comments from my friends and family, and my overactive mind convinced me that he wasn't making any time for me. I felt this was confirmed this morning when he wasn't able to Skype with me. During the Reiki session I thought if he can't find the time for me, instead of feeling there needs to be any conclusion, I need to treat it like a flower and stop watering it. It will die slowly and gracefully. Instead of a harsh finality, with a definitive end and beginning, I instead have a graceful and progressive finish and beginning, similar to how a dancer moves instead of the drastic curtain drop and lights on that I was looking for.

The Reiki master used his energy to move all this negative energy down my body, and I could feel the weight of these blockages as my feet suddenly felt heavier. He opened the window and in three returns he grabbed the negativity and threw it out the window, ensuring to wipe himself clean on the last time. He then told me to not take a shower until at least 10PM and prepare myself for some bad dreams as the last of the negative energy escapes.

Sean and I discussed our next move. I said that I would be more disappointed to not see Buddha's temple than to have more time with the group. We hired a tuk-tuk and took it to the outskirts of Varanasi. This temple is located in the spot where Buddha gave his first sermon to his disciples. The spot is commemorated with a full-sized statue under the tree that Buddha sat under. In Hinduism, Buddha is considered one of the incarnations of Lord Shiva, and is called Lord Buddha.

We met the rest of the group for an evening boat ride, lassies and a Bollywood movie.

Namaste, India

It was my last full day in India. Many of the people on my tour group were continuing on for another two weeks to complete the South loop. For me two weeks was enough. If "India grows on you" is true, I would need to separate myself from the country to fully appreciate it. In the meantime I get to leave India on a high note.

Our tour group had us on buses, day trains, sleeper trains and ending it by putting us on a flight from Varanasi to Delhi. Even though it was a domestic flight, and we aren't able to check in until 90 minutes before our departure, the airport asks that everyone arrive three hours before, so we followed the rules.

I was in a mad rush in the morning. I had my flight booked to Dubai, but every time I tried to book my flight out of Dubai to Istanbul I was receiving errors on the webpage. It was driving me insane. Within the two days that I had been trying my flight had already doubled in price. I borrowed Sean's laptop and booked it as everyone was loading up on the bus to go to the airport.

I woke up feeling an incredible rush of joy from my Reiki session. I didn't have any of the bad dreams the master had warned me about, but I did have one where I was a princess with my choice of high potential suitors. I could live with that.

I felt bubblier and open to everyone than I have in a very long time. I spent the ride to the airport in enjoyable philosophical debates. I felt I love who and where I am. I didn't care if there was something that actually happened in the Reiki session or not. The point was I felt incredible and that's all that mattered.

When we arrived at the airport it was a lot of sitting around and waiting. I tried to catch up on my last three days of missed blog entries, but found myself far too easily distracted with conversation with everyone around.

My unfinished love story sent me a message last night. He had said he does miss me and he loves me. He said that his company fired over a hundred people yesterday. He also apologized for reading my last couple messages as demanding. Before leaving for the airport I sent him back two messages. I told him not to be stressed about his job, he is smart, and he could do his own thing. I told him to believe in himself because I believe in him. I also told him about the Reiki session and how I was feeling so much happier and excited about my life. I then offered to book some sessions for him, maybe for August if he is not coming to see me.

The flight to Delhi was only an hour. We collected our bags and headed back to the hotel where we started our trip from. I went up to my room and continued to write and edit photos. After an hour I found that my head was getting burnt out and my writing was turning weak. I needed to go for a walk, eat and recharge my body.

Sean joined me and we walked over to a small little hole in the wall, street food restaurant. The portions were massive, and when I couldn't finish anymore I gave my left overs to a beggar on the street.

Sean and I continued to walk down to the market so he could buy some cheap sunglasses. As we walked I was stopped by the beauty of a dress hanging up in a stall. It was stunning. The seller pulled out a packaged dress and put the dress over my head, over my clothes, and guided me to look at myself in a mirror. It was really pretty. I took it off and asked him how much. He quoted a price, and then gave me a 30% "wholesale discount". I said no thank you as I tried to walk away. He was insistent and offered another 10% discount. I didn't want the dress, and I had a hard time giving a forceful no. "I have to ask my husband", I said. Sean was around the corner and the man grabbed him. Sean could see I was having a hard time and tried to help by saying we should go to another store. The owner was already packing the dress, and in a desperate attempt offered a ridiculously low price. I had no room in my bag. I bought the dress.

It was my last dinner in India and despite the dress being far too glamourous for a simple dinner I decided to wear it. I looked like an Indian Princess.

Eddie sent me a couple of messages before I headed out and then called me. He told me about all the fun he was having. I told him about my Reiki session and how I felt like my head finally shut-up for a little while. Then he asked the question I didn't want him to ask, nor did I want to answer. When can he see me again?

I told him I still didn't know. My heart was still devoted. I was still waiting to hear back from my unfinished love story. He hasn't completely dismissed coming to Greece.

Then the phrase I heard so many times since being on my trip, "Kimmy, if he wanted to be there he would be".

I tell him I need more time.

None of this is right. I would love to allow myself to fall deep in love with Eddie. I feel like I am sitting in the middle of a crack in the universe. Eddie is supposed to go back to his wife and then my unfinished love story comes to see me. I don't want to say it; I look away so that I don't cry. "Eddie, I started this trip alone, I need to finish it that way".

"Kimmy, if you change your mind, I already told you I would be your singing partner".

I did the right thing. I know the universe will reward me.

Dubai Mirages or
She Loves Him Not,
She Loves Him

Dubai, United Arab Emirates
July 20

Dubai Mirages

My flight to Dubai was oddly complicated. My seat was taken by a husband and wife that had spread out their items over the entire row I was sharing with them. The flight attendant told me to sit in the aisle seat in the next row. This turned out to be a poor decision, as did the two more times I had to change my seat. As I watched the cabin crew finish up their run through and take their own seats, I saw my window, literally, a seat in the upper row.

Flying over Dubai was amazing; a true desert. Complete blankets of sand, with a city or a whole lawn created in the middle of nothing. The day was hazy, but I could still see the top of Burj Khalifa.

The customs officers were dressed in traditional Arab wear, white from head to toe with the black crown holding it together. They were friendly as I came through, laughing and joking with me. My fear that Dubai was going to be one of the more difficult places for a solo female traveller quickly vanished.

After the heat of the day subsided I headed out. I took a long walk along the marina hoping to find an open restaurant with a view of the sunset. Because of Ramadan many restaurants are closed during daylight hours. By law there is no public eating or drinking allowed during fasting time. I decided to cut my losses and head back towards Burj Al Arab hoping to find a place for dinner.

I rode the metro until the Mall of Emirates stop. I could see the building. The buildings here are so tall they look deceivingly closer than they actually are. I walked for 2.5km in what felt like a rice steamer. I couldn't find a restaurant that would give me a nice view of the building so I cut my losses again and I took a taxi to Chili's. It's been so long since I've had a burger.

She Loves Him Not, She Loves Him
Last night before meeting the group for cards I checked my email. My unfinished love story sent me a message. He said he was still unsure about the Reiki and didn't want to make any plans until he is comfortable with what is going on. He was down because he didn't hear much from me last week. He's glad I'm having fun and meeting new people but he heard some good and bad things from people that were reading my blog postings. He then said he had plans for the first weekend in August to help a buddy out. I was crushed to read that last line. I felt he was stringing me along. He wasn't coming to Greece.

I wanted to be clear with the direction I was going to run at with my love life. But over the last week the conflicts both within myself, the love triangle I put myself in and the multiple outside opinions of family and friends reading my postings were making everything feel like I was stuck in a bog and I needed to take a fast movement to get myself out.

I felt how I did when I made the decision to breakup and travel. I needed my unfinished love story to *do* something! I was afraid that when given a second chance at love with us he was still all talk and no action; a series of empty promises. I needed to prove to myself that he either was not the man I thought I was in love with, he was never going to commit to me, or in some amazing move he could be capable of a grand romantic gesture. I know there are men out there that are, I had one tell me he would come to me only hours before, and he has only known me for a few weeks.

I sent a long response to my unfinished love story as soon as I received his message. I told him I still didn't feel supported by him for my creative outlet. I was really concerned since he was taking second-hand information about my blog postings, when he hadn't taken the time to read them himself and form his own opinion. I told him I was really concerned that nothing has changed between us. I still didn't feel like a priority in his life. There were no Skype chat dates booked and there were no plans of him visiting me. I wanted to be touched by him. I wanted to be with him, be us, but I felt his conversations always brought up work. I told him I was tired of putting in so much effort into so many areas of my life. I felt weighed down in my life back home. I want to always give, but I want to be more conscious about my time and energy to make sure I am not feeling exhausted. I told him that our relationship is a flower, he is the sunshine and I am the rain. We both need to give, but too much or little of one of the other will make our little flower die. Then I told him to not be afraid. Take a leap. He will never regret it.

Then I closed off: "I still love you. I always have. I always will. I believe you are my soulmate. My only prayer right now is to one day kiss your lips, hold you close, and make unbelievable passionate love to you like we both remember it. But until then I keep myself busy and find a creative outlet to release all my thoughts, good and bad".

He responded back a couple of hours later. He said that he wasn't concerned about losing his job or money but it was about not knowing. He wanted me to keep having fun, but "if you feel that me not coming to visit you or reading your blog or being your friend on Facebook is so important to have in order for us to continue then that's a bold statement". He said he is guarded against me, that I have changed and he would rather get to know the new me once I was done travelling. He recognized that he did make mistakes, "but maybe there's a reason for all of this". He closed off by saying when I figure out my time zone we could set up a Skype chat.

I read his response and I was angry. I was angry because I felt I felt he was constricted by fear. I felt his fear was hindering his entire life. He has always had the potential to make so much out of his life. I responded to him the moment I arrived at my hotel in Dubai. I told him leaps of faith allow us to do massive things with our lives and if he holds himself back he will never be any better off than where he was. I was angry because he said he never wanted to lose me, but here I was, halfway around the world. I felt he was more concerned about the things he would lose that weren't me.

I told him being my Facebook friend and reading my blog were important to me. I want a partner that is engrained in my life and we create one together. I apologized for hurting him, but I told him he had the potential to stop his pain, and he has the potential to change my stories to amazing romantic ones staring him.

My aggravation with him was increasing as I wrote the email.

Me: You could do whatever it takes to create a wonderful life for us. Aren't you tired of seeing your friends married with kids and you're still on the sidelines? You could be one of them this time next year. What actions are you taking today to make that happen to be with the woman that you love?

I say all of this with the utmost love for you. I say it most importantly as your friend and supporter.

I will try to encourage you as much as I can, but it goes back to my last email about effort. I can't give more effort than you are willing to give yourself. Do you truly feel that you are doing absolutely everything to give yourself a happy life? Do you think your job cares if you want a family and a loving wife who makes love to you passionately every night? Or do you think your wife cares that your same energy is going into a job that keeps you up at night worrying if you will have a job tomorrow.

Take a really bold risk. Make this life yours. Design it and capture all of it.

I am also really sad that I won't see you. It's actually incredibly heartbreaking. I don't say that to give you guilt, I say that because that's how I feel. I wish I was enough that you would do anything to be next to me. I'm sure I will get over it in my own way.

I then closed off the email telling him that I would be open-minded about teaching our children about Catholicism. I asked him again to be more open minded about the Reiki, he had nothing to lose except a couple hours and a bit of money. But it never really was about the Reiki.

I sent him two more messages asking him if he could chat. I forgot it was a Sunday. I sent one just before 6AM and another at 6:20AM his time, then I took off to explore for the day.

He had a short response when he woke up. He said he was in a successful position and was enjoying his celebrations. He would rather chat online but because he was still staying with his best friend and he didn't think he would be able to until the week. He closed off telling me to enjoy my exploring and the neat things I would see.

I felt like my head was going to explode and my heart was being ripped from my chest. I had spent the day re-reading our entire email string. I received a message from Sean, from my India group, asking if I would like any company in Dubai. I told him not really, but since he already booked a flight, we should meet up. I knew Eddie was waiting on the sidelines for me to give him a date when we could see each other. I had spent the day responding to emails from friends and family telling me to stop with my unfinished love story and to focus on Eddie: "Don't confuse your unfinished love story's jealousy with love", "Eddie is so in love with you", "You're going to sabotage a really good thing if you don't let go of your unfinished love story". My spinning thoughts were out of control. I felt like I was standing on the edge, I wanted to be talked down and all I heard was the crowd shouting, "jump"!

I sent my unfinished love story another message only minutes after he sent his last one. It was like my suicide note before making the plunge. I was desperate. Come and get me. Catch me. Him. I wanted him to either stop me from jumping or be there to break my fall.

Me: No Problems. I'll be in Turkey next week.

Maybe we should take a break from the emails for a while. I get the impression that I'm doing more harm than good. But along those lines since it won't be another 10 weeks or so before we see each other, maybe we shouldn't get ourselves too wrapped up into something if you're still feeling unsure and guarded towards me.

I have no intentions of adding any tag-alongs to my trip, except those that have received exclusive invitation, which was only you. However, coincidentally enough today I received two messages from people that want to join me. Since you're not interested, I may consider some alternatives. It's really flattering to have someone want me in return.

I waited a couple of hours asking if he was available to Skype chat. I told him I would keep my Skype on all night. I would wake up in the middle of the night for him.

He responded. He said he knew there was something up. He said that if I have other travelling companions I have obviously had other encounters and am still keeping my options open. He was upset that my trip was supposed to be for me, I told him I wouldn't get involved on my trip and I did; he knew I would. He now doesn't want to see me come back after my travel flings still convinced that he is the one for me. He is feeling really confused where he is right now in his life, but he is in no position to make any changes; he's not in a rut, he is looking for options, but for now he is enjoying the rest of the summer.

There was nothing more I wanted to say. I was tired of emails. I wanted to scream. I wanted him. I wanted to feel connected with him. I wanted to feel that he wanted to be with me. I wanted to Skype him. I wanted him to hug me, stroke my hair, kiss my lips, and hold me tight. I would cry it all out into his shoulder, he would tell me that he is here now and he will never, ever leave me.

I was angry that it had been over a week since we last spoke. I was angry that I missed him as much as I did. I was angry at myself for giving my love to him and I felt he wasn't in a position to receive it. I wanted my heart back, but it was no longer mine. I already decided it was his.

I needed to vent. There was no one I could talk to, so my next best option was to write. I wrote a long blog entry. My heated head and broken heart saw the facts differently than they actually were. I paired up mine and my unfinished love story's conversation in tit-for-tat fashion; I forgot about time zones and delays in communications. I had read the email string so many times I could repeat every email without chronological order. I added colour commentary after every line of text.

Then between tears and rage I threw a match on the bridge that I was standing on. I announced in my blog that Eddie was falling in love with me.

I finished off by saying, "or I could wait for the one that I have called for months my unfinished love story to give me a time next week when he will be able to Skype with me for 15 minutes.

I know which one I will not choose".

Arabian Nights

Dubai, United Arab Emirates
July 21

The busyness of travelling, early mornings and late nights have finally caught up to me. I couldn't bring myself to get out of bed until three hours later than my standard natural wakeup, despite gaining an hour and a half time zone.

Before getting up to take a shower, I exchanged a couple more messages with Sean. He was arriving in Dubai tonight. We agreed to meet for a drink after my sand dune safari was completed.

I then exchanged some messages with Eddie. I told him I was having a change of heart. Even though I said I wanted to do my trip solo, if he was still up for meeting me, it would be really nice to see him again. We did have so much fun hanging out. I told him it was my fear and complete uncertainty about our potential future that is holding me back from allowing my heart to be completely captured by him.

Maybe that was always the case. Maybe the universe wasn't pulling me back to my unfinished love story, maybe it was pushing me towards Eddie and I was the one pushing back. Eddie wasn't brought to me as a distraction; he was actually the one I was supposed to meet. When faced with two options, I typically go with the one I know and maybe this was part of my first meditation: be open to possibility.

Eddie looked excited. Then he pulled his excitement back. "Are you sure"?

His question brought back my cloud of uncertainty. "I don't know", I said. Why don't I know?

"Go meditate on it", he said. "Get back to me when you're ready. There's no rush".

That's actually a really good place to start.

I started my meditation by deciding to be completely done with my unfinished love story. I imagined standing on top of a large skyscraper with a stack of papers. Each paper was a memory, an attribute, and anything else that reminded me and held me to my now and permanently off-again ex. I folded each paper into an airplane and released them into the sky. They are no longer mine. I let them go. Watching these paper airplanes fly in the sky had a beautiful departure from my hands to wherever they will now lay. It was a softer ending than imagining a burning or a cutting of the cord. For me there was a beauty in thinking that each piece could still exist, but it was for someone else to collect, not me. With that release I could now focus again on my prayer of having love come to me. He already said he would.

With a late start, I made my way to the Dubai Mall. Before heading there, I had seen a Tim Horton's on the street one metro station before the mall. I finally get to relieve one of my home sickness cravings: a Timmy's coffee and a honey cruller donut. Tim Horton's was closed for dining, but offer take-away. I ordered my items, plus a turkey sandwich, and asked the cashier where I could eat.

His eyes widened, "uh, nowhere. Back at your hotel room"?

The tragedy! I finally get my Timmy's coffee and donut and I can't even eat it.

The cashier then said, since there was no one else in the restaurant right now, if I am fast, and stay hidden, I could eat there. I was nervous. He said that he is Catholic, and it didn't bother him. I ate my donut in one bite, drank my coffee in record time and put my sandwich in my bag.

The Dubai mirage effect had its hold on me again. I could see Burj Khalifa easily from Tim's, and knew that the mall was right beside. I covered my head with my scarf and walked for over 20 minutes in the hot, humid sun-filled day. I felt like a Bedouin in the desert, I saw my destination, I just couldn't get there.

Tickets to Burj at the Top had to be bought in advance and the only time that worked for me was later tonight after my night safari. Since Sean and I already agreed to meet tonight I bought us both a ticket.

Around early evening I was picked up in a 4x4 to head to the sand dunes. As we made it to the dunes the driver popped a Bollywood DVD into his navigation system. The music bopped while the driver made fast climbs and skilled spins on the dunes. It felt like a rollercoaster ride cruising over the top and around the dunes. Then before heading back to the city I was taken into the middle of the desert for a buffet dinner, shisha and dancing show.

Sean and I met in his hotel lobby. His hotel didn't offer alcohol so we took a cab to a beautiful bar close to the Burj, for a couple of excessively taxed drinks. The bar was at the top of a 5-star hotel and in hindsight I enjoyed the views there more than the "top" of the Burj, which at only 424m was a far cry from the 800m that the tower actually stands. Sean and I headed to another basement bar for a couple more drinks, him asking questions about my decisions in love. We chatted well past midnight then it was time for us to permanently part ways. Tomorrow I was heading to Istanbul and he was off to Kuwait.

Starting Something New

Eddie sent me a message last night. He said after our exchanges yesterday he did some of his own reflecting. He decided his heart is too important to him to give it to someone that didn't give hers back to him fully in return. He didn't want to be a puppet in another man's love story and if I invested in us I had to be fully ready.

He was right. It hurt to hear. I wanted to give my heart to someone who is fully willing to take it and give me theirs in return. I want to be able to give my heart to Eddie. My head is telling me that I should be with someone that wants to be with me. Eddie has shown that he is willing to come to me. I always look forward to seeing his messages and hearing his sexy British accent. I cried when I left him. So why does my heart still not feel it? Where is my truth, my head or my heart?

I knew I needed to send him a message. Even though he told me to take my time responding, I knew he was waiting. I didn't even know what I was going to send yet, but when I opened my iPad the hotel internet was down. I breathed a sigh of relief. I have extra time.

I checked out of my hotel, sent a package home and visited the Dubai museum. It all took far less time than I hoped it would. I then slowly walked to the metro station. I was going to the Dubai Mall for free Wi-Fi.

I sat in a plush chair in the mall, my iPad open, still not clear on what to write Eddie. I was scared that if I told him that I needed more time to think he wouldn't be willing to wait for me. I was scared of disappointing my friends and family by not choosing him. I was worried that my hesitation would get in the way of potentially amazing happiness. I was scared that my lingering love for my unfinished love story was clouding my judgment.

I felt hypocritical. I pressured my unfinished love story to make a decision to decide on me and here I am paralyzed to decide on Eddie. It seemed right. Could it eventually feel right?

I sat for an hour trying to figure out what I wanted to say to Eddie. Eddie saw that I was online and immediately called me. I still didn't have my answer, but I felt compelled to tell him something, even if wasn't a complete thought yet. Something is better than nothing.

I told him that I knew I needed frequent, physical affection. I needed to be touched and held and kissed. I told him that's why I think things couldn't be resolved between me and my unfinished love story, I needed him next to me.

"Kimmy, I would do all of that for you"

I then told Eddie that I would rather delay a start than to start something I couldn't finish.

He said he got all of that. He has no timeline on when he has to be home, but he would love to know what his next destination is. Then, "Kimmy, I haven't been able to stop thinking about you since you left".

Without thinking about it before I said it, "Eddie, you made me feel so good when we were together. I could go years dating people only to be searching for what I felt when I was with you".

Then he asks, "So, where do we go from here"?

I tell him I am leaving for Istanbul tonight, and will be in Turkey for the next two weeks; after that Greece

"Okay, let me work out some flights. I promise you, I am coming to you".

It was about midafternoon, and despite it being a couple hours too early to go to the airport, I was now done with Dubai. Besides, the airport will be serving food, and I was starving.

Get Naked

Istanbul, Turkey
July 23

Sometimes the cheapest flights are not worth it. My flight was to arrive in Istanbul around 1AM and the airport I chose was not the main airport but an hour away from the city centre. I still needed to purchase a visa as I entered but once I arrived none of the kiosks were open. There was a mass of people yelling at a few officials in Turkish. One official told me to stand in the customs line anyway, which is poor advice. I would get to the front of the line and be sent back. No visa, no entry. Finally it looked like the visa line was back in action and I jumped right in. Maybe someone finally came back from their break. The visa price as quoted in Euro, which I didn't have so I asked if I could pay in Turkish Lira. Nope, they don't accept that. Of course not, why would the Turkish government accept their own currency? I had USD on me, which they did accept.

I slept most of the morning away. My hotel was only a 10-minute walk from the Blue Mosque and some of the other highlights in Istanbul. As I walked around the area outside the mosque I came across a hamam. Every Turkish experience must include a trip to a hamam, so everyone told me.

I booked a treatment and was given a sarong-like towel and a pair of sandals to wear. I had no idea what to expect. I stripped down, debating whether to wear my underwear or not, and last minute decided not to. I was guided into an all-marble room that had 3 subsections of half-walls that overlooked a main platform. Each subsection had a bench and 3 marble sinks with gold faucets and bowls. The woman sat me on one of the benches and took off my towel. I was now fully naked. I tried to avoid eye contact with the few other women getting the same treatment. The woman who guided me took a gold bowl and dipped it full of water from the marble sink and poured water across my body. I thought to myself that there is no room for shyness anymore. I was also glad I didn't wear my underwear. I saw a few other women still in theirs and could only imagine the uncomfortable experience of leaving the hamam with either soaking wet underwear or going free.

Eventually an older woman came by and took me by the hand to another marble room. She scrubbed my body with an exfoliating glove, then placed mud all over my body and face. She told me to relax, which I did my best to, but the clay was getting hot against my skin. After probably only 10 minutes the older woman came back and washed the clay off my body, shampooed my hair and led me back to the large, main room where she laid me down on the main "viewing" platform so she could soap up my body. I went for a final cold rinse before being taken to the lounge for some Turkish delight and aromatic tea.

I sent Eddie a message over dinner then finished the night off with a night boat tour between the channel that separates Istanbul from Asia and Europe. It was a lovely ride as the sun set and the city lit up.

Problems of a (Solo) Constant Traveller

Istanbul, Turkey
July 24

I had to force myself to wake up at a reasonable time. I'm starting to feel lazy. A funny statement for someone who hasn't worked in over four and a half months. I thought I could leave Istanbul tomorrow, I was also indifferent to staying, however if I did leave I needed to arrange a flight or a bus or whatever. I still wanted to visit Hagia Sofia, the Topkapi Palace and the Grand Bizarre. A full day no matter how I looked at it. Yet I still took my sweet time getting out of bed.

Somewhere along the way to Hagia Sofia I either turned when I shouldn't have or the road turned on its own and I didn't notice, but every time I looked at Google Maps I was no closer to my destination. I felt like I was in Vietnam all over again. Walking and walking and never arriving anywhere.

It didn't take long to go through Hagia Sofia, and fortunately right around the corner is the Topkapi Palace. It took me over two-hours to walk through the entire palace, by which time I started to feel bored from the history and tired of the crowds.

I found a café close by and sat drinking a Turkish coffee and eating a sandwich. Then I was lucky enough to receive a call from Eddie. It had been at least a couple of days since we chatted with one another. He wanted to let me know that he was still intending on seeing me, but had to arrange a flight change and before speaking to me a couple of days ago he had committed to James that he would join him on a fitness camp in Bangkok. It had been a while since I had been travelling solo for this long. I was actually starting to feel lonely. We had to decide where and when we would be able to see each other again. I laughed at our conversation. It was the epitome of the jetsetter lifestyle: Cairo Aug 21? Athens Aug 6? Bangkok Sept 21? Maybe Singapore? Are you kidding me? Who has those conversations? Finally it was decided that we still had a week to decide. Then there will be the big question that Future Eddie and Future Kim would eventually have to face: A Canadian and a Briton meet in Indonesia, where do they live? There was so much yet to plan, but more urgently, for me, what do I do tomorrow? Should I stay or should I go?

After visiting the Grand Bazaar I figured I had delayed my decision long enough. I was just feeling lonely and before I had always defeated the loneliness by staying on the move. A new location meant new things to see and do, which meant no time to think about anything else. Despite Eddie and I having discussions about seeing each other, that was more than likely not going to be for at least a month, and my mind was already racing as to what that all meant. I was now getting scared on top of lonely.

Sometimes life likes to give us a little surprises and mine came in the form of a thoughtful email from my third love, who is now engaged. He told me he was enjoying reading my posts and wished me all the best. He said he knows I will eventually find love. He never thought he would ever get married and now he is planning a wedding, so it can happen to anyone. I hope he was right.

It's probably a good thing that Eddie and I wouldn't see each other for a while. It would give us time to have conversations, get to know each other, and I don't lose my original intention of travelling alone. At the same time, those hard days when the loneliness does set in, I get to see someone, hear their voice and words of encouragement. I get to do this solo without being alone. That's all I wanted. There will also be a special person that I can rely on that will give me time when I need a cheerleader in my corner, a coach to pump me up and tell me to continue the good fight.

I finally gave in to my laziness of booking my next destination and walked into a travel agency. I was ready to leave Istanbul and was happy to give someone else the reins to book something for me. The cheapest option was Antalya, on the Southern tip of Turkey. A beach town along the Mediterranean. That sounded pretty good to me. I booked the flight, with a shuttle. Then as a thank you the agent invited me to come back when his family would be breaking their fast for the day and having dinner. I graciously thanked him, but decided to find a rooftop and enjoy my last night in Istanbul.

Giving Myself a Pass

Antalya, Turkey
July 25

I went to bed early and still had a hard time falling asleep. Eddie called me late that evening. He had been out with his boys, came back to the hotel early, saw I was online, and wanted to chat with me. We chatted for over 90 minutes, about nothing. It was just nice to have someone to talk to.

I arrived in Antalya, found a café just outside of the airport, ordered breakfast, and looked online for a hotel. Eddie was online again and called to say hi. Every time he reaches out my heart flutters. It's what I prayed for: someone that wants me to be their number one, he takes the time and the opportunity to let me know, and someone he would drop everything when I reach out to him. We treat each other with constant affection, despite the distance, until we see each other again. I never wanted to do any distance in my relationships ever again, at least with now there was an end date. Nairobi. Sept 7th. Then we take it from there.

Dress Up to Cheer Up

Antalya, Turkey
July 26

I've been feeling generally down for the last several days, so I thought some pampering would help. I gauge my haircuts based on the country and my last one was Kuala Lumpur, about 6 weeks ago.

I walked into a busy salon, figuring busy means good haircuts. The hairdresser spoke no English, so in charades I actioned I needed my roots dyed and my fringe trimmed. As he coloured another woman came by and I agreed to have my poorly maintained eyebrows waxed. I then agreed to a manicure and pedicure. My complete makeover didn't make me feel happier but at least I looked better.

I continued to walk around, unfortunately my mind doing more of the wandering. I have been getting itchy to get back to work. Since India I have been really considering the potential of never moving back to Canada, especially if Eddie and my relationship blossoms. I wondered if my ex missed me, because I was missing him. My self-doubt crept back and questioned if I could ever be a good partner to someone, and maybe I really am not enough. I thought about just going home, and at the same time just sticking it out. I was meeting my friends in a couple of days, and I would hate to leave before that.

My sadness spiral brought me back to my hotel where I called my mom. She told me my dog was sick, and they were taking her to the vet. She then said, "cheer up. If you really want to come home, then you should. But before booking a flight, put on a pretty dress, go to a pub, and have a couple of drinks. I'm sure you will feel different after tonight". Maybe that's pretty good advice.

I walked around the Old Town, sat down on their patio ordered my comfort food, pizza and beer. Within a few minutes

302

I was invited to join a table of three guys and a girl from Italy, Russia and Turkey. As we were chatting Eddie called me. I quickly dismissed him. My annoyance with him was starting to build. The last few days we had been chatting it always involved him being out "on the piss" with the guys, and now it was my turn. My new friends asked if that was my boyfriend, and I said yes. They said I should call him back, I came across really rude. I called Eddie and apologized. I told him I would call him when I got back to my hotel. I really didn't want to ruin this relationship too. I did feel lucky to have someone in a time zone 5-hours away and he is still interested and finds time for me.

The group and I finished our beers at the first pub and then walked across the lane to another pub for a couple more drinks. One of the guys bought me a wishing lantern that we lit and released into the sky. Mom was right, a pretty dress and a couple of beers really can cheer anyone up.

No Regrets

I spent yesterday at the beach, sun-tanning and reading old blog entries. I couldn't believe how far I've come as a person in four months. I even forgot it was my trip anniversary a couple days ago.

I was still in a funk though. I wasn't having a terrible time in Turkey, I just wasn't enjoying myself. Something didn't feel right.

I laid in bed and gave Eddie a call. I hoped there was something he could say to make it all better. I sometimes forget that he is going through his own breakup struggle. He has been so strong and a perfect example of moving on and forward, especially while keeping his head high. "Get out of bed, lazy ass", he tells me. I know he's right, lying in bed helped nothing.

I ask him how else are things. He tells me that it was a hard day for him yesterday. He received a nice note from his wife's mom and sister letting him know that they feel bad for him, and are glad to hear that he is doing well and making himself happy. He told me that was a great ego boost. I completely agreed. I wondered if my ex's family thought positive thoughts and wished the best for me too. I hoped if nothing else they sympathize why I couldn't stay with someone whose priorities were work and friends then me. Not that it matters. I made the only decision I could at the time with the information I had and what I knew I was capable of.

I scrolled through Facebook hoping to see something new when I came across a Ted Talk about regret. For a long time, and still now, I felt regret about my decisions, about the timing, and feeling that maybe there was still more or different actions that I could have taken. The Ted Talk made me realize that my feelings are because I knew I could to better for myself. Throughout my blog postings I received a lot of feedback that my actions were justified, and granted there is only one side of the story being presented, I was now starting to believe it. I accepted my actions around the catalyst for my trip, my breakup.

I have no regrets for what I did. It's not that I felt I could *do* better; I still believe he is an unbelievably wonderful person, and I truly do hope and wish the absolute best things in his life. I do however believe that I *deserved* better. I deserve to have someone tell me 1) I pick you to share the rest of my life with, and 2) you (and our future family) are the most important thing in my life. The reason I tried to make it work with him (albeit a very distant go) was because I believed him when he said his priorities changed. I know what I deserve in my life. I am lucky to be where I am and have the strength to say, "yes, I am a wonderful person, and I deserve to be happy and have someone in my life that finds it enough to be with me". Work and friends are important, but they should never, ever come before the overall happiness of me and the person that I want to spend the rest of my life with.

I played a song that I was introduced to in India, I Lived, by One Republic. I instantly felt better about me, every day since being away, and the days that lay ahead. If it was to ever happen that I never, ever found myself with another person again, I would be satisfied knowing that one day I woke up and said "I deserve love and I deserve to be somebody's number one".

In the early evening I walked down to the marina to see about catching a boat for a sunset tour. On my way I passed by the carpet store owner and his young apprentice that I met the night before when I took interest in frank fruit. I sat with them drinking tea and eating the exotic fruit. They stopped me again today and invited me for another tea. I graciously accepted. We chatted and the owner invited me out for dinner. I refused at first, and then on the second ask, I accepted as long as he knew that I had a boyfriend. He felt insulted that I would have to clarify, but I would feel terrible if I didn't.

I met up with Mustafa again after my boat ride and we walked over to a very nice vegetarian restaurant. We drank most of a small bottle of Raki, which added to water turns the clear liquid into a cloudy white. We chatted about business, immigration, global job opportunities, love and following your heart and passion. He was the first person in a long time that encouraged me to listen to my heart over my head and be with the man I thought was my soulmate.

Just Chill, Kimmy

Antalya, Turkey
July 29

I was bored with Antalya. I normally move every third day or so, and to spend five days in a single city, especially in a country as beautiful and diverse as Turkey was a tragedy. Eddie said to me that it would be good for me to sit and chill in a single place for a while. My anxiety needed me to be on the move, but with only one full-day left there was no reason to look at any other locations. One more day meant I could find something to do, even if it included more beaches and cafés.

I rolled out of bed, went for a shower, sang Roxette's ballads and prepared for the beach.

I sat on my beach chair with the occasional dip in the Mediterranean Sea. My mind wandered to my unknown future, being back home, and then to my heart. I accepted the release of the things I cannot change, and I wished it was just as easy to release the daily thoughts and memories, but I know those will just take more time. Every night I go to sleep I hope to wake up and not have that certain person's face in my head. I have accepted that I will always feel nothing but love for him, but obviously I know that feelings of love are not enough.

Coming to this realization started to put me in a calmer state. I didn't want to struggle to resist these demons. It takes too much energy and leaves me feeling guilty for having the feelings to begin with. Instead I see them standing in the corners, asking me to play, teasing me to go down those "what-if" paths that I know leave me exhausted and emotionally destroyed. I acknowledge their presence and simply say, not today. I have more wonderful things to think about and explore. Not necessarily a new love, but I get to go back to focusing on my own happiness and self-love. My journey that was started and interrupted by so many amazing detours. But now with just over two months left, I'd like to climb this mountain as high as possible and be even more amazed how far I've come.

Crazy Is As Crazy Does

Fethiye, Turkey
July 31

I was so excited to arrive in Fethiye yesterday. I was meeting up with a couple I knew back in Calgary. They moved to Saudi Arabia in February and they asked me to meet up with them before they were finished their Turkish vacation. We, with a couple more of their friends, all went out for dinner and drinks last night.

I ended up drinking too much last night, made some poor decisions, which included calling and emailing my ex. I felt terrible when I realized what I did in the morning. The worst part being one of the emails I wrote last night didn't send until this morning after a Wi-Fi hiccup. I wanted to send an apology, but then thought best to leave it. I am not the first person to make poor life decisions in an alcohol induced state, and I won't be the last.

My email apologized for hurting him and for the rapid breakdown in our communication. I said I had read through our string of emails and although I felt really hurt when he said he wasn't coming to see me I felt like I was understood where he was coming from. I told him that the love I need includes being next to someone, where I am touched and kissed and without his touch I forgot how much I truly loved him. I told him I wanted to publish my blog as a book, but only after completing the story by inserting our communications and some selectively left out events and thoughts. Then I said the hardest part is that I still dream of him every night, always in some future state. I told him that I wanted him to pick me.

The day continued getting better when I received my first blog troll. A long-winded rant that summarized my trip as best as I would put it myself: broke up with my Canadian boyfriend, quit my job, sold my house, went on a "soul-searching" mission, all the while still believing my ex was "the one", met a guy from the UK, meeting up with the UK guy later on my trip. However it was the end of his rant that really stung: "...but as a man, a regular guy with regular relationship issues, you come across as bat-shit-fucking-insane... I really wanted you to know that you probably should spend less time meditating and more time with a psychiatrist".

I thanked him for reading; he's obviously read a few posts to know all that information. I thanked him for having an opinion. I said that maybe I do need a psychiatrist and that will be something I will look into when I get home. Then I finished by saying I'm sure his opinion is coming from a place where he hopes I get my "happily ever after", and I wish the same for him.

He thanked me for being a better person.

I'm not the first person that has felt the "crazy" overcome her (or him) when faced with a breakup. I held onto my thought, hopes, dreams, and memories, much longer than I probably should have. Instead of just letting it be and allowing things to naturally play their course I fought and expended constant effort to make my dreams come true. I refused to open myself up to possibilities because my mind was set on how I wanted my story to end. I deceived myself multiple times believing I was allowing things to "come as they may", but quickly became impatient with the "natural" pace. In my impatience I caused more pain to myself, my family, my friends, and my ex.

I met up with Kim and Darren for the afternoon. They wanted to go exploring some ruins nearby, and the walk was definitely going to help me clear my head and my severe hangover. As we walked we talked about their new life in Saudi, the difficulty of staying in touch with friends when being so far away, but for the most part it was nice just to be around someone without having to say anything. I was reminded of long-term love and the definition of marital bliss: two best friends that love hanging out together and support each other through adventures and challenges. Someone to hold onto after a bad day. Someone that will say, "yes, I will travel anywhere in the world for you. You are my friend, my family, and I am happiest when I am with you, no matter what we are doing or where we are".

We went for dinner and then after we grabbed a couple bottles of wine and sat on Kim and Darren's balcony overlooking the yachts in the sea. They both had strong opinions about me, my situation, my travelling experience and my heart. Darren said I give far too much in my relationships, I end up with men that don't try as much, because they don't have to because I'm there to do it all, then I feel exhausted. He said that's why it also takes me longer to let go, I've invested so much that I don't want to just walk away from all that effort. I then said I would love to get to the point on this trip where I'm not spending my time stuck in either the future or the past. I would love to be here. Right here, right now.

We chatted for a while longer then I decided it was time to leave the past where it is. I deleted my ex from my contacts.

Summertime Sadness

There has been a dark cloud hanging over me for several days. Part of it is because I am going to Greece tomorrow. Greece itself doesn't make me sad, but it's what Greece meant. I was certain that my ex was coming to see me. I dreamed about him meeting me in Athens. I convinced myself my dream was a premonition. He always spoke of how he wanted to see Greece. My mom told me that he was planning on taking time off in August. I had a palm reader and tarot card reader tell me that my love was coming to me in August. Now I am heading to one of the most romantic places in the world by myself.

I do not want to be sad. If I wanted to start practicing being in the moment, what better time than the next two and a half weeks? Sailing between islands, watching sunsets, gorging on food and wine. Being open to saying "yes". This is still my story and I am not finished or ready to turn it into a tragedy. Maybe I do find my love in Greece.

Maybe the self-love journey I started in June continues and brings me to a new level. Maybe I fall in love with Greece or maybe I finally learn how to fall in love with the moments. It would be lovely to have a day where I realize I was enjoying being right here right now and I didn't spend a moment thinking about the past or the future. That's where I want to be.

I reflected back on the last couple of months. Before arriving in Thailand I had so much love in my heart for everyone. I felt consistent calmness and clarity. I felt absolute certainty about the ending to my story, the correctness of the path I was taking, it felt so good and romantic. How could I do a complete 180-turn with my heart when I arrived in Indonesia? Thinking about it made me want to get sick.

I don't regret meeting Eddie, and I don't regret the moments I spent with him. We had such a wonderful time together. He showed me that love has no boundaries, no time zones, and no distance too far. He has been close to me even after we parted ways. Our daily conversations have made him a really great friend. He opened my eyes to long-term love, someone who can commit to the person they love through the hardest times. He proved that there are people out there that when their partner is having a difficult time you step up and say, how do WE fix this? When his wife needed him to be there, even though they are broken up, he said she is still his best friend and he needs to be there for her. He said that he wanted to do everything he could for her so that they could eventually part ways in a happy and loving place. As he would tell me his conversations that he was having with her, he always sounded like he was still so in love with her. I know there is probably a lot more to it, but sometimes I wish I could just tell him to go back to his wife.

I really don't think I would be here if my ex could have just provided me with the same support that Eddie provides. I was going through a tough emotional time and I needed someone to hold onto me really tight and say it will be alright, just tell me what you need. Instead I felt like my ex turned his back on me and I fought and begged and cried just to hear, I still love you, I still want to be with you.

To be fair my ex did so many things right. When we were together we would laugh all the time. I knew how much he loved me and our dog. He had so many ambitions for us. He would love to talk about us moving to Australia, and our future life. Every now and then he would surprise me with a beautiful dinner or a concert. He loved being the "man" and taking care of man-type duties around the house. He loved to BBQ while we would both sit on the patio, drinking Coronas and waiting until it was dark. But the best part was when we were together he made me really happy. The thought of him and of our love still warms my entire body. The few times that we did chat since I was away I became overwhelmed with giddiness. Out of all my relationships I was happiest with him.

I read an article saying the difference between a relationship that lasts and one that fails is often how the two partners look at it. Those that see their relationship as "soul-mates" or "the one" are likely to fail. The partners can't understand that when times become difficult there will be differences of opinions and fights. They believe if they are "meant to be" the relationship should move flawlessly. However those that saw their relationship as a growing opportunity were likely to last. They saw their discrepancies as opportunities to learn and grow. Mistakes made become lessons and are viewed as the chance to strengthen the relationship.

Kim, Darren and I went out for dinner again. We talked more about my heart. They encouraged me to allow Eddie to love me. They said based on the stories they really liked him and thought he would be such a great person for me. I told them that it somehow doesn't feel right. I said my heart only feels healed when I allow it to be committed to my ex. Thinking about him not in my life makes me feel broken and if my ex responded to my email, if he agreed to have a conversation with me, I would be done.

I told them about what my buddy Blair said to me when I chatted with him earlier in the day. He told me I should not be in a relationship at all.

I then had to weigh the different advice I was getting. Two different sets of friends, two completely different opinions. Differing opinions about where I should go and what I should do when my travel is complete. Differing opinions about my love life. However they both agreed on what my goal should be over the next two months: focus on myself, live for the moment and do whatever makes me happy.

Doing It For Myself

When I woke up I was feeling pretty confident that I was going to tell Eddie not too book his trip to Africa. But when I saw him on FaceTime my mind became muddled, thoughts of my friends and their advice started flipping through my head. The only thing I was capable of doing was to start to cry. "I'm not going to go back to the UK with you", I said.

He said that was okay. There were no expectations. But then he asked about Africa. I couldn't bring myself to saying no. I thought about what Kim and Darren had said about just having fun and allowing it to be. I told him I would let him make that decision based on what I said about me going to the UK.

I caught the ferry from Fethiye to Rodos. When I arrived at my hotel I opened Facebook. I felt like I was going to have a panic attack. Eddie had posted his status as "going to Africa at the end of the month". It was suddenly so real and I didn't feel ready. I called him up practically in tears. He said if it made me feel better he would come just as my friend. That made me feel slightly better, I agreed and let him go. But my heart was still unsure.

He then said, "but be prepared, when I see you at the airport I am going to kiss you".

I've wanted to hear thought those words for so long. They were coming out of the wrong person. I didn't want this to become something it wasn't.

A short while later I received a message from Eddie. He was feeling confused after reading my recent blog posting. Was I as over my ex as I was telling him? I felt myself become defensive. I didn't respond.

I realized my blog had taken on a life of its own. I was creating a story. I wasn't being honest with Eddie only because I wasn't being honest with myself. I was with Eddie because so many people said I should be. I wanted my trip to be a love story and that was going to happen with our without my unfinished love story. I was writing for the sake of the story and not the journey that I was supposed to be in. I realized I completely lost my focus. Then I decided it was enough. My blog had caused too much pain and hurt. I will be true to myself when I can write unfiltered. I am no longer posting.

My heart knew who I wanted to spend the rest of my life with. I didn't want to hear that he wasn't the man for me. My mind was constantly on my unfinished love story. I have never been able to stop thinking about him. I missed him so much. I prayed he would reach out to me. I felt like I did in Indonesia. One call and all the hurt could be over. Yet my head said my unfinished love story doesn't want me and it insisted Eddie is the one I should be with. Who was right, my head or my heart?

As I walked home after dinner I stared up at the night sky and prayed out loud. "Dear Universe, please show me the way. Please paint a path that is easy for me to see". I repeated my mantra several times. I prayed for an answer soon. I am tired of my heartbreak. I am ready for my love story to have a happy ending.

I Will Travel Anywhere In The World For You

Faliraki, Greece
August 3

I woke up in the morning and felt certain what I needed to do. I had a dream that I wanted to go out for a coffee with my unfinished love story, but I couldn't because I chose Eddie. I had to tell Eddie not to come to Africa. None of it felt right. Deep in my heart I knew that if my unfinished love story called me and said he was coming to see me, I would drop Eddie in an instant, and never look back. It wasn't fair to either of us. I sent Eddie a message: I need to talk.

My prayer from last night was answered, Eddie replied, "I would love to FaceTime you, but it would be too difficult for both of us".

He has been back in regular communication with his wife to try to make things work. She was now willing to work on their issues, but she knew she had to be there in person. She told Eddie that she would travel anywhere in the world to be with him. She booked a flight and would be with him within two weeks. She was even willing to quit her job if he needed to just travel for a while. She wanted to be there for him.

I was so happy for him. He deserved that happiness. He thanked me for being a wonderful person. Then I told him goodbye. The end of the story of Eddie. Eddie, who got the story end that I wished for desperately, and wanted for myself.

And like a wave of relief I was now opened up without clouded confusion. I could now focus on my one love. The one I've wanted all along. I screwed up plenty. Maybe he would be willing to make it work. I immediately sent my unfinished love story a message.

Me: I don't know what you heard, but I want you to know that I'm not having anyone join me on my trip. Eddie was interested in joining me in Africa, we talked about it, but it never felt right. Told him today not to come. Africa was originally for you and me. This trip was about me finding my missing pieces, and I lost focus in all of that.

I misread that last email you sent me where it said you would have time for me in "the week". I thought it said "next week" and I lost it. Sorry.

I have not had any other encounters with anyone else. I have not opened myself up to that possibility. I also won't for a very, very long time.

I have also considered coming home right away. If you wanted me to, I would book the next flight home without hesitation or regret. I am done with my journey. The thing I have been searching for has been in Calgary all along.

I love you and miss you.

I couldn't do much else the entire day. I cried. I sat by the pool, tried to read, but then found myself crying again. I went for a nap. Maybe when I wake up I'll feel better. Unfortunately my dreams and my tears woke me up. I cried because I fucked up so bad. I knew in my heart Eddie was not the one I was supposed to be with, yet I played with that idea because his words were the ones I wanted to hear from my unfinished love story.

My head spun with questions. Why in the world was I not more patient? Why couldn't I hang on to the thought of love when I was in Indonesia? Why couldn't I take the time before responding to my unfinished love story's emails? My meditations told me to wait until after India to reconcile, yet my impatience decided I didn't need to listen.

It was still the middle of the night for my unfinished love story, but five hours later I sent a longer email. I told him it was a horrible day. It had been weeks since I heard anything from him. I didn't know if there was any love in his heart for me. I apologize again for the breakup, for my frustration, and for being broken. I told him I needed him then to hold me, tell me he loved me, be my friend and be with me. I told him how hard it was to confess my love, hold onto feelings of love from him when I was getting nothing in return, then see him with another woman and hear that he saw no future with me. I apologized for Eddie and flipping in my heart. Then I said we will never talk about either again. I love him so much, and I had been waiting for someone to tell me that they love me so much they would travel anywhere in the world, but today I was saying it to him.

Then: "I'm going to come home. You are my home. Let's talk about everything. Let's understand where we broke down. Then let's never, ever let each other go. We will have our problems. We will have communication breakdowns. We may even be faced with one of us wanting to call it quits in the future. But let's say no to all of that. If you try to break away I will hold you tight, I will hug you, kiss you, be your friend and say what can WE do to make it better? You will do the same for me, and I will never feel like your back was ever turned on me. You will never feel like I abandoned you."

I walked into town to have dinner. But I didn't want to be there. I didn't want to be anywhere. I wanted to be back in Calgary, cuddled up next to my unfinished love story and being happier than I have ever been before. I came back to the hotel and booked a flight to Athens.

Coming Home?

Rhodes, Greece
August 4

I woke up from a dream. I was looking for the pieces of an engagement ring that had shattered. The pieces were everywhere. It was somehow my ring. As I picked up the pieces I handed them to a man that was going to fix the ring for me. He asked me if I was happiest with the man I was with. I said no, my perfect match was my unfinished love story. The sound of his full name in my dream woke me up right away. It wasn't quite sunrise.

I sat on the bed and meditated. I went back to my complete focused one. I am thankful for the day, I give love to everyone around, I give myself love, and I sit with a clear and open mind.

I walked down to the hotel reception. I sat on a couch, watched the sun rise over the sea, and checked my emails. My unfinished love story responded.

> Him: Stay there and finish what you started. I'm not going to say much but I'm trying to move on. But please don't give in because you're going through a hard time. Pull yourself together and enjoy your travels. It's a once in a lifetime opportunity and you've made it this far. So keep on keeping on. You're not a quitter. Finish your trip, please.

> Me: Thank you for responding. The hardest part is not knowing if you are getting my emails or not.
> Okay. I hope she makes you incredibly happy. I hope you've been happier than you ever have in your lifetime. You deserve that.

320

I'm so, so sorry we broke down in our communication. You are and forever will mean the world to me.

I will continue because you asked me to. I will always be here for you if you ever need. I will wait for you.

I walked back up to my room, and started having flashes of an old dream. The one where he got the girl he was seeing pregnant and they decided to get engaged. I started hyperventilating. I couldn't handle it. I walked back down to the reception as I madly wiped away my tears. I had to call my mom.

There is nothing left for anyone to say to me anymore. So the story goes, girl loves boy, boy doesn't respond to girl, girl moves on, boy gets hurt, girl comes back, boy's moved on, girl still loves boy.

I can't handle the pain anymore. I am ready to throw myself into the sea and never resurface. There is only one place in the world that I want to be, and his cuddles are reserved for someone else. I went for a nap. Please, please let sleep be the solution.

I checked out of my hotel and was booked into a new one in Rhodes Town.

As my cabbie was driving me to the new hotel I kept thinking to myself, be in this moment. Be right here. The driver told me about the different sights in Rhodes and we discussed seeing those this morning.

My mind wandered between my two former loves. Then in Eddie's voice I heard "Stop it, just stop". I breathed deeply. I focused on exactly where I was while I was sightseeing.

Back at my hotel I chatted with my mom, but every time the question came up how I was doing the tears started pouring. Like a floodgate that I had to use force to close. I don't want to talk about me. The only thoughts I had were non-serious suicidal ones. I could drink to the point my liver collapses. I do have a lot of sleeping pills. Maybe I slit my wrists. I wanted to be anywhere but where I was in this moment. Even a plane ride didn't seem right. I went from having two men love me to no one. No one.

I went for a nap. Please let sleep heal. Please when I wake up let it all be better. Or please let me never, ever wake up.

Unfortunately, eventually, I did wake up. After a lot of self-motivation I made my way out of bed and spent two hours watching my email inbox hoping in some time-lapse my ex replied telling me he wants me home.

I went for a walk. I didn't want to be in public. I grabbed some beers and went back to my room.

I then came to a conclusion. I'm done. I'm quitting my trip. My head and my heart have always been in one place - my unfinished love story. I will no longer live this dichotomy of being here and there at the same time. If the goal in life is to find someone that I could say "I will travel the world for" I found mine. Why am I wasting another day being anywhere other than with him? If I thought I was better off without, at the very least, I would have found that place. Instead all I wanted to say was fuck the world. I choose him. I pick him.

I sent him a couple more messages. Travel can wait. My heart and love for him cannot. If we could just talk I would book the rest of my flights home. I am done.

Dark Paradise

Rhodes, Greece
August 5

My sleep was terrible. I decided to get up and see if I had received any response from my unfinished love story. I did. It felt curt. He thought the only reason I felt this way was because my trip was coming to a close. He didn't want to talk about any of it right now. He closed, "do us both a favour and enjoy the trip you are on". But I haven't been. My mind is elsewhere.

I responded back super apologetic. I told him I feel like I have been gone too long. I said that I was most sad that we went from talking to everything going bad so quickly. I felt that had we just had one conversation it would have allowed us to both understand where the other was coming from. We would have never had let our stubbornness get in the way if I was back home, yet we did when I was so far away. I closed, "I will continue my trip because I love you. Because you asked me to. Because, hopefully, time will heal".

I was broken. I felt so unloved. I wanted someone to love me. Love me back. I hit rock bottom.

I milled around. Went for breakfast. Came back to the room. Stared at the ceiling. Forced myself to go for a shower. Checked my emails again. I concentrated on only focusing on my current moment. I somehow got through the day. I felt like I was in a haze. Like the shell of a person, but it at least stops the tears.

I told myself I deserve better. I deserve someone who is going to love me in return. Someone who is my friend first and my companion second. Someone who will say, yes, I will go where you need me to. I was willing to stop my trip tomorrow and I didn't know if he would take off the Friday I would arrive.

My heart was bleeding. I felt it bleeding non-stop. I wanted a pill to get over the pain. It was too unbearable.

Had it not been for me needing to check out my hotel today I truly believe I wouldn't have found the capacity in myself to leave the hotel. I narrated my walk. There's a tree. Walking down stairs. That store is having a sale. I continued to talk in my head about exactly what I was seeing and what was in front of me. I didn't have the thought process to think about being anywhere else, thinking of the future, or the past, or of anyone other than me.

I stopped at anything that looked slightly interesting. I walked around a dried up moat around a castle. I went to a museum. I had lunch at a café. I called my mom and told her I wasn't coming home. I doubted my ex wanted me back and I decided to just ride it out. Instead of buying a flight from Athens to Calgary I bought a ferry ticket to Mykonos from Athens. I told myself I am stronger today than I was yesterday.

I stopped at another café and finally received the email from my ex that brought everything to an end. My expected finality. He was tired of me throwing my other relationships in his face and he can't handle any more of the hurt I've put him through. He's given me enough chances.

"Enough chances". That hurt the most. Not the words, but the way he could be there. Why couldn't I be "done"? I always think I am and I somehow dig deep and find another chance, another opportunity. Effort I had no idea existed.

He then told me again he is moving on and wished me "Good Luck".

Should I have responded, I don't know. I clarified a couple of things with his "other relationships" comment. There was only one relationship. I said I felt terrible that we had to have this conversation over email and we never had the chance to talk about it. Then I told him I love him, because I do and always will. I felt good to be capable of giving love even when I felt love wasn't given.

I sat at a seaside pub having my comfort beer and pizza. I told myself that I am a wonderful person. I am in love with myself and eventually when the love for me spills over I will be able to give the excess to someone else. He's out there. He's taking his time to find me.

My Second Angel

Eddie. My second angel. Neither he nor I would know the impact we would have on each other's lives the moment we met. Neither he nor I would know that what we carved is something that would change the trajectory of what our lives were divinely planned to be.

I hadn't heard from him since the morning he said he wasn't coming to Kenya. I didn't want to disturb the natural order of things by sending him one of our now habitual daily messages. But I missed him. More than I would have expected.

I cried when I received his random morning message.

Eddie: Our lives are not measured by the length of our years, but by the number of lives that we touch. From our time together I know that you will find love. Trust me.

His message opened a flood gate with me. I told him everything I was doing over the last two days. I was touched by his romantic story. I told Eddie that I reached out, again, to my unfinished love story and told him I was ready to stop my travels to be with him. But not to worry about me, Eddie, I will be fine.

Eddie: Stop chasing him, he's not worth the heartache.

Me: Here's to hoping I have a wonderful love story to share in the next couple of months.

I knew in my heart I was just waiting out the day for a nail in the coffin response from my unfinished love story. I felt I had let Eddie, and the promises I had made to Eddie, down. I sent him another message.

> Me: I will be fantastic. There is nothing a new, pretty dress, a deep conditioning treatment and a smile won't fix. Plus if I'm currently attracting men of your quality, I know I am in for more happiness than I have ever received.

> Eddie: You're a hot chick. Just try to chill. Don't push anything too fast. You will be fine. Love yourself first.

The first day we met Eddie and I had a lengthy conversation about self-love and I believed it was the most common reason women either can't find love or their current relationships end. I was currently completely empty. No matter what I was never going to have any love come to me in my current state. I needed to focus on filling up the vessel of love that is me.

Six months to the day I said the words "I can't do this anymore". For six months I tried to revive and continued to keep my relationship with my unfinished love story on life support. Every now and then it would sputter and cough, and I would be filled with hope, but it always went back to the same unresponsive state.

Maybe it was my need to have an answer. It could have been my impatience to bring it back to life that pushed it over the edge. But I also know it was Eddie's random message to me today that made me feel okay when my finished love story told me: I'm moving on. I responded back to my ex with love and compassion then deleted his message.

Today, I open my heart up to love. It is open to the places I am willing to call home. It is open to life. Today I am finally open to possibility.

Saying Yes

Somehow the space-time continuum doesn't apply when I have had a couple of drinks and then try to make trip itinerary plans. I booked a series of ferry tickets and once the confirmation page came up I realized I gave myself one night in Mykonos and a week in Ios.

When I arrived in Mykonos I decided to rent a scooter. I could explore the island, or just do something different that would take my mind to a new place. As I was getting the low-down on the scooter, the guy asked me if I have driven one before.

"Yes, one time, in Cambodia".

He looked at me to see if I was joking.

I was disappointed when he suggested I go with an ATV instead. I didn't think I would look as sexy driving it, but went with the ATV anyway.

I zipped around town for the day, lounged by the pool in the afternoon, and had dinner at the hotel.

After dinner I walked to a nearby restaurant that was having a traditional Greek performance. I was seated at a table and started chatting with the server about wine. The woman sitting at the table in front of me turned around and asked where I was from. Canada. Calgary. She said they were from Toronto, on their honeymoon, and asked me to join her and her husband. We spent the night chatting, laughing, and drinking far too much wine. Then as we were saying our goodbyes for the evening we made plans to meet again for lunch the next day.

We chatted more about them, their work back home, and their families. I realized I probably spent too long talking about myself last night and I need to focus more on learning more about others. I'm here to open my eyes to new people and experiences, and I can't do that if I'm taking over the entire conversation.

Eventually we parted ways and I was taken to the port to catch my ferry to Ios. I am grateful for new friends. I am excited about new experiences. I feel like I am focusing more on the moment I am in. I am being the best version of myself.

When I arrived in Ios I walked and found a little restaurant by the port for dinner. As I sat down at a table I was approached by a nice woman asking me to join her and her man for dinner. At first I said that I was alright and then I second-guessed myself and said that I would love to. We chatted over wine about sailing, the UK, education systems and travelling.

I am so lucky. I feel like my heart is healing and I am attracting love and loving couples.

There Is No Rush

Ios, Greece
August 8

I'm making small progress in my patience practice. I am working hard to focus on the current moment. I have tried to not be consumed by future or the past thoughts. Although there are things I wish I could desperately change, I have accepted that I needed to go down this path to finally learn the lesson that I needed. Slow down. Don't be in a rush. It will come in its own time. It hurts desperately that I had to go through this much pain for both myself and the people I love the most. But I am here now. The rabbit that tried to make it to the finish line has now seen that she has lost the race.

With a week in Ios I have no rush on any activities. I have nothing but time with whatever I want to do. I get to sit back and enjoy the beauty that is around me. I get to move at a really relaxed pace; a pace that I am not used but with more practice I could become accustomed to.

I had a great chat with my friend Joanne this morning. I love her optimism and her take that everything happens for a reason. I believe I will have a happy ending to my story, but first I need to heal. I need to allow time to do that. I will no longer look for quick solutions. My heart will tell me when it's time. It's not up to me anymore. It never really was.

I had a breakfast of yogurt with honey and a coffee while I overlooked the rolling hills and the sea. I debated taking my meditation before or after my shower and decided I should match my clean mind with a clean body. After my chat with the British couple last night I may try to integrate a second meditation into my day.

I took a walk into the village. I stopped a couple of times just to enjoy my surroundings. At one point I sat and watched a bird in flight. I stopped and noticed the bird was flying and gliding all over the place, but it rarely flapped its wings. It used the pockets of wind to carry it where it needed to go, and sometimes where it didn't, but it always came back. I want to be more like that bird. Let the wind carry me wherever I need to go.

I followed the many winding paths around town and made it to the top of a hill where a church stood. It had beautiful views of the island.

I had lunch, walked through a few stores and went back to my room to read.

I've been considering buying my last flight home. I went from ready to book an immediate flight to now not being able to bring myself to buying that final ticket. I'm going to wait some more.

I'll head out eventually for dinner. There's no rush.

Small Changes

Ios, Greece
August 9

Last night as I was making my way to dinner I stopped into a store. I have wanted to buy a new dress for a couple of days now, but haven't seen any that I like, for a price I would be willing to spend. I walked in, browsed through the racks and found a few that were worth trying on. As I was chatting with the saleswoman she was impressed that I was travelling alone. She said that she meets about one person a month that is doing that, and it is definitely something a lot of people can't do. "You spend a lot of time really looking inside yourself", she said. I definitely have been. Specifically the last couple of days as I have completely removed any chance of a love interest to occupy my mind and my time. Suddenly I was feeling really good, and really pretty. I bought two dresses.

I made my way to a small Italian restaurant for dinner. The service was terrible. It was ridiculously slow, but as I sat there, I thought there is absolutely no where that I need to be, so why stress out about it. I stayed kind to the wait staff. I ate my meal and focused on enjoying it. Really enjoying it. Tasting the flavours and the textures of the pumpkin and sage risotto. I don't even know the last time I sat and enjoyed my food for the simple pleasure of enjoying it. Not chatting. Not writing. Not reading. Just eating. Focusing on portioning my bites and allowing the flavours to take over.

I woke up around sunrise, meditated then went back to sleep. I had some vivid dreams. One was about not losing hope. I've been having images of the movie "5 Year Engagement", specifically the scene where they break up and he calls her on her birthday. Maybe it's too hopeful that I will hear anything from my unfinished love story on my birthday. I try not to think about it. It was really difficult today when I woke up and was really missing him again. It could just be the habit trying to break free. I work hard to push those ideas out of my head.

Recently I've been exchanging messages with one of my friends, Mandi. She has been going through her own breakup with a man that she is still desperately in love with. The mutual words of encouragement have been helping us both along.

She explained more of her breakup and all the things she was doing to try to make the relationship work. I told her she sounded exhausted. I told her to read her last couple of messages that she sent to me and imagine it was me sending it to her. I asked her the advice she would give to me. Then to close her eyes and imagine she is the mother of herself. She would hold onto her child, she would tell her she's beautiful and she would give unconditional love. She would say she is so proud for trying so hard, but she's even more proud that her child can decide when it's enough.

Then I told her to stop overanalyzing all the conversations and messages. We trained ourselves to become busy minded people and we have to now train ourselves not to be. I closed off by telling her to do what she needs to become better. She needs to allow her man time for him to miss her. Sit back and wait. Allow things to happen.

I came to a thought I had before. I am obviously not ready to be back with my ex, if that is what happens, but maybe he's not ready to be back with me. I am still working on my patience. I am learning to be okay with the slow process of things. Maybe he has own things that he wants to be better at too.

I used to place judgment and figure out what I would need him to be better at, but with my Buddhist readings, that is not the way. "The faults of others is easily perceived, but that of oneself is difficult to perceive".

I need to be okay with whoever my partner is. I can only change myself. If my partner ever wants to change, I need to be okay with that, but if he never does, I need to be okay with that too. I have to accept him for all that he is all the time. I need to look into myself at what I can do to be more patient, more accepting and kinder to the people around me.

This is the path that I need to be on right now. I need to practice these habits until I feel they come naturally and no longer require conscious thought to bring me to this place. I sometimes wish I could call my ex up and tell him all the progress I am making and how I am becoming a better person, but I know that I shouldn't. I will become that better person, the one that I want to be, the one that I am proud to be, and my heart will open up wide and call to the person that I will love unconditionally, and he will love me the same. My heart knows who it wants; I have to trust that it is doing its job, no matter how long it takes.

Finding Inner Peace

Ios, Greece
August 10

Some of my days still feel like I am in a constant haze. I am nothing more than my never-ending mental questions and slow movements.

Last night I put on one of my new dresses and treated myself out to a nice evening. I went to a sunset bar and drank a cocktail called "love story" while eating an alternative "meat" ball dish. After dark I walked around town until I was drawn to a lounge playing soulful music. I sat, had a couple of martinis and chatted with the server.

As I walked home I prayed to either please relieve me of the thoughts of him, or please help him heal so he can come back to me. As I prayed I realized my prayer was wrong. I should pray for him to heal and then he can decide, but better yet, I should focus my prayers on my healing.

I woke up with the sun. I tried to fight it, but decided to do my meditation before putting it off any longer. My meditations are always good. They start out calming. I am at peace. I love myself. I have kindness and compassion in my heart. I am sharing that love with others. I am love and light and everyone around me is also love and light. I can feel a smile come to my face and my chest feels full and warm with the amount of love inside me. I sit with that feeling for a while. My mind is blank. I don't want to think about anything else. Then the meditation ends.

I went back to sleep, but it wasn't a good sleep. I was startled by a dream that my younger cousin got engaged. I dreamed that when I found out I broke down. I woke up breathing heavy. I cannot handle this. I am better in a team. I would love to be the person that increases someone else's happiness. Breathe. Be patient. He's out there.

I came to a realization yesterday about why I have been on this mission to slow down. It's because I do want to be married. I do want to have kids. I don't want to rush through that moment of just being engaged, forgetting those sweet, tender moments. I don't want to rush to the point of getting to the wedding to realize I was so frazzled I didn't even enjoy the moment. I don't want to be in such a rush to get pregnant that all the fun is taking out of trying. Then when my child is born I don't want to be at a point where the years flew by and I can't remember the moments of just holding him (or her) in my arms. The moments when I am watching my husband care and look at our baby, at me, so proud of what we created. I need to slow down now. This moment. Remember the pain of heartbreak so that when the time comes for my heart to say, "okay, it's time", the love I give and receive will feel sweeter than anything I could ever imagine.

I find myself napping a lot during the day, which reminds me of my time in Vietnam and Thailand when I would try to nap during the day to match my unfinished love story's sleep time, hoping that we could share our dreams. I woke up after dreaming that he wrote on my Facebook wall: "It's not that I don't believe I will like you when you are back, it's that I liked you so much before. You didn't need to change".

Being Right Here

Ios, Greece
August 11

I woke up this morning with anxiety. I didn't want my day to start.

In my morning meditations I've been working on creating equanimity and using compassion for people close to me, enemies and neutral people. I feel that it is starting to work and it is bringing a sense of calm to me and my thoughts about my ex. However it has recently felt like I feel him again. It feels like he is holding me close when we are lying in bed together. I love that feeling so much that I don't even try to resist it. When I finished my meditation, as I tried to go back to sleep, it felt like he was holding me close, my face in his chest, our legs wrapped around each other. I then dreamed of us playing a game of twister and laughing.

I woke up startled. It had been almost a week since I heard anything. My obsession with him increased. I wanted to see if he did have an active profile on Match.com like he said he did. I needed to look right now. He was last online 24 hours ago. I started to set up my own profile then he would see I can be on there too. I was able to activate a profile from several years ago. I started to update the information but it became overwhelming. I didn't want anyone to contact me, no one except him.

I need to get out. A long walk to the beach would distract my brain and hopefully stop the obsession. The views were beautiful, but the walk was too long. My mind wanted to slowly search for answers.

I deconstructed the entire failed reconciliation. When did it all turn so bad? Why couldn't we make it work?

I then had an aha-moment: a 12-hour time difference, patchy internet and email as our primary form of communication. We were setting ourselves up to fail, and fail we did.

I asked the universe to send him that message. I wondered if, and hoped, he searched for his own aha-moment. Maybe then he will be willing to see me when I get back.

I then tried to rationalize what it would mean if he did find a relationship. If he gives his heart away to someone else then our relationship was equally not meant to be for him and me. There can't be one-sided soulmates. We both deserve happiness and I hope we both find it with each other again or other people. Be open to possibility. Anything is possible.

My head continued on with commentary. I am glad he asked me to stay. I feel further along today than I was a week ago in my calmness and acceptance for the things I cannot change. Please let me continue down the path of patience and please let me bring it home with me.

I couldn't stay at the beach for long. I tried to focus on the beautiful day, the glistening sea, the sun and the sand but my brain wouldn't quit on the rotating thoughts.

When I arrived back at my hotel I had a message from Eddie. I wasn't expecting to hear anything from him ever again. He wanted to know how I was doing. I didn't have anything to say. I thought sarcastically, "I'm doing well, how's your wife"?

I know his intention was from a friendly, caring place, but my heart is bleeding. I need to take care of me. I just can't have these daily conversations anymore that I enjoyed so much. I want someone to be my confidant and friend, it just cannot be him. We exchanged a couple brief notes and then ended on "take care of yourself".

After dinner I came back to my room and made a drunk Facebook status. I was angry and heartbroken. I rambled through my head for months. Today I couldn't find the answer I needed when I needed it the most. I am willing to do everything for my ex. I would jump on a plane. We know we have good love, when we are together. Why the hell is he still looking for something else? What is it about me that wasn't enough? Why am I forced to wait, and wait for him? I have been patient! Universe, I am done waiting!

I waited until I saw his sister come online. I hoped she read it. I re-read it and took it down in exhausting defeat. If the universe is trying to teach me patience my posting sounded like the woman standing in the queue huffing, puffing and stamping her foot saying she is waiting, but nothing's happening.

Patience, this could be my greatest lesson if I can wait long enough to get through it.

Expanding Love

The second I calmed my mind down for my meditation I felt like I was being pulled to my unfinished love story. We were holding each other. I love that feeling. I didn't even care if the only time I will ever have this moment is for a few minutes with my eyes closed. Please don't have this moment end. I finished the rest of my mediation focusing on the love and light that I am and concentrating on sending compassion and love to others. I feel my heart filling up with more love all around.

I am starting to feel calmer in the mornings. My thoughts are always with him as soon as I wake up, but I'm working hard at refocusing my energy. I forget that my days here feel double or triple the same amount that time does back home. I get an entire day to work on myself whereas at home I would only have a few hours, if I had the energy. I'm putting myself right here right now. I'd like to think if I can get to that point then my love will come to me when I am ready. I am prepared to handle the days. I won't get overanxious about the future or next steps. I can enjoy the moment that it is and I will be in a far better relationship, be able to provide my partner more support, and be able to accept love far more easily.

I rented an ATV to explore the island. Anything that looked even slightly interesting I decided to stop at. Take a couple of photos. Enjoy the day.

I stopped at Homer's tomb. I made my way to the East side of the island. I was heading to another beach when a fortress caught my interest. It looked so beautiful sitting on top of the mountain. There was a steep and narrow pathway that led to the top. I walked in the hot sun, hoping it wasn't further than it looked. When I made it to the top I was stunned to see a little church there. There were a few white, stone benches around, but the yellow, fiberglass one called me over.

I had been fighting the thoughts of my ex all day. I needed to stop playing head games with myself. Stop thinking about him. Stop thinking about the past. Stop thinking if he will or will not meet me for a coffee. The only thing I need to think about is how do I make myself a better person? How do I calm my mind so that I can truly become the wife and mother that someone would love to have in their life? Focus on becoming more patient. Enjoy the day I am in, the moment I am in it.

I stood at the mountain-top fortress, looking at the church. One of my meditation books said sometimes the best answers come at the top of the world. There is no noise to prevent what is being said.

I sat down on the little yellow bench staring at the pure white church with the blue dome roof. It contrasted the blue sea and the silhouetted islands in the background. I closed my eyes and opened my mind. "Keep doing what you're doing", I heard. It said yes, it was wrong for me and my ex to try our relationship again when there was so much distance. More distance does not solve the problem of distance. It said that there will be more things to say, but I don't need to say them right now. Nothing can be made better from here. I have to wait until either he is ready or I am back. Then it said that if I want him, I can have him again. I have not ruined everything.

I then asked if there was someone else, and it said yes. It said that there would be another option in Egypt. But I will need to choose wisely because I can only have one. I cannot waffle on this decision. Choose wisely.

Suddenly I was reconsidering my determination to be with my ex. He will love me and he would be an excellent father to our future children. We would have a wonderful life. But do I really want someone that won't talk to me? Someone who would rather shut the door on us than have a conversation? Someone who I struggled to book a phone call with? Someone who when I was struggling with our relationship and said

I needed a change, he decided to turn his back on me as opposed to fighting with me to make it work? Will it always be a struggle with him?

I cruised around the island a bit more and then went back to my hotel room. I took a shower, had a short meditation and went for a nap. I started feeling at peace with myself and my life. I felt like "you got this". Just keep focusing on me. Every time my brain wants to replay "love stories gone bad" or the "what-if" game, it brings me into a negative space. I keep reminding myself to think about what's in front of me, what I can do to improve my life and expand the love that I have. It's working. I'm getting there.

Deep Seeded Emotions

Ios, Greece
August 13

I woke up in the middle of the night from a dream. I was getting dressed to go to a birthday party for my ex. His best friend asked me to show up and surprise him. I didn't know what I wanted to wear and I was trying on every dress I owned. I was already late for the party. As I was changing dresses my ex's friend was telling me that my ex has been on 30 dates since I've been gone. Hearing the number woke me up in a panic. I needed to have someone talk me through it, but I couldn't get a hold of anyone. Where was everybody? I wanted to go back to sleep but couldn't stop thinking about the number. My mind asked if it was true, would I be upset about the 30 dates or that he met 30 girls and not a single one was worth a second date? With 30 dates he would be hoping to play the numbers game without putting any thought into who he was dating. Relieved at the thought I fell back asleep.

The second time I woke up it was to a wonderful dream. My ex and I were visiting wine country. We were laughing, touching and having a good time. We went into one winery that had since been renamed from the last time we were there. We had history.

I decided to meditate on this love. I sent him my dream in the meditation. I have wanted to contact him for so long, but I know deep down I need to let it be. When he is open to forgiveness and love he will connect with me. Or maybe I will have a new love come to me in Egypt. Or maybe I should carry my patience lesson until I am home.

I'm feeling okay with that. I find myself feeling better about waiting. Love will come. It was silly to think we could have revived our love while I was in India. I wish I would have said, yes, I am committed to you, yes, we will have to wait, and we would both be in a far better position. My ultimate lesson. Now I will wait for whatever love will come my way. I will not rush. I will not be impatient. I will allow it to naturally come and progress. That will be good love.

I am able to hold my peaceful thoughts until mid-afternoon. After that the constant stream of questions about my unfinished love story start coming up: Will I ever see him again? Will I ever have a chance with him again? Will he ever contact me again? Did I make a mistake? How would I make it all different? It becomes so hard to make it all stop. Then finally, I poised a question to my overactive brain: Could I wait a week? If my meditation is correct I will have a new option introduced in Egypt. I took a deep breath. Yes, I can wait a week. Nothing significant will happen between now and eight days from now. I can wait. But my mind wasn't completely letting up, so it was time to leave the beach.

I read when one starts mediation practice for the first time a lot of deep seeded emotions are eventually brought up. I thought I was pretty lucky that no unexpected thoughts or feelings have appeared yet. Turns out my deep seeded emotions were pushed so deep that it would take months to bring them out. Today was the day. Not in the meditation, but on the walk home.

It was the recent story of my dad. Probably an unaddressed contributing factor as to why I broke up with my unfinished love story. I held back the tears until I reached my room, then I had a massive urge to break down and cry. I had a lot of issues with my father that I never dealt with. Today my mind decided it was time. Address them. Say goodbye to all of them forever. Let it all out. I meditated on it first then I wrote.

I called my dad for the first time in ten years. Ten years. Less than two weeks before I broke up with my unfinished love story something in me said it was time to reach out to him. I didn't make it out to be a big deal when I placed the call one Monday afternoon, but it was. It had to be.

The conversation was decent. He asked me what was new. I told him I would be lying if I said nothing. The entire conversation lasted no more than twenty minutes. I texted my unfinished love story immediately after. I dismissed the significant deal that I just went through. I told him it was fine, but what I really needed was a hug, and him to tell me I will never be abandoned and rejected again. It was a big deal and I denied that.

The entire process just brought up more of the "I am so broken" feelings. I am so tired of feeling like I am broken. When does it end?

I know I should go out but even that is a struggle. I know I will get hungry enough and eventually it won't even be a negotiable.

Lows and Highs and Lows

Ios, Greece
August 14

Last night I could only convince myself to leave the hotel room by believing my unfinished love story was going to be at home, waiting. My realism kept saying no, I will never have him again. My anxiety and thoughts of my ex carried me through the night. I wanted to break down.

I was doing so well yesterday morning and today I can't get out of bed. I convinced myself that I am feeling this way because of my psychic connection with him. His family probably told him about my latest Facebook status updates, and in succession, it sounds exactly how it is, how I didn't want it to sound, I cannot live without him. I now sound so desperate that he would never come back anyway because it would sound like he did so out of pity for me. I am now a pity case.

The dreams I had when I went back to sleep were no better. I want off this island. I want to be home. I have nothing there for me. I just want to run and run and run with no direction.

Thank God I am in a tour group next week. I need company. I've been on this island too long. When I arrive in Santorini tonight the change in atmosphere will do me good. I need stimulation. I have been taking really good care of my body. I haven't been drinking overly much, I've been doing a lot of walking, relaxing, morning pushups, eating healthy, and all in moderation. Only my mind is my enemy.

I had breakfast and decided to explore the town. I was positive there were areas that I hadn't explored yet, and that quickly became true. I wandered into areas that I saw no one, up and down goat paths. I found myself on the edge of the ancient city wall. I climbed to the top where there was a church. I sat in the shade and watched a couple of butterflies dance. That set the tone for the rest of the day.

I walked through every side street, sat on the partition that separated the road from the central square, walked some more then had a beer and chatted with my mom. Somewhere in between I thought maybe my Egyptian love was going to be my unfinished love story. Maybe he was capable of doing something super romantic. We're all capable of grand romantic gestures. The thought provided a spring in my step. I knew it probably wasn't likely. My head asked, "is that what I really want"? It is. I do. I want the Eddies of the world. I want someone to catch a plane or a boat for me. I want someone to say, I will come to you. I would for him. I have said it. I would have done it in an instant and I would do it again.

I said out loud to the universe, "book at ticket. Book a ticket today". I posted on my Facebook where I will be next week. Maybe the powers that be will surprise me. They will one way or another. He will be there or he won't. Then it will be someone else. I pray for him. I want him to be the one that makes it all possible. Please, please, please. My prayer had been put out there. I wait.

I am getting to a good place. I feel that once my unfinished love story went to sleep I did become good again. He does affect me. I hope he sees that I affect him too. We are meant to be. I hope in this lifetime. But, God, I feel it. I feel love is coming to me. It's coming to me faster than I realize. I promise the love that comes to me I will accept with open arms and say yes. I am waiting. I am not fighting. I will not doubt. From my lips to God's ears to angels deliver, it will be so.

I caught the ferry to Santorini and the shuttle to the main town of Fira. I dropped my bag off at my hotel and received directions for the best sunset viewing. I walked along the pathway that graced the cliff's edge then found a café where I drank a glass of wine and joined the many other thousands of people to watch the sunset. It was beautiful.

I wanted to share the moment with someone. That someone was my ex. The alcohol, the people in love, the jewelry stores, all of it was making my heart bleed again. I found a nice restaurant for pizza and beer. I wanted to continue to explore, but I drank too much and now couldn't fight the spinning, incessant thoughts. I needed to know.

Am I going crazy? Is he really completely done with me? I couldn't contact him, so I did the next best thing; I sent a message to his sister. I am sure she will be honest with me and tell me that I need to move on if I have to. I wrote her a message, crying as I did. I needed to know the answer, but at the same time did not. I needed to know if I was holding onto something that I was never going to hold me back. My impatience and busy head is getting the better of me now. I cried. Go to sleep. Nothing can be done this far away.

Love Without Attachment

I felt better when I woke in the morning. I was in a better state of mind. My ex's sister responded. She was incredibly kind. She said the most perfect things. The exact things I needed to hear and be reminded of: "you need to release him to the universe and embrace happiness alone before you can be happy with anyone".

In my mediation I expressed gratitude, I practiced unconditional love for myself and others, then I opened the cage to my heart that was holding him inside and told him to be free. I want him to find happiness and love. Maybe that is not with me, but neither of us will know if I don't allow him to seek and find it on his own. I also need to find that love and happiness.

I explored Fira and found a bench to pull out my book and read. The chapter was appropriately on love without attachment. That would be my newest contemplation for the next while. Everything must come to an end. The man I hope to one day marry will be with me until death do us part. I have to allow him to be with me for just this lifetime and then move on. I can love him unconditionally knowing, eventually, we will part. Therefore our moments, while we are here, are cherished and loved, and I will one day release him when his next calling comes. I will love my children knowing they will leave my womb, and my arms and eventually my home. I will love my friends and my pets and my material life knowing that nothing in this world or this lifetime is permanent. I will love knowing that attachment closes both me and the people that I love off to higher purpose and more life. We are all meant to impact and then be free. It would be silly for me to think that the people and the places I have enjoyed will be permanent in my life. I cannot be upset when I check out of a hotel or when I leave another newly met friend. Therefore I cannot be upset when I am so lucky to have someone touch me so profoundly and our time to part has finally come. I cannot limit him. I cannot limit myself. Together, and apart, we must soar and land where we need to be again.

I felt lifted. I felt my heart fill with love and compassion. I looked at everyone around and knew they were all seeking happiness and love, the same as me. A smile crossed my face. I was happy. I was at peace. I walked and was pulled into a jewelry store by a very charming sales person. He tried to sell me a beautiful necklace for the one-time low price equivalent to a flight back home. I could really use a beautiful necklace...

The peace I felt continued on. I thought about all the things I have to be grateful for and about how love is here for us temporarily. I thought that I am here. I am in this moment. My heart is filled. I am so grateful that I have the chance to not just be taught a lesson by reading about it, I have the opportunity to live my life, the highs and lows, until I feel it and understand it. Oh, my, Buddha, I am here.

As the day turned to evening I was immediately drawn to a lounge playing Ben Howard. Maybe it was a sign. Meant to be. I ordered a glass of champagne and enjoyed the night.

Leaving the Crowds

Santorini, Greece
August 16

As the sunset finished last night I noticed another young woman sitting by herself. Something in me said to say hi. Have a conversation. I leaned over in my chair and did just that. She and I started chatting about travelling then I asked her if she wanted to join me for some food. As we were about to leave another couple said that they overheard our conversation and asked us if we would instead like to join them over a bottle of wine and chat some more. We did, laughing and talking about everything. We then decided as a group to go for dinner, and as that finished we went to a nightclub together for a great night all around.

Within the couple, the man, Joe, somehow read me like a book. He told me all about my history with my unfinished love story. He said the guy just couldn't commit, and he doubts he ever will. He said my ex probably struggled to move in, was feeling smothered, started to push back more, and this created fights as he would find excuses to not come home. Hence the increase in boy's trips, solo snowboarding trips and extra work hours. Eventually I had enough. Seriously? That pretty much sums it up.

Joe said it was more than likely because my unfinished love story had his heart broken years before ever meeting me and until my ex heals that old wound he will never be able to give his heart completely to anyone. He said every woman that tries to give her heart to him will end up suffering in return. Joe's words rang true. It hurt.

I then told Joe all about Eddie. Joe said Eddie was going to go back to his wife no matter what. There was too much history there. I reminded Eddie just enough of his wife, but I was different enough that it was fun and exciting for him.

I told Joe about my meditation on top of the fortress. Joe thought that I more than likely would have another chance with my unfinished love story. "But are you sure that's really what you want? You've more than likely have outgrown him".

I asked the woman that Joe was with if he was a psychic. I couldn't imagine someone that I met only a couple hours before would know this much about me and my history.

After rolling into the hotel at 3AM after the night club it was a tough go this morning. I headed to the Old Port. I was going on a boat trip today.

The boat looked like a giant pirate ship and stopped at several places around the island. The first stop, a volcano climb was far tougher than it needed to be. The day was hot, and my hangover headache was throbbing. It took 30 minutes to get to the volcano summit, a crater filled with volcanic rock, only to have the super passionate guide go on about elements, magma and tectonic plates. I didn't have the patience or desire for any of it.

We sailed from there to a "hot springs" spot, which was a slightly warmed water area in the sea, and then to a little island for lunch at our choice of restaurants.

Our final stop was back to the town of Oia. I rode a donkey from the port to the main town site then walked along the beautiful marble streets admiring the white washed buildings that graced the cliff side. Every scene is completely picture perfect. I wanted to chill out and found a little café away from the crowds, and unfortunately away from prime sunset viewings, but that's okay. This is my trip and only I can decide what will make my day amazing. As the sun went down I could still hear the crowds of people erupt in applause. It made me smile. I know there is an encore performance tomorrow.

Black, Blue, White and Red

Santorini, Greece
August 17

I had a really good sleep. I kept dreaming that I was really calm and that everything would be alright. I was no longer stressed. I was no longer worried about the day. I just was.

It was my last day on Santorini and I was determined to end it on a high note. I was going to rent an ATV and drive it around the island. I'm always surprised that it takes far less time to drive around the islands than I would expect. My first stop was to Kamari beach, known for its black sands. I walked along the beach front, stopped at a little café and had a frappe.

As I left the beach I saw signs pointing to the ancient town of Thira. I decided to make the uphill drive to the top of the mountain. It was steep, and I was so glad I had an ATV. As I drove I saw a middle-aged woman making the walk. I asked her if she wanted a ride. She asked how much, and I said free, since I was going that way anyway. She was so thankful and accepted. We passed her two daughters along the way, and she shouted at them that she would see them at the top.

The ride was long, but eventually we made it. The day was so hot that I couldn't imagine doing the walk up. The woman and I parted ways, and I continued up a further walk to where the ancient city existed. Most of the ruins have since been destroyed by time and earthquakes, but many of the foundations and framing of the building still exist. It was interesting to see how vast the town was back in BC time, but for the most part it really did nothing for me. I like history to a certain point, but I find once it gets into history of the millennia my interest is completely lost.

I started driving again with no direction in particular. I drove up and down the hills of the vineyards. I waved to people as I passed them. I made a stop to a wine museum and vineyard. The museum is built inside a cave formerly used for keeping wine when the vineyard was first created. The mannequins inside were super creepy so I quickly moved through to the wine tasting. I tried a few different wines in varieties that I have never heard of before. As I was being poured the different samples I chatted with the hostess about how interesting it is that grapes in Santorini are still hand harvested and are free grown as opposed to structured rows. She said many of the wine producers believe in the tradition of grape collection, and very few vineyards are provided with proper irrigation.

I found a café at the mountain top town of Pyrgos for a lunch stop. The views were stunning as I was able to see the sea and some of the surrounding islands.

I drove again taking turns and different directions until I found myself on a road that looked to be used more by the locals than by tourists. The road was narrow and winding. Often times there were retaining walls on either side. The fields were filled with grapes and donkeys, and as I got closer to the sea it turned into massive sand banks. I kept driving and made three more brief stops, one to take a picture of the "new beach", which was filled with yachts, another to get a picture of the Red Beach and finally one more to check out a Victorian castle, which was beautiful, but disappointingly didn't photo very well.

I drove west to Oia. I kept driving. I didn't want to stop anymore. I made another turn and instead of returning on the high road that I took to get to Oia, I ended up on a low road on the North side of the island that grasped along the sea. It was beautiful. I could drive forever. Just enjoy. Feel free. Be in this moment. Sucking up the last time I will be on an island for this trip, and maybe again for a while.

My head did a little bit of wandering today, but I only wanted to feel free and open today. I don't know what will happen in the future, but it's not worth worrying about because that sets me up for expectations that could leave me feeling disappointed. I would rather just let it play out and be. Be here. Right now. That was my goal for Greece, and I think I am almost there.

Lingering Expectations

Athens, Greece
August 18

The last several hours stretched my travelling skills. I took an overnight ferry from Santorini to Athens. The water was terribly choppy causing people to get seasick all around me. I then caught a taxi from a man that kept saying he knew where he was going, but then would stop constantly and ask for directions. I had almost no sleep and when I walk into my hotel I ended up taking a patchy one hour nap on the couch in the reception while waiting for any room to be ready. But by the time they checked me in it was mid-morning and I decided to power through the day instead of going back to sleep. I could always come back in the afternoon for a nap.

Just outside of the hotel I see a stop for one of the hop-on-hop-off bus tours. I buy a pass. It sounded like an easy way to see the different sights of Athens. I get off at the Acropolis point and the line ups were already ridiculously long.

The sight was definitely worth it. The height alone makes for a spectacular view. I walk around for a bit, but soon can't handle the crowds and the heat any further. I wander through a mixed neighbourhood of chic shops and run-down buildings covered in graffiti. It's a bit early, but I decide to go for lunch.

Earlier in the day I received an email from my step-dad: "Your mom was telling me that you are still talking about your ex. In my opinion this is getting out of hand and it has now been five months of you talking about him. From my seat he has moved on and you have to move on with your journey. You have wasted far too much energy worrying about something not in your control. Maybe it's time to come home and deal with this rather than seek answers from everyone. Maybe you're the one that should be travelling to your love to see if it's still there instead of waiting for your love to travel to you".

As I sat in the café my mind was playing through what he said. I was angry at all the outside opinions. I believed it was because of everyone's commentary I was in my current situation to begin with. I should have been a stronger person and only listened to my heart and not everyone's advice. I thought of the perfect response:

Me: Thanks, Tom. I do agree that I need to move on. I did offer to come and see him and he did say no. I'm going to continue my journey because I am a better person today than I was two weeks ago. And I know the habits I am building will make me a better person overall. I did have a moment of complete loss when I emailed his sister, but that was my mistake that I recognize.

At the end of the day this is still my journey. This has been the hardest breakup that I have ever had to deal with and thinking about it still makes me want to break down and cry. But I am getting stronger. I am getting more self-confident and I am starting to believe in the love I have for myself.

I was not seeking answers from anybody. I know where my answers are and they will be found when I can find patience, lose my expectations and not let my head spin me out.

I know your words are coming from a place of love because you do want to see the best for me. It would have been nicer for you to say, you got this. You're stronger today than you were yesterday. No one else knows what's going on in your heart, therefore no one can tell you how long it will take for you to heal.

I would drop everything and be home in a second if he was ready to see me. I need to be patient and wait. He'll either let me know or time will just pass and I will meet someone new.

It's nice to know that you care enough to take the time to send me a message.

As I sat there I continued to stare out into space I decided for my own happiness to just go back to the hotel and rest.

I don't know why I convinced myself for so long that by Greece my unfinished love story and I would reconcile, reconnect and everything would be right in the world again. My hopeless romantic heart holds onto so much love and the idea that love stories still do exist. I became desperate for love and anything besides my high expectations just wasn't acceptable. I could have allowed myself to be really surprised. To let go. Instead I cried more than I have in months because I just couldn't let go of the pain. As difficult as the last couple of weeks have been I realized that my best moments were when I was in love with simplicity. Love with being happy for what I am given, not what I wanted.

Angry With The World

Athens, Greece
August 19

Come on, get moving. Enjoy my last full day of Athens, I told myself as I woke up in the morning. I then had a very calming meditation. It told me to keep waiting. Be patient. You may hear from your ex, but be prepared it is not what you are going to want to hear.

I saw my sister was still up. I asked if she would stay awake to chat. Sure, she said. We chatted about her. She was trying to make me feel better by letting me know that all relationships have their problems. The last couple of weeks have been very difficult on me emotionally and sometimes I feel like I am getting no further ahead. It was wonderful to just chat with her. Her kindness made me feel okay again.

I put on a dress, grabbed a cappuccino and waited for the hop-on-hop-off bus. I didn't have any plan. I just thought I would ride it around and see what peaked my interest. But I wasn't into it. I rode it. Played games on my iPad. I wanted to be as far away from everything as possible. My head and heart weren't here. They were in a place that they didn't belong, nor were welcome. I started to understand why the tragic love stories of the past would include a woman plunging to her death for a lover that never comes for her. I felt I could join that company.

I jumped off the bus at the Temple of Zeus to snap a couple of photos, and waited for the bus to come around again. The bus driver was in a good mood and he wanted to joke around with me. I entertained the company, but I was feeling anti-social. I didn't want to go back to my hotel room just to sleep more, so I decided the best place for an anti-social person would be a museum. If I was lucky I could waste several hours there.

I walked through the archeological museum, stopping at pieces that looked interesting enough to read more about them. Once I finished I headed across the street to an outdoor café. I had a glass of wine and a salad and thought that it has now been two weeks since the last time we spoke. Two weeks and my heart is still in pain. It felt longer than that. I looked at my calendar and tried to figure out how much I could cut my trip short. Maybe a week? Could I leave out Kilimanjaro? Would I regret not doing it?

I slowly walked back to the hop-on-hop-off bus holding back the tears that are constantly in the background of my thoughts. I got off at another stop, an old neighbourhood known for its eclectic and preserved Greek culture. I looked at the different stores, bought my aunt a souvenir, and sent it off in the mail. I'm just wasting time. Maybe I could find a place to get a pedicure. Maybe some new paint on my toes would cheer me up.

I saw an advertisement for a place in a building and without registering what floor it was on I wandered up the building. I made it to the first floor when I stopped at a hair salon. That's it. I'm going to get a hair treatment. If my hair looked nice then maybe my funk would be lifted. She didn't offer deep conditioning, so I asked for lots of highlights. I need to lighten my hair. I need to be fresh and new again. She said she would but it will take several hours. Okay, I have nothing but time.

I sat in the chair thinking more about making it home. But to what? I have no plan. I would be going home to someone that doesn't want me. My thoughts shifted. He doesn't want me. I gave him my heart and he threw it away. I kept giving it to him, and he never took it. He just pushed me away. Even when we were together, he never wanted to be with me the same that I wanted to be with him. So who am I really angry with? Am I angry with the world for bringing me someone that it didn't work out with? Am I angry at myself for working so hard to become a better person and I can't share that with him?

Or am I angry at him? It does nothing to be angry at someone, but for my purposes it felt really good in that moment. Yes, I am a good person. I am amazing and with my new hair colour I am more beautiful than ever. Let's rock this!

I bought a new outfit. I helped an old woman cross the street. I grabbed a sandwich and took a couple of beers back to my room. I could have thrown a dance party. I am not someone's second. My heart is not going to be thrown back to me anymore. If I give it, you will receive it, or I move on.

World, bring me clarity and peace. I am happy.

Adventures in Cairo

Giza, Egypt
August 21

Yesterday was the first day that I felt good in a long time. It felt like I was finding happiness again. I took the day to fly from Athens to Cairo. But the peace I found yesterday was suddenly taken away.

My meditation from two days came true. I checked my email in the morning I saw my ex's name among the list of new messages. I opened his last. I didn't know if I wanted to read it.

> Him: Please don't bother my family with your thoughts on us. They have no say in the decisions I make. You knew nothing about the relationship I had and yet you compared it to one you had with someone else. I gave you chances and you did not accept them. Now we are here. You mentioned crying after reading you past messages but I had to experience it every time. And it had led me to move on. I am seeing someone now.

I've grown so much. I would have immediately responded to that. I would have pled my case and tried to justify my actions. I would have probably made myself sound desperate as I asked him again if we could talk. I would have said something harsh like "that was quick, wasn't it? Only a month ago you gave your heart to me. You were a man on a mission".

Instead I read it a couple of times. I wrote him a response that I wasn't ready to send then I filed the email away. I will not respond yet. I am hurt. He sounds so angry. We would never be able to progress if he doesn't move past his anger. Plus I'm not interested in getting into an email exchange with him. I want a coffee with him in person. I would rather just wait it out.

Time will help me heal. Time will help him. Nobody knows what the future holds, maybe it's not him. My meditation did tell me I would have a different option in Egypt. I thought at first that meant that I would meet someone but looking at the group list that is very unlikely. Maybe my option is to choose him or not him. The answer will, no matter what, be the love for me. I feel that already. I love myself enough to not get pulled down that rabbit hole. I will only talk with people that are deserving of my love, not ones I have to try to convince to love me in return.

I left my hotel to check into the hotel that my tour group would be meeting at later in the day. I was taken to the room where my bunk mate was already checked in. Not surprisingly the woman that I was rooming with refused to open the door. I then said I was her roommate from G Adventures, and then she opened it up. I introduced myself to Elizabeth and asked her if she would be interested in joining me for the day. I told her that I wanted to check out the Citadel and the Bazaar. We then left the hotel and negotiated with a couple of drivers for a day of service.

When our driver took us to our first stop of a high-end store, we told him that we weren't interested in any extras. He drove us around pointing out the different sights, and when we told him we were hungry he walked up to a hole-in-the-wall restaurant and picked us up some falafel pitas wrapped in paper. They were excellent. We went to another store, picked up a few bottles of water, and then went to the Bazaar.

He parked across the road and gave us strict instructions not to talk to anyone. Make sure we watch our bags. He'll meet us in about an hour at a café across the street. We walked through the Bazaar enjoying the sights and sounds, the spices, the clothing. Before meeting with our driver again we passed by another small, but very impressive mosque. We decided to go inside and take a look around. We were given robes to wear and a nice, young man escorted us around the site. We asked to go up to the minaret, and the young man got a key to a padlocked door and walked us up the many flight of stairs to the top of the mosque. The views of Cairo were incredibly impressive.

Elizabeth and I spent the evening on a Nile River cruise, enjoying a buffet, wine and belly dancing. As we walked back to the hotel we stopped to drink "Nile River" tea from a vendor selling it on the bridge on the way back to the hotel. We were too tipsy on the wine to think about the likeliness that the water did or did not come from the river.

Tomorrow was going to be an exciting day visiting the Great Pyramids, Sphinx and a night train to the Southern tip of Egypt.

Birthday Wishes

We arrived to Aswan yesterday by night train. We visited the Philae temple, which was moved to higher ground after it was flooded when the Egyptians build a dam that flooded the plains where the temple was originally located. Today we were waking up at 3AM to join the daily arranged police convoy to escort tourists to the Abu Simbel temple, 40km away from the Sudan border.

I had to do my meditation on the bus, and decided to mix up my gratitude. Instead of giving love I became grateful for what is yet to come. I thanked the universe for my husband. I said I loved him so much and my heart can't contain the love for him. As I said these words I could feel him, almost touch him. He is out there. I know he is coming and I will be grateful when he actually does arrive, but for now I am happy to know he is on his way.

After visiting the temple my guide and I chatted about travelling, love and patience. I am so impressed with how far I've come in my mindset and learning to just allow things to come.

I wasn't really excited to be celebrating my birthday, but when Elizabeth mentioned we should go to a spa my eyes lit up. I asked all my Facebook friends to help celebrate with me in a virtual party and to post photos of themselves with a drink or in front of some food. I am so loved that I already had a few people grant me my Facebook birthday wish. I needed to respond with my own cocktail picture, and getting a massage at a high-end hotel with a cocktail would be the perfect treat.

Before dinner my tour group asked me to meet them on our hotel roof for views of the Nile while they surprised me with a birthday cake. The ladies of the group and I then headed to a five-star restaurant. We shared a bottle of wine on the terrace watching the sun set on the Nile. The restaurant gave us the best table in the house. We each ordered the set 5-course meal which included shrimp, lobster medallions, fish from Lake Nassar, and a chocolate cigar. I have not had an exceptional meal at all during this trip, and it was exactly what I would have loved for my birthday back home. It was perfect, almost. The only message I wanted to receive on my birthday I didn't get. It is definitely a birthday I will always remember.

Feeling Death by Temple

Luxor, Egypt
August 26

I woke up on a felucca after a lovely, calm ride down the Nile yesterday. The day was hot, but the night was cool. I spent the day reading the in shade.

I've been reading a lot of religious texts, including the Dhammapada and the Bhagavad Gita. Both of them bring me a sense of peacefulness and they have been guiding me along my path of calming my mind and finding peace within myself. One of the walkthroughs that I read used the phrase "Just this moment", and for some reason it really stuck with me. I am finding it easier to be in the present and nowhere else. My mind still wanders a bit, but I find it is far easier to bring back. It doesn't speed away like a race horse anymore. It will wander off at a slow pace, but I can always call it back.

When I woke up the day was already starting to warm up. I sat and meditated as the sun began to rise. I can feel my heart and body filling with love with every meditation and I know great things are in store for me ahead. My mind is more focused on the here and now, and from my reading my latest mantra has been: Just This Moment. It has the same context as right here, right now, but somehow the words hold and harder insistence on where I am at this exact moment. My meditations also thank the universe for bringing my future husband to me and having him share the love that I have for myself and others. I thank him for providing me love that I can't provide myself, such as cuddles, touch and kisses. Whenever I do this I feel my heart fill up with joy and warmth for him. I begin to feel that full body love that I had with my ex and I feel my heart calling to someone again.

We visited 2 more temples today. By the end of it I couldn't remember any of the history or the differences between them and the many others that we have seen over the last few days.

We continued to drive for another couple of hours until we made it to Luxor. I was tired and just wanted to get a bit of Wi-Fi. I had a dream that my ex had finally accepted my friend request on Facebook because he was curious about me and wanted to look at my photos. I was so happy, I needed to check to see if it had actually happened. Of course that wasn't the case.

I met the rest of the group at the top of the hotel for the sunset then we hired a couple of horse carriages to take us to Karnak temple for a sound a light show, and a bit of variety from the hot daytime temple viewings.

Nothing to Lose

Every morning I have be meditating on my ex, asking if he would contact me. The response was always "yes, be patient, you'll hear from him". It's been giving me that response for several weeks now. Today was a different story. I was in a deeper meditation. Far deeper than I have been in for a very long time. I asked the question again. My heart was ready to collapse. It told me "no, you'll never hear from him again. He's trying too hard to move on. He has no forgiveness in his heart". I felt broken all over again. Why is the message all of the sudden changing? I believe this morning's, since I was in a heavier state of unconsciousness, but why the change in the message? Why does my heart have to break here? I want to cry all over again. Why does it always make me cry? Why do I think about him every single day? Why is he always the first one that comes to mind? Why can't he just forgive?

This idea that I will never hear from him again provided me with the darkest cloud over my day. I wanted to be back into my "Just this moment" phase, but I didn't want to be. I tried so hard to practice love without attachment with him, and here I am feeling so attached. I am not ready to let him go. I am patient. I will wait for him, but I think my waiting will be fruitless. Despite the love he has for me, he has sealed it so tightly in his heart that he will never open up to me again. Was he ever fully open?

We had a full day of adventuring. The morning started out with a hot air balloon over the farming fields. Once we landed we were met with a convoy of donkeys that we rode until we hit the entrance of the Valley of the Kings. We then spent most of the morning, until it became too hot, visiting a couple of the original Pharaoh tombs. It was so impressive walking through

369

the tombs as the colouring used in the hieroglyphics were still entirely intact and it covered the walls and ceilings of the tombs as they went deeper and deeper underground until the final burial chambers.

Back at the hotel I chatted with Bruce and Elizabeth from my group. We talked about men and relationships.

I told them about my meditation and how I was feeling about my ex. Talking it through gave me some additional clarity. My meditation in Greece said that I would be given a different option in Egypt, but I haven't been given an option yet. It did tell me I had to decide, and once I did I couldn't be flakey. I had one shot. I told them that I drafted an email to my unfinished love story and I was thinking about sending it. I told them there are probably only a handful of people in our life time that we are willing to say "you are worth it. I want you and I will do everything in my power to work together with you". He was definitely the one for me. I have been thinking about him every single day since I've been away. I've had lots of opportunities to turn that off, but I just couldn't. I don't care if he's seen other girls. He is mine. I will always dedicate my heart and love to him.

Bruce told me to send the email if I needed to then he added maybe the option in Egypt was to not choose him. He asked if my mediation this morning said there is no forgiveness, why would I choose that?

I didn't want to hear it. True love should prevail. I stayed at the hotel for an hour waiting for the power, and Wi-Fi to be restored.

Maybe he will respond and maybe he won't. I was already preparing myself to never hear from him again, and I am on the path to get over him if I need. But if I hear from him, that's it. I'm done. There will never be another man in my entire life. I pick him.

I felt good after sending the note. It was honest. It felt right. I had no regrets.

A Different Side of Cairo

Cairo, Egypt
August 28

I needed to take a break and experience a bit of modern Cairo. I was leaving the group and going to check out a shopping mall. Seven stories of shopping, and there is a nail place. I can finally get my much needed pedicure. It was bliss. I walked into a Hagen Dazs, had a cappuccino and grabbed some internet. Although most of me is expecting to never hear from my ex again I still had a pang of anxiety when I went to open my email. I felt nervous that there could be a response. It could have been good or bad. But after a quick scan of my emails I saw that there was nothing from him. That was okay.

I updated my travel blog and then decided today was the day. It was time to book that final flight home. I have been thinking about it for a while, and today just seemed perfect. I booked the shortest and quickest way home I could get. 21 hours, 2 stops. I'll be home on October 1. It felt like a huge relief had been lifted off me. I was actually excited to go home. I don't know what will be there. I don't know what I will be doing when I get there, but hasn't that always been the case since my travels? Show up to a location and make a go of it. Stumble and it somehow works. This will just work.

There are a few luxuries that really can make me feel good again, and a manicure pedicure combo is definitely one of them. In my head I am already making a list of all the things I want to do as soon as I get home: mani-pedi, hair colouring, and a new outfit.

New Cairo felt different. It was a modern city. Where we were coming from in Giza was more of the expectation of stares, cat calls, and harassment. Here is was calm and peaceful. We were allowed to just be.

Elizabeth and I found an outdoor restaurant district. We sat on the patio, shared a grape shisha and a cold Lebanese appetizer then sat there until it was dark and time to go.

After a 45-minute cab ride in the ridiculous Cairo traffic, where two lanes actually means that you can fit three cars across, we made it close enough to our hotel. We told driver to drop us off on the side of the road and we took the shorter walk of five minutes to the hotel.

Mountain Meditations

My sleeps have been getting better. I am waking up more relaxed. Since the morning after sending the last note to my ex I have been really releasing him. I still dream about him, but the dreams always have a detachment to them. They have a feeling that I am really going to be alright. There will be other alternatives. There will be never-ending happiness. I will be taken care of as long as my happiness starts from within.

My habits are finally starting to feel ingrained. I would like to take the final month to feel completely secure that the lessons I have wanted to learn I can say without doubt that I am the person that I wanted to become. I feel that already. The last month will be the final wrapping on the gift that I am.

Today I was heading to St. Catherine's to climb to the top of Mt. Sinai, the famous mountain that is believed to have been climbed by Moses where he heard the message from God and announced the 10 commandments. If Moses heard profound things from God, maybe God will have something to tell me too.

When we made it to Saint Catherine's the day was already hot. Our group explored the cathedral and then made our way back down to the car park where a few shops and cafés were open. We sat down at one, had mango juice and cheese sandwiches and waited for the day to cool so we could start the mountain climb and reach the top by sunset.

The walk up was beautiful. The mountains were spectacular. There were patches of green space. There were plenty of places to stop, specifically in the shade to catch our breath. At the top there was a small cathedral sitting there. It immediately reminded me of the little church that was on top of the mountain in Ios, Greece. I found a nice spot, knowing that I had lots of time before sunset and committed to a long meditation session. I decided to push myself to 45 minutes. I set my iPad timer, sat on the cliff edge and closed my eyes.

My first pause was right at the 20 minute mark. Not surprising, my normal sessions only last 20 minutes, always on the dot. I closed my eyes again and made it through another 10 minutes. It was somewhere between the 30 and 40 minute mark that my head really cleared. I pictured being with my ex.

I was lying next to him, but he was just not interested in sharing his love. I kept trying to hold him, but I felt like I wasn't being held back. My mind told me that it will take a lot of patience and time for him to open up his heart again. But then I started picturing a new man. I felt like he was an option. Almost like my life was introducing him to me to ask me if I wanted one or the other. I felt this questioning inside of me. Choose my ex and I will never be introduced to this new man.

I felt my stubbornness as I said I still wanted to wait for my ex. As I held on to this idea it felt like my future with him was becoming more and more uncertain. As if choosing this path will become more difficult as I continue on. It felt like his feelings. He feels like I am pushing him to be different. I am not, but I feel like he feels that. It asked me if I still want to wait.

I know right now I still would take my ex in an instant. There is something about the love of a soul that is so difficult to severe, but sometimes I feel like my ex has already decided to cut that cord with me. Maybe it's because he has.

If after this entire journey that is who I choose, then the world needs to accept that. However by the end I felt my meditation letting me know it is possible, it just won't be easy. I am not afraid of long, difficult struggles, especially if the outcome is worth it. But I now understand it is as much his decision as it is mine, and I have to continue my personal journey. I cannot wait for him to come around. I don't want to miss an opportunity with someone else that could be just as spectacular.

I felt calm and accepting afterwards. I felt like I am still on the cusp of something big and at a crossroads that only exists in this higher "power of intention" level. I continue to try to live love without attachment, but the truth is I love the attachment and pleasure I receive from it. Maybe I can find a moderate amount of attachment without going overboard.

By the time I awoke from my meditation everyone else had arrived. I went down from the peak to a level where there were a few of make-shift shops and cafés. I ordered a tea and sat on a pillow and drank. Later I sat with the rest of the group to watch the sun fall behind the mountain.

Egyptian time

Aqaba, Jordan
August 31

I slept so peacefully throughout the night. I don't even know what I dreamed about.

In the morning I sent Mandi a message. Misery does love company. We are both trying to be supportive to each other and share our individual experiences of the highs and lows involved in the tearing of the heart. I told her my biggest hurt is that many of my friends that I have given relationship advice to over the last few months, including "love more", "be there for them", "they are still your important person", are all in happy relationships and I am still waiting for a response. I'm not really waiting. It's more that I just can't understand why. It's because I have to accept the peace on my own. I have to accept that he will always be my heartbreak. Maybe I will always cry when I talk about him.

I was going diving this morning. The coral reefs are walking distance from the shore, so we gear up and walk into the sea. The first group went while I stayed back and chatted with a young Russian woman. We chatted about long distance love and my tears came immediately back. I wish that I wouldn't cry when I talked about him anymore. I wish it was so easy to completely release him. But as she said sometimes the soul knows more than anything and in those cases not even time will be the doctor.

Then it was my time to dive. I was amazed. The fish were stunning. There was so much coral and variety of fish. I even had the chance to see a sea horse when we were first making our way out. I was much calmer on this dive than I have ever been on any of my other dives, which made me feel really good. My practice, my breathing, trying to be Zen, started to finally come together.

We were originally told we would be back at 9:30 and even with Egyptian time I assumed that would mean closer to 10:30, but by 11AM we were being brought out tea and asked to sit and relax. I still needed to pack, shower and check out of the hotel. I don't stress out about time anymore. I noticed that on our way back one of the ladies couldn't focus on just enjoying the moment. That was me. Filled with anxiety over punctuality. Not anymore. If I can't change it, I just go with it. Plus there is always room for buffer. If it is Egyptian time to get us back it will be Egyptian time to get us to the ferry, and for the ferry to take off, and so forth.

The ferry is "scheduled" to leave at 3PM but doesn't leave Jordan until it is full, and it doesn't leave Egypt to return until it is full. We were told it would be a lucky sign if the ferry was at the port when we arrived. It was.

We were given a private police escort through the immigration process and expedited to the front of every line. Elizabeth said she felt terrible that we were queue jumping, but I told her not to hate the players, hate the game. If it wasn't acceptable for tourists to get priority they wouldn't be doing it.

The police office walked us onto the ferry, ensuring all other passengers were a safe distance behind us. We walked to the boat and guided up the stairs as some of the first passengers. We found some seats and started playing cards. And played. And waited. And played. And waited. We got on the ferry around 1:30PM and left the port around 4 PM. It was a three-hour boat ride.

Once we had all our bags we were guided again to meet our new Jordanian tour guide, Zuhair. At this point I was hungry and my hunger was turning me incredibly cranky. I couldn't handle the multiple personalities of the many different people. I just needed some food. Our group was taken to a restaurant and I ordered quickly. I ate until I was tired. I was hoping to sleep right up until I was hungry again.

Visiting Petra

Petra, Jordan
September 3

Yesterday morning Mandi and I exchanged a couple of messages. I told her things were getting better. Maybe I finally found the joy in solitude I was looking for. I still felt my unfinished love story and I could be so happy together, especially with all the growth I've experienced over the last several months, but if he cannot accept my love and is not allowing his heart to open up to forgiveness, do I really want him? My meditations are feeling more and more detachment. I am also starting to believe that he will never come back. I need someone who will accept my love.

This morning I could have easily slept for another couple of hours. I drank too much tea last night and ended up being overly caffeinated for bed. It must have been about 11PM by the time I finally feel asleep. The hotel had a wakeup set for 5AM. I know I need 8 hours, so I was feeling cranky when I woke up. But the water in the shower was hot and at least I could start the day off on the right foot. I prepared my day pack for a full day of hiking, met the rest of the group for breakfast then walked the five minutes to the Petra Visitors Centre.

We were the first ones in the area. We would probably have several hours before the other tourists come through and we could enjoy the cool of the morning before the day got too hot.

The walk along the path was impressive. The sandstone has so many different elements it looks like swirls of colours in the mountain ranges. Many of the mountains are close together creating narrow paths giving a mystical feel to the area.

We continued to walk through the path when our guide asked us to turn around and look at the top of a mountain.

When no one could see anything he then asked us to turn around. In between a sliver of two mountains we could see the Treasury, the most famous of all the Petra carvings. The height, scale and details of the carving are nothing short of impressive.

We were then given the choice to take a break for a bit or do a higher climb; see some of the higher tombs and a viewpoint of the Treasury looking down. It took about an hour and several stairs to get to the top. By this time many other tourists had arrived to Petra and the way the mountains are positioned it created a loud echoing effect. I wanted to enjoy my hard earned work up the top, so I stepped back from the group for a bit and found a quiet spot on top of a rock and did my daily meditation.

I slowly walked down the mountain by myself and enjoyed the many wonders of nature. The colours of the sandstone, the wildlife of birds and lizards, the bleating of the goats as they crossed the path I was walking along.

After a short break I continued to hike up to the Monastery. It was a direct uphill climb with snaking stairs the entire way. It took almost an hour to get to the top. I crossed the final area and saw an empty space and a café. I didn't know what I was looking for. As I walked closer towards the café I turned around and saw it: a stunning display of ancient design, as tall, if not taller, than the Treasury. Maybe it's because of the believed religious aspect, or perhaps because of the height, or that I found it to be in such amazing condition, but I loved it. The entire café was set up with benches all facing the Monastery, and realistically despite the amazing views of the valleys and canyons slightly higher, it's the Monastery that anyone would really be interested in viewing.

I headed up to the peak of the mountain to see the impressive views from the top. From there it was a complete panoramic of all the highs and lows of the country side. The shop owner at the top of the mountain pointed out the directions of the Red Sea, Dead Sea and the Israel/Palestine border.

I was exhausted from such a long day and decided to head back. I took my time coming down. As I made it to the bottom I was chatted up with a Chinese Naval officer. It was flattering despite the fact that I tried to shake him a couple of times. Maybe I am starting to attract love again.

Driving the Promised Land

I woke up twice. The first time I didn't like. I woke up from a dream about my house. I felt that I still had it, but the new owners were living in it. I thought about it and I think my mind was telling me it was time to move out. Move my mind out of the old house. It was no longer mine. It was a metaphor for my thoughts. I couldn't get back to sleep, so I sat and meditated to calm my mind. It worked.

The second time I woke up from a dream about the last episode of show Mad About You. The whole show was about the marriage of Paul Riser and Helen Hunt, but the last episode they were now divorced. I felt it was another metaphor for me. I made the right decision. I should never doubt that. If I keep focused on what I want my life to look like the right man at the right time will come.

I am lucky to be able to redesign my life. I don't need another person to fill in my gaps. I've already decided that I'm not going to date for a long time. I have too many things to finish and start first. Once I have everything in place I can enjoy someone entering without me feeling like I have to try. There will be no effort. We will be a part of each other's lives and I will feel confident that when I know I need something, or he needs something, we would love to meet each other halfway. I already love this man I haven't met only because I have so much love for me, I feel secure and focused on this current moment, on being patient, waiting for him, and knowing that he is coming. He is waiting for me too. We are both working hard to make ourselves better people individually that when we finally meet it truly will be a match made in heaven.

It was a long driving day. We were working our way from Petra to Madaba. Our first stop was the Karak castle, built during the crusades of the 11th and 12th century. On our way to the castle we stopped to meet a man living in a cave. He converted a Volkswagen Beetle into his bedroom overlooking the castle. The man invited us in, served us tea, and showed us his collection of rocks and antiques that he has collected. After looking at a couple of his items I found myself drawn to a beautiful bracelet. He said that it was made by the Nabatean women of the lands, but it looked very well made and perhaps real gemstones and diamonds. It was incredibly dainty. I couldn't say no. I negotiated very little and bought the bracelet.

We made it to the hotel shortly before supper time. I was still thinking about the Mad About You dream, so I had to look it up on Wikipedia. Turns out the two characters were separated but once they saw each other again they immediately fell in love all over.

Walking Through Amman

Amman, Jordan
September 6

We spent the yesterday morning at the Dead Sea. This was going to be one of my Jordan highlights.

As I walked into the lake the rock hard salt deposits on the beach eventually turned to sand and it became soft on my feet. I continued to walk out but then that's it. The floating takes over completely. I could stand directly vertical and still float. There's no swimming, the water was just too thick.

Elizabeth and I lathered up with Dead Sea salt and mud, which apparently has healing and age reducing benefits because of the mineral concentration. We were completely black with mud, and everyone wanted our picture taken with them.

The group departed ways last night and I went back to being a solo traveller. It felt odd to be alone again. Only a few months ago I cherished the moments that I would be able to wander the streets, deep in my own thoughts, no rush to the day. This morning I woke up feeling mixed blessings.

Amman looked to be such a beautiful city. I was looking forward to relaxing, enjoying cafés, reading, walking, and getting my last chance to feel the temporary mellow of Arabian shisha. However I was going to miss the company, even the mixed group of personalities that helped me to improve my patience. I learned to relax as others talked around me, as they moved at a frazzled, indecisive pace from me. New people that have helped me shape the person that I now am. Conversations that helped me release the things and thoughts that I no longer wanted to be. There was so much beauty and gratitude in my daily meditations for all of the experiences and individuals that are now in my memories.

I was solo again and suffering from a bit of loneliness. Thank you for the teaching to receive love I need to give love. I sent several messages to several friends. They were all in my

383

thoughts. Thankfully I was also in theirs. I went for breakfast: pancakes, eggs and coffee. I went back to my room and packed my bag to Ben Howard. As I checked out of the hotel I received two gifts, a book from a woman in my tour group left at reception and a message from Kim asking for a Skype chat.

Kim and I chatted about my "plans" for when I get home, which are still up in the air. Every now and then my old anxiety starts to sneak up. I want to plan what the weeks following my return will look like, but as I've learned from being on this journey nothing can be really planned. I need to relax and the future will come, as it always does, and I can make a decision when the time is right, not before then. When she asked about my love life I told her I still was not ready.

I know that I am comfortable with me right now. I am in love with this person that I have become. I have a truly amazing life. Maybe that's enough. I got to this point. I still get to continue the development of this amazing woman when I return home in a few weeks. Love has come. If I found myself to be solo for the rest of my days I could be happy. I didn't become someone new, I un-became everything I wasn't. I found simplicity and harmony in this moment.

I left the hotel and walked. I love to walk and enjoy the sights and sounds. Rarely do I listen to my iPod during my walks. I don't want to drown out the beauty of everything around me: the music with words I don't understand, old men chatting over chai street side, the honking of horns. I made me grateful to be here. My destination was not the passport stamps, but the feeling of wherever I am, here I am.

I couldn't believe how far I came in one month. One month. Desperate to return home to find something I was searching for when it was with me all along.

I walked through the market of Souk Bakharia on King Talal Street. When I was hungry I walked up to Rainbow Street and sat at a café. I ordered a peach shisha and a fatoush salad. I started reading the book left for me then I started writing again; writing my thoughts and not the events of a touristy day. Thank you, Universe.

I left the café and visited a modern art gallery. I miss looking at art, and thought this would give me a bit of culture. The Jordan gallery is one of the largest in the Middle East and caters to art specifically from artists in the region. As I walked through the two buildings much of the art was really sad. Understandable when the artists are from the war regions of Syria, Palestine, and Israel.

I still had 90 minutes before catching my airport transfer so I decided to find another café. As I walked I was unable to spot any places, but in the distance I saw some ancient ruins that I had read about, so I decided to head in that direction. Amman is filled with hills and turns and somehow I made two wrong turns and was completely lost. I felt like I was walking up large flights of steps constantly to try to get back on my route according to Google maps. I didn't even think I went that far downhill, but apparently I did.

I walked through residential streets, the people staring at me, knowing as well as I did that I was completely lost. I could tell from the map that I was close to the hotel, but somehow couldn't make it there. I had been walking for an hour; I needed to go back to my hotel. Why did I say earlier that I loved to walk? I finally said to myself that I was going to catch a cab if I couldn't get on a street that I recognized. I was afraid of missing my airport transfer. Thankfully I arrived at my hotel at 5:12 to meet my already waiting driver for my 5:15 pickup. I sat in the vehicle, thinking gracious thoughts for a wonderful time in Jordan. The world of travel still waits. Next stop: Nairobi.

Phoenix in Kenya

Nairobi, Kenya
September 7

I made it through Nairobi in record time. The flight from Amman to Cairo was redirected to avoid the Syria and Israel borders. My flight from Cairo to Nairobi landed at 3:45AM. When I arrived I had to clear an Ebola health check screening before reaching immigration. The security guard before immigration was still asleep so I didn't bother waking him up as I walked through the checkpoint. I was the first one to arrive to the immigration line and my only delay was to wait for one of the six officials to wake up from their desk. I paid for my $50 visa, watched the official put the cash in his pocket then issue me a receipt. My bag was the first one out. The driver that was waiting for me didn't even have time to pull out his sign that had my name on it. I made it to Jaime and Denzil's before 5AM. Thankfully baby Phoenix woke up his mom and dad before I did. We chatted and drank tea as the morning sun started to rise.

After my shower we left to Jaime and Denzil's favourite breakfast spot. I borrowed a sweater from Jaime. It was a cold 12 degrees and only warmed up to slightly more than 20 degrees. We were joined by their friend Laura then headed out to do some grocery shopping and banking. It felt so good to do some domestic, normal, things again.

I moved my bag over to Laura's flat, where I will be staying while I am here. We all met again later in the evening to enjoy dinner and watch cooking shows.

I loved watching Jaime and Denzil interact with the newest family member. It made my heart warm up. I feel excited for my own chance to have my own little family. I can't wait to experience the love of a husband and allow it to grow by creating a new life with him. One day. It will come in its own time.

When Yes Means No or Trading It All Away

Kilimanjaro, Tanzania
September 10

When Yes Means No

It was the day before my Kilimanjaro trek. Jaime, Denzil and I worked all of the evening before to arrange the trek, a shuttle and transport to the shuttle pickup point. I spent the rest of the evening packing a duffle bag of gear for the 7-day hike. I set my alarm. I was ready.

My taxi driver picked me up at 6:30AM to take me to the Silversprings hotel. On the way there he asked me again if it was Silversprings that I wanted to go to. I double checked my email. It was.

"Okay", he says as he pulls into the Fairview hotel, "this is it".

Maybe there's a name change, but before getting out of the cab I ask one of the hotel staff, "is this Silversprings hotel"?

"Yes", he answers back.

I'm early so I go into the hotel for breakfast. My shuttle is expected to arrive between 7:45 and 8AM.

At 8:10 I start to get anxious. I'm sure it's just the Nairobi traffic I tell myself to calm down, but to be sure I decide to email the trekking company. They are based in the UK and aren't awake yet. I have no phone number of the shuttle company. I look up Google maps and see there is a Silversprings hotel about 15 minutes away. One of the security guards asks me if he can help and I tell him I need to get a shuttle to Moshi today. He has a number of someone at the Silversprings hotel. He calls them and tells me my shuttle is still waiting. If I leave right now I can make it. He then arranges the hotel airport shuttle driver to take me there. I tip the man and jump in the van.

When I get to the shuttle office I go in and say someone had just called and said there was still a shuttle waiting for me.

"Oh, no", says the man, "that shuttle left 30 minutes ago".

I ask him if there are any other shuttles, and when he tells me no, I ask him if there is still a 1PM shuttle.

"Yes", he replies.

"Can I get on that one?" I ask.

There is room but it will only take me to Arusha, which I have been told is 45 minutes away from Moshi, where my trek starts. I decide to book the shuttle and then spend the rest of the morning working with the trekking company to arrange a private car to drive me the rest of the way.

The 1PM shuttle arrived just before 2PM. My bag was loaded onto the roof of the matatu. We stopped only briefly during the six hour journey at the Tanzania border to pay for our visas. I was redirected a couple times before finding the correct one. I went to pay for my visa and the man told me it was US$100. I laughed and said I was pretty sure it was only US$50. He laughed back, and said I was right. Ha, there's nothing but love for Africa. We were loaded onto the matatu quickly before too many beggars and peddlers approached.

I can't wait to get up this mountain. If seven days with no internet and nothing but my thoughts doesn't clear away the clutter I may be a complete lost cause.

Trading It All Away
I woke up sometime around 4AM and despite my best efforts couldn't get back to sleep. I tossed and turned for a while but finally when it was about 5:30 I just decided just to be up.

I sat on my bed and meditated. Once my brain shut off I felt close to someone. Like that moment just before a passionate kiss when I could feel the other person's face close to mine, but our lips haven't touched yet. It is like the entire world disappears for that moment. The only thing that exists is right here, right in front of me. I held onto that moment for as long as I possibly could, which I think was several minutes.

As my trip comes to a close I've done a lot of thinking about possibilities. Part of me thinks six months may have been too long. Had I returned home at the three month mark I could have avoided all the confusion that Indonesia was to my heart for those two weeks. Even if I would have gone home at the four month mark I would have stayed on my relationship reconciliation high knowing that I only had to wait a couple of weeks before I had the touch of someone again. It would have saved me from the rock bottom heart break that Greece was to me. But, no, for some reason I chose six months. An arbitrary number that has moved me across incredible highs and lows, both in location and emotionally.

My ending location before going home was to be visiting my cousin, her husband and their beautiful baby boy. The three things that kept me trekking on. But as I spent the last couple days with them, being a silent observer to their love-filled relationship, the question I had several times throughout this trip came back again: would I trade it all away for what they have?

To decide all the places, things, people, conversations, and growth, could be traded away. *The growth*. All of it gone for a loving husband and a baby. If someone snapped their fingers would I say yes?

Early on in my trip my answer would have been a very strong and definitive no. But as the time passes the answer is becoming cloudier. Mostly because at that time I believed this trip would make me a far better person. If I was a better person I would have and give more love than I could ever imagine. However right now I will be returning home feeling not even close to emotionally ready to put myself out there again. I will focus on my career, maybe turn to determination to immigrate to Australia sooner rather than later. Then if I'm lucky a year out I may finally be ready to put my heart out there again. I have always been lucky in love so within 6 months from then I would meet someone wonderful. We would have my historical standard two year courtship before getting married, and within another year be ready to try for children. I'm now 36. My biggest fear is now my looking at me directly in the face. I missed my fertility window.

Although I hear it often, I still have time, I don't have to worry, lots of people have children past the age of 35, for now I have to look at what I have right now, did I chose wrong today? Should I have just gone home? Or really, if I could today, would I give it all up?

I suppose it's not even a question worth asking. There is no answer. The person today is not in the same headspace as the girl that made the decision to be here in the first place. So I guess in lieu of the "what-if" question and answer games that used to occupy my head for hours or even days, I will instead concentrate on an ask to the Universe to please, please bring love to me. I will maintain my promise of focusing on me, making me a better person, doing what I can to help make the world better one gesture at a time. I have faith that this is exactly where I needed to be. I have nowhere to go but up.

Bottoms Up

I eventually made it to Moshi last night. After an hour delay with the shuttle, construction on the road leading to Arusha, and the milk run stops before our destination, our shuttle pulled into the parking lot at 8PM. Thankfully I had my private driver waiting for me. I told him I was absolutely starving. He took me into the hotel restaurant and I order a pizza, he had rice and chicken, of course I paid for both.

It was a 90 minute drive to Moshi, not the 45 minutes I was originally told. I checked into the hotel just before 10:30PM. I changed the settings on my iPad to the dimmest setting, turning off Wi-Fi, and hopefully, if I am very conservative, I will have enough battery for the full week. Just enough to write my daily entries.

As I made my way to breakfast my trek manager arrived. He checked to make sure I had three-layers of clothing and winter-wear items for my summit day. He also mentioned the effects of altitude sickness, which includes headaches, loss of appetite and light-headedness. He talked about the process of going up the mountain: the camps, the different climate zones, the daily washing pan, the meals, and to ensure that I am sleeping with my electronics so they don't freeze, especially my camera on summit day.

I filled my camel pack with water and stored my passport, money, cards and other non-essential items at the hotel waiting for my return. Samson took me to my van, where I met the team of people that were going to take me up. I had a guide, a main porter and another team of 4 cooks and porters; me and six men going up the mountain.

We drove for 45 minutes until we finally reached the Machame starting point. The porters got organized while I sat back and waited. My brain was starting to go active and I reminded myself that this was my test week. Could I go seven days without getting too lost in thought? Could I enjoy the moment and focus on my here and now? Whatever is waiting for me at home will be waiting, and what is not, will not be. This is my time. My chance to forge new memories. Focus on the trees. Watch the wind move the leaves. Calm.

It seemed like I was waiting forever. I did well trying not to get myself too overly anxious. I had to conserve my energy. Today was going to be a 5-hour hiking day. Finally, we were ready to go. My guide and I walked along having brief chit chat from time to time. I asked about his family. He asked about my age. I focused on the trees, the flowers, and in my head I kept saying "slowly, slowly, pole, pole". I am in no rush. My mantra for my life.

The trek was going smooth and eventually we caught up with our lead porter, who decided to keep pace with us. The three of us all walking up together.

We made it up to camp in almost record time. My guide told me I am strong like lion. They started calling me Simba, Swahili for lion. As I entered my name into the record book I saw that there was another already there. Since the only other people to sign in were a French couple that I saw leaving the registration office, I found the Canadian and we started chatting for a bit. Simon and I talked about travelling, our families, and work. Then we chatted about relationships, or specifically breakups, and how he was here because he was with a woman for two years and he didn't feel ready to commit when she was asking him for one. He kept an eye out for the sunset and the adjoining glow on the peak of Mt. Kilimanjaro. It was my first time seeing the peak.

When my dinner was ready, Simon headed off to his tent while I enjoyed a mountain gourmet meal of potato soup, fish, vegetables, tea and a banana. My tent view was beautiful trees and mountain peaks. If camping was like this all the time I don't think I would do anything else on my weekends.

What Was I Thinking?

Kilimanjaro, Tanzania
September 13

As I was going to bed last night I thought to myself what was I thinking? I have five more night of sleeping in a tent in the freezing cold. Am I absolutely nuts?

I woke up around midnight. My stomach was aching. At first I thought it was the altitude sickness starting to kick in, but when the pit in my stomach didn't quite feel like nausea, I realized it was a symptom of over gorging myself over the day. My porters are insistent that I keep eating. I have let them know that I don't even eat this much normally, there is no way that I can keep eating. It turns out it's not just me, in the morning I chatted with Simon and he said his team was doing the same thing to him.

It took me hours to get back to sleep. Somehow I did only to be awoken again by the thought that I finally fell asleep.

I made myself a cup of the 3-in-1 instant coffee I brought for myself. I found Simon's tent and gave him one, like I promised, then I found Ryan's tent, who I met the day before when I saw him attending to a blister. Ryan is travelling with a group of Americans working in charitable organizations. I let him use my blister stick the day before and I found him again in the morning to give him a chance to use it again before the hike. Yesterday was 5-hours and today was going to be a 6-hour climb to Lava point and then down to our camping spot.

My guide and I took off around the middle of the pack of people and we made good time. Steady, one foot in front of the other, climbing. Just keep trekking, just keep trekking. Hakuna matata, dada. Hakuna matata, kaka. No worries, sister. No worries, brother.

The trek up to Lava point was difficult, long and repetitive. The terrain had turned from grasses to rocks. Lots of rocks. Some big, some small, but all black volcanic rocks. Just before ascending up to Lava Point we crossed a small creek with the first signs of ice. Then I thought I must be stupid. If I wanted to climb a mountain with snow and ice I could do it any day in Canada. Yet here I am, taking a week out, and paying to do it. I don't even like the cold.

I thought a lot about this trek being my final exam for my months of travelling, soul searching, and learning to slow down my body and my brain. I walked with more consciousness of my surroundings. I spent little time thinking about the future and more in what can I do today, or what could be the potential outcome of my recent actions.

The final part of the hike was a nice descent and the scenery became more and more beautiful. I stopped to take plenty of photos, just taking it all in. Reminding my head that I am supposed to be here right now and not thinking about anything else. If this trek was my exam to see if I could clear my head, today I barely passed. But that's okay, because I think I came to some really nice thoughts at the end, including "I am ready". I am ready to put my heart out there again. I will find a wonderful man that will give me the time I never received in my last relationship. He will fall in love with me and will not wait to start his life with me, like my other ex did with his current fiancée. I am worth it. I am a wonderful person and someone will find me and know how lucky they are.

I arrived at camp early and decided to go for a nap. It was raining outside and the sound of the rain on the tent sent me right to sleep. I was awoken by someone calling my name. It was Ryan. He was standing outside and wanted to see if I had walked over to some of the viewpoints. I had not. I quickly organized myself and we took a short walk. As the clouds moved into the mountain, we walked back towards my tent and sat and drank tea as we chatted. It was through our conversation I decided that I no longer wanted to do the 7-day when I could easily do it in six. I was feeling strong and hadn't had any altitude sickness. I told my guides and they tried to convince me that I shouldn't. It would be better for me to do seven days. I told them I had no desire to spend an extra day in a cold tent, and I really felt like I could do this. This went back and forth for a while.

I couldn't understand why it was such a struggle to have these men get one extra day off. I thought they would be happy to have the extra night. Maybe they thought I would be tipping them less. Maybe they don't want to go home to their wives. Maybe I am better off being single if many married men are trying to find reasons to not come home early.

Eventually after a few phone calls, unnecessary conversations and delays it was decided I would be trekking to base camp tomorrow.

I Can Almost Touch It

The altitude must be affecting my dreams. I had some odd ones last night around coming home. I was feeling that I may have to wait a couple of years for my Australia dream. I might need to be in Calgary for two more years or so. However, no matter what, I am excited to finally be coming back and embarking on my next adventure over the next couple of months.

I think my mountain guides were upset with me for reducing their time on the mountain. I was supposed to be served breakfast by 7:30 AM, but it didn't happen until much later. They wanted me to wait inside my tent until the sun crossed over, but I refused. I had everything packed and was ready to go for the day. So instead I sat on a giant rock, slowly sipped on tea and contemplated my recent thoughts about balance and moderation, between taking action when I know action must be taken and enjoying the moment, slowing down and being right here when there is still time. But how would I know when to do either? Somewhere there is a balance between moving fast and being patiently slow.

I then realized that one sentence is the entire central theme of the Bhagavad Gita, the Hindu story of Krishna and Arjun. That's when my guides were ready to go.

I have been really good at conserving the battery of my iPad, so I decided for a special treat I would play some music out of my day pack as we walked along. I just had to make sure I would still have enough battery for the ascent up to Kilimanjaro tomorrow. Music might be one of the few things that keeps me going.

Today's trek was a lot more rock climbing. I felt more in my element. I kept up the steady pace. We made it to the point where the Lomosho and Machame routes combine at a nice plateau peak point. I started chatting with a guy sitting there. Hemad told me his story of how he won a $25,000 grant from Dos Equis to live the most interesting life in the world. He was just getting started and was doing a Kili climb then flying to India to meditate with the Buddhist monks then off to Japan to try weird and unusual food.

My guide and I continued on our trek, this time the mountain and the trails getting steeper and steeper. I kept going in my head, just keep trekking, just keep trekking. As we made it up the final climb I could see the tents all sitting above. I was excited and just wanted to get to camp. I found a burst of energy and was ready to just get there, like a horse seeing the stables. My guide kept yelling at me "pole, pole". I swallowed my pride and incredibly slowly followed behind him, but I felt like a stubborn child and didn't want to talk to him for the rest of the night.

I had an early dinner with a super early bedtime. The Kili ascent starts at midnight to peak for 6:30 sunrise.

Top of the World

Kilimanjaro, Tanzania
September 15

Wake up was at midnight. I was served tea and cookies, which I couldn't eat at that time. Thankfully I still had a bunch of nuts that I ate. That would give me both protein and calories. With the expected six hour climb I didn't want to sugar crash on the mountain. Then when I was sure that I had everything packed we made our ascent.

I figured we were somewhere in the middle of the pack when we started. We walked up in a steady pace. It was so dark the only thing I stared at was my guide's heels as he walked in front of me. Every now and then I would hear him say "hakuna matata, dada". Or he would tell me that I was strong like simba. We pressed on. The start of the climb was nice. It was calm. There were no clouds, but somewhere around the second hour the winds started to pick up with force. It brought a cold that just wouldn't quit. It could have been the equivalent of -15C or so, maybe even colder. I put on a third pair of socks. My feet were freezing. I couldn't feel my toes. I put on the balaclava to cover more of my face. I went through an entire package of tissues my nose wouldn't stop running. I pressed on. One foot in front of the other. When I looked down I saw a trail of head lamps coming up the same switchback path that I just did. When I looked up I saw more head lamps and a little bit of hope that I could almost see the top. It looked brighter like the sky and not solid dark like the rocks. Hopefully this wasn't an illusion.

My guide and I stopped briefly a couple of times. We couldn't stop for long. Movement prevents hypothermia from kicking in. I shared my protein bars with him. We both needed energy to keep going. My camelback line froze. There would be no more water for me for the rest of the hike. As the hours continued I sang in my head. Turns out I was singing and people I passed sang along with me. Anything to keep moving. My sugar level dropped. My body was exhausted. It reminded me of my marathon run and how I just had to keep going. Picture things in my head that would help me along. What's waiting for me at the top?

The altitude started to get to me. I could feel my hands were retaining water. I could barely move my fingers. My arms were getting tingly. I had a headache. Then my mind started flashing images. Without ever having one, and hopefully never will, it felt like watching my life flash before my eyes. It was the things that were most important to me. Four moments. It was my unfinished love story's and my first Valentine's together. I was sitting on his kitchen counter and he was feeding me Grand Marnier-soaked strawberries. The second was one of our last moments together. We were already broken up and the house was getting emptier by the week. We were driving in his truck taking a few items to the e-recycling depot. We were holding hands. Then I saw my dog, Tila. Then I saw my mom. That's it. It was simple and pure love. I didn't see my trip. I didn't see Eddie or any of the moments we shared together. There was nothing about my stuff, my vacations, or anything else. I wanted to cry. I held back the tears mostly because I had no more tissues and I didn't want my tears to freeze. It felt like a pinnacle moment inside of me. I knew before, but now I really knew who is most important to me and my life. I know what I want my life to mean.

I asked my guide if we could please stop. I needed to eat something. He pushed me to keep going. But, I need to stop, I insisted. No stopping, we were almost at the top. I kept taking steps. One foot in front of the other. Then there, like magic, the summit of Kilimanjaro, Stella Point. I cried. I did it. This may be one of the most physically and mentally demanding things I have ever done. I sat for a moment and just stared at the sign. I took off my boots, tried to warm up my feet and then put my feet back in, this time with looser laces. The stop was brief. It felt like there was not a lot of time to enjoy this moment. My guide pushed me on. The sun would be up soon. I could still make it to Uhuru Peak, Freedom Peak, and see the sun rise from there, if we are quick.

We trekked on and then I had to stop despite my guide's urge to keep going. I had to have a juice. I felt faint. I felt like I was going to puke. We pushed and pushed. Another 30 minutes. The sun was beginning to rise and it cast a stunning red line across the horizon. I shuffled my feet. That's all I had the strength to do. Shuffle, shuffle, shuffle. Then I saw the people, the celebrations. People were congratulating everyone around. My heart wanted to burst into tears. Millions of people dream of this. I woke up early and made it happen. I challenged every part of me to put me here. This is more than just a mountain. It was my test. It became my inspiration. This is the moment I will go back to when I am home. I know what I want to do, who I want to be, the person I want in my life.

The moment was brief. There was not a lot of time to enjoy and take pictures. I stood in front on the sign and had my picture taken and another one with my guide. I didn't walk off the platform so much as just let my body drop. People started to line up. They all wanted their photos. The clouds moved in and the air became icy. There was no sunrise to be viewed today. With the clouds a snowstorm was being brought in. I had my window and it was now over. I did it. Time to move again. We started our descent.

As the day became brighter we were able to move much more quickly. I found a burst of energy with my elation. My guide and I practically ran down. I high-fived people that were making their way to the top. I cheered and clapped them on. I told everyone that I passed that they were a champion. I left for the ascent around 12:30AM, was at the peak at 6AM and back at camp at 7:35AM. I was exhausted. I made my way to my tent and passed out for an hour until my lunch-like breakfast was served. I couldn't eat any of it. I was overly hungry but far more tired. A bit of soup, two bites of toast, the orange slices.

I couldn't even eat the spaghetti or the sauce. I drank two cups of Milo to try to get some liquid calories. Then my team urged me to get ready. Get packed. I was exhausted and dehydrated. I didn't know what the rush was, but they wanted me to move. I slowly put my gear together and pulled myself together. Turns out the snow storm was moving down the mountain.

We went down a different route. I couldn't believe how fast we were travelling. Once I hit my tent I completely crashed. I was done.

I must have slept for about three hours. It was raining outside and when I left my tent the entire area was covered in a fog. Many of the groups that made the summit this morning were just arriving for the day.

Coming Down

I told my guides I wanted an early wake-up. The sooner I could get down to the bottom of the mountain, and to a shower, the better. I was expecting to wake up around 7AM, but the other tents around were already up and making chatter, I couldn't sleep in any longer. I took a moment to reflect on my Kilimanjaro experience and had a proper meditation. I am very ready to go back home. I am ready for love.

I am ready to act. I am ready to be patient and wait. I am stronger today than I have ever been in my life. I know I will have amazing things in my life. How could I not? I am an amazing person. I feel love for myself and the people around me. My time will come.

I packed my bag while I drank my coffee and slowly ate my breakfast. I still didn't have much of an appetite from the altitude sickness, but I've also never been a massive breakfast eater anyway. I tried a little bit of everything because I was told that it is insulting in African culture to be served something and not at least try it. I ate a small bowl of porridge, a single piece of toast, fried egg and mango.

As my team was packing I took a few minutes to say goodbye to the friends that I had met on the mountain. I said goodbye to the group of Americans then I said goodbye to Simon. The air was cool and slightly drizzly. It was perfect for the last of our descent. I told my guide I loved running in the rain. When I was marathon training my best times were in the slight, easy rain. I stayed cool and the air was always freshest. I watched my footing as the rocks on the path became more slippery and we trekked down at a moderate pace.

I chatted with a few people along the path. I took some time to talk to a group of New Zealanders. They were all part of a charity organization, and with the number of people that I met from NGOs and charities, I knew my mind was set. I am ready to impact more than just my life. I want to do something bigger than myself. Be a part of something amazing. I am determined to find an organization that needs me to help them raise funds and awareness for their cause.

My guide was in front of me, so it was time to pick up the pace. We continued down further through the rain forest, the misty air keeping the hike down cool and light. Then my guide introduced me to the next couple of people; another solo female that hired Absolute Africa as well. Charlene and I chatted until we made it to the gate. We talked about our travels and about love, relationships, self-confidence and the experience that Kili had on each of us. Somehow it was brought up that I felt like I had a life-flashing-before-my-eyes moment. She looked at me, breathed deeply, and said, "thank god, you said something, I felt like I had the exact same thing".

Kilimanjaro obviously has a bigger effect on people than anyone ever says. We talked about the odd dreams that we had on the mountain as well. Maybe it's the altitude, the cold, or the physical exertion, but I believe no one leaves a hike up Kilimanjaro without feeling some life-moving moment. Everyone cries. Everyone is so happy to complete it. It doesn't matter how many times each person does it, I saw even the guides being affected by the altitude. I saw strong people become weak and the weakest find deep strength. The most important things in my life I saw up there. I can't wait to return home. I am ready for the love in my heart to be received.

Shortly after making it to the gate the group of New Zealanders that I passed came down. They bought a round of Kilimanjaro beer and one of the men shared his beer with me while we all relieved our experience one final time before hugs and goodbyes we said. Charlene and I loaded up into a van and were driven back to our hotels.

Since I was down a day earlier I had to be booked into a different hotel. I picked up my items at my original hotel and was dropped off at another. I agreed to take my entire team out for lunch as a celebration, and we arranged a time for them to pick me up, after a much needed, and very much enjoyed, shower.

As our car left the hotel I saw Hemad walking down the street, who I hadn't seen since before base camp. He and I had such a great conversation; I wanted to continue where we left off. I asked the driver to turn around. As we came close enough I told the driver to cut him off. We opened the rear passenger door and I yelled "get in the car" in a deep voice. I think the moment would have made anyone void themselves with fear. But once he realized it was me, he unsuccessfully objected, and jumped in as we all went to a traditional African BBQ place that my guide chose.

I treated the entire group out for a buffet lunch with a couple of beers. My team presented me my official Kilimanjaro certificate. I was a very proud simba. Then we had the driver take Hemad and I back to the hotel that we both happened to be staying at.

I met Hemad back in the lobby a little bit later while we tried to upload photos on a very, very slow internet connection. The hours somehow just flowed and suddenly it was dinner time. We decided to stay at the hotel but switch to the patio. We ate pizza, drank tea and chatted about ourselves and our experiences. Without me realizing it he saw me at Stella Point. He asked me how I was doing and my response of "hanging on by a thread" made him laugh.

As I told him my story as to why I was travelling, because it's a question that always comes up, his opinion is the same that I've heard so many times before from people that hear my story. I was with a man that couldn't commit at the time. I travelled the entire globe. I heard it from Anjulie in Vietnam and Joe in Greece. Maybe this time it will finally stick.

However I believe if I've changed over the last six months he probably has too.

We had a lovely evening and then it was time for me to finally go to sleep in a much longed for proper bed.

Border Crossing

When I couldn't find a reasonably priced two-day-one-night tour to the Ngorongo crater I decided it was probably best to head back to Nairobi. I still was going to be doing a Masa Mari safari, and that might be more than enough for my needs.

When I went down for breakfast Hemad was already sitting at a table. I grabbed a coffee and a bowl of cereal and joined him. I told him that I would be leaving today. I think he was a little sad to be without company for the day.

I walked over to the reception desk and asked about arranging a shuttle to Nairobi for today. The man at the reception let me know that one was already arranged and a car was picking me up at 11AM. Good thing I asked. I had no idea. There seems to be a huge lack of communication in Africa.

Until the shuttle came Hemad and I hung out in the hotel restaurant. He showed me his video that he used to enter the Dos Equis contest. We talked about his restaurant, Movida, and again about travelling and the things he could likely expect on his next two destinations of India and Japan. He again wanted to talk about my love-life, or really my possibilities when it came to future potential. I just listened and took it all in. Who knew a self-proclaimed George Clooney, playboy, could be so wise beyond his years. He was convinced that I will have a coffee with my ex when I am eventually back, but when I do eventually meet him I will realize I've outgrown him. I told him I will send a message if that ever happens. I think everyone wants to know the outcome of the likely/unlikely meeting if it ever does happen.

The internet was patchy and we had a blackout for about 30 minutes as we sat there. I received so many notes of love, encouragement and support throughout my trip, and for some reason yesterday I received more than usual. I am so lucky to have the people in my life that I do. I can feel their love for me and I hope they feel the amount of love that I have for them in return.

At about 20 minutes after 11AM a car pulled up. The driver grabbed my bag and told me I had to hurry. We were late for the shuttle. We? Okay, I'm not one to argue. I jumped in the car and we stopped quickly at the bus ticketing office only to be told, again, that I wouldn't need a ticket for the shuttle, so we went directly to the shuttle station. One other man and I were on the shuttle and we took off to the hotel that I was supposed to stay last night at. We picked up Charlene and two other men. It was so great to see her again. Charlene and the men we picked up were on their way to a 4-day crater tour for less than I was being quoted for the 2-day tour. I seriously considered getting off the bus wherever it was going to drop them off and seeing about getting on their tour with them. Then I changed my mind. I had already told my cousin that I was going to come back, plus all my clothes in my bag were in desperate need of a washing. I don't think I could last four days with only sink laundry.

The bus dropped off the three of them then the driver told me to stay on for Nairobi. We drove another 50m, then he dropped me off, along with my bag, and told me that I have an hour to wait, so maybe I would be interested in walking back to the hotel that we just dropped the other three people off at?

I walked into the hotel and went to the internet café when I was approached by a woman from the shuttle office and another man. They weren't expecting me to be going to Nairobi today. I told them neither was I, but apparently everything was already arranged and here I am. There was nothing more to say to either of them.

The shuttle back to Nairobi was long. We didn't get back to the city centre until past 8PM. I sat, and wrote, and read, and stared out the window. I was happy. Truly happy. I felt complete with myself. I knew what I wanted to do with my life and where I wanted to go. I felt happy waiting for the reaction to each of my actions, and not pushing for anything. I felt like I was right where I needed to be. I am looking forward to being home. I hope my dreams become reality.

Irony

Nairobi, Kenya
September 18

I woke up to the voices of the security guards outside. They must do a shift change around 5AM. I couldn't get back to sleep. I tried to meditate.

I have been struggling with my breakup since the very first day. Some days are better and others are worse. I keep myself going by saying that whatever will be will be, and if he is meant for someone else that means I am meant for someone else too. The images I again thought about my experience of the most important things I saw on Kilimanjaro. It was not my trip. It was not the items I owned or the vacations I went on. I am grateful to be here and have met and touched the people that I have, but there was one person that struck me in that moment. It was tenderness, simplicity and pure love.

When I got down from the mountain and climbed into my sleeping bag I cried. I let it all out. I pictured those moments that I saw on the top of the mountain again and I wanted them. I then fell asleep. I dreamed about sending my ex an email: "Are you in Calgary this weekend? Would you like to go for coffee"? I have had the same dream every night since.

Today my meditation was cut short. Change your flight, it said. I couldn't concentrate on anything more. I debated on waiting. Maybe talk to Jaime. See what is available for safaris. Change your flight, I heard in my head again. I called up my flight booking company. I decided to come home early, before the weekend. I am back on Sept 26th. I immediately sent my ex a message. The long awaited coffee. The one everyone promised at minimum that I would have. "Something in me said to change my flight. Are you in Calgary next weekend? Would you like to go for a coffee"? I sent it off. I hope he gets back to me. I am home in a week.

I drank a coffee and caught up on the events of Facebook. Somehow through the listing of events I missed is that my cousin got engaged. The same one that I dreamed about a month previous. I was happy for her. That now leaves me as the last one to either be engaged or have a baby. I have two younger sisters, and three female cousins. I am the second oldest of the group and now the official last. Laura came in from her morning gym session and we chatted. I told her that I changed my flight and I let her know the reasons why. I still can't talk about the breakup without crying. It's been months. My heart definitely knows something that my head is trying to block.

As Laura went to get ready for work I decided to go back and do a proper meditation. Was changing my flight the right thing to do? It told me that he still loves me. I am still the one for him. Take things slow. Pole, pole. You will hear back. Then I pictured all my love and dreams, everything. It is all meant to be. I feel good. I made the right decision.

Before I got into the shower my mom called. I picked it up. I hadn't chatted with her in a long time. "Are you okay?" she asks. Yes. It's nice that Alex got engaged. Then she tells me that she deleted my ex from her Facebook. She doesn't want to tell me why. Well, now that means you have to. She says my ex is currently on vacation with his new girlfriend in San Francisco. He posted a picture of them holding each other. People were commenting that they were so happy he finally found a great girlfriend. She said she couldn't stand to look at it. She knows how much I still love him and it hurts her to know that I would hurt from it. She said she sent him a nice note, she was kind, but she couldn't look at it anymore and had to delete him.

I broke down. Completely. I couldn't breathe. I felt my world collapse. I couldn't believe that I had just changed my flight and sent him an email. I am an idiot. I ruined my life. I can't believe that my meditations, the psychics, my dreams, all of it, it all told me that him and I will be. He's moved on. I couldn't talk to mom anymore.

I took my shower and walked over to Jaime's. I felt like I was in a haze. A haze that I am all too familiar with. I have felt this same heartbreak feeling far too many times since being on this trip. Now I am finally going home and a simple prayer of a coffee will never happen. He's in love with someone else. I am in love with someone that will never love me in return. How could it all be so wrong?

I couldn't stop crying while I told Jaime the ironic set of events that occurred this morning. After all this time, months, I still cry.

Jaime and I decided to go for pedicures. A little pampering helps the soul. We stopped briefly at a travel booking office, where I booked myself a 3-day safari for Monday. I will be back by Wednesday night. Counting down the days until I am home. We ae lunch while we waited for our pedicure appointments. We chatted about love and relationships. I need a plan A. Maybe Australia is calling my name sooner than I thought. But as her and I sat and discussed, the only thing that was certain was I really wouldn't know what my plan is until I am back home.

Maybe I will get that coffee, maybe I won't. Maybe a flood of emotions will come back upon seeing him again or maybe I will feel I've outgrown him. I've never prayed so hard for a coffee.

Jaime and I then went to a craft market. My mind was turning so sour. Every moment I wanted to cry. I worked hard to redirect my thoughts. I've been training my mind for months to keep in the moment. Just this moment. Love without attachment. If he and I were really not meant to be it's probably because something bigger is waiting for me in Australia now. I have come so, so far. More than my miles. I have grown. I have more love than I have ever had in my life. Someone is waiting for me. He has to be.

Coffee Response

Nairobi, Kenya
September 19

Jaime had to stop by her school in the morning, so I agreed to go with her. She gave me a tour of the school that she teaches at, and I had a chance to take care of Phoenix for a bit, visit Jaime's classroom, visit with Laura in the art room, and sit in on Denzil's lecture including a Ted Talk video that he wanted to show his IB physics class. I can't believe how far away high school was for me. Back then I had so many hopes and dreams, and I am thankful that many of them never came true. There's something to be said for unanswered prayers.

Jaime and I decided to visit an art park. Artists rent space in converted trailers and sell their art in hopes of making it big. We walked around each studio, each person displaying something a little bit different. I loved the iron work eyeglasses that one artist made, but I completely fell in love with a colour block design. The painting was unfortunately far too big, especially considering I don't actually have a place to live when I get home. As well, I've spent a lot of time thinking about moving directly to Australia once I am back, but something in me is saying that I should wait for a bit. Spend a couple years in Calgary first.

I don't know what it was about today. I was feeling good. Overly confident. Like my dreams were going to come true. I wanted to run with these emotions. Something good was going to come out of today. I could feel it. I wrote a note to the Universe. I have been praying and meditating for so long. Maybe my letter will allow it to be put out there with even more conviction. One wish. I believe it will happen.

Jaime and I then decided to head to the Masai market before heading home. All of the Masai people sell a variety of craft wares. I walked around for a bit then poor little Phoenix

411

went into a crying fit. Jaime had never seen him like this. I felt sorry for Jaime as Phoenix struggled to be comforted. I figured he must have had a bad dream with the way he woke up in such a panic. Once he calmed down we finished walking around the market. I didn't see anything I liked until I came across some glass etched shot glasses. I bought the set of six of them. My ex would collect shot glasses and Hard Rock café pins from all his travels. It made me wish that I collected something.

We came back to the compound and headed over to the compound bar. It was nice to sit and have a drink. Jaime introduced me to a few of her friends and we partially watched Denzil and his team play football in the field just behind the parking lot.

I was starting to get a bit tired and Jaime and I made her way back to her flat. I opened my email and finally saw the response that I was waiting for. His name in my inbox. My day was feeling good. I was confident it was a good response. We were going to meet for coffee. Then I read it.

Him: Unfortunately I cannot. Glad to hear everything is well.

I couldn't breathe. I cried instantly. I didn't tell him I was doing well. Why would he mock me like that? I sat back and thought. It took him two days to come up with that response. He thought about it for a long time. I wish he would know that if we just saw each other everything would be all figured out.

I wrote back saying I know he has a girlfriend and a coffee and a brief conversation will not change anything that is meant to be. I don't think I will ever hear back. My conclusion is one that will never happen. My dreams and meditations set me up for more heartbreak. Someone please take my heart. I do not want it anymore.

Touring with Hippos

Nairobi, Kenya
September 20

We were going for a day tour to Lake Naivasha. The lake is known for its hippo tours, and since it is about an hour to 90-minutes outside of Nairobi we decided to make a full day of it.

I had a difficult sleep last night. My dreams kept me up. I am less than a week away from coming home and the one thing I was hoping for will not be there. It's a tough realization. Even tougher when my dreams and mediations still show me things that will never come. I am tired of heartbreak. I am exhausted of trying, yet I can't find it in me to stop. I know that once I am home it will all be done. I can't be home, where I pictured coming to a fairytale ending, and go day-in-and-day-out without the fairytale. Yet my meditation told me to send a last email, again. I summed it up with "don't be afraid to go for coffee". We regret the things that we never do, not the things we do. I am prepared to never get that coffee. I will never have the hope or the closure. I will have my unfinished love story hang in a state of limbo that will slowly die with age.

My meditation said to send my email, but wait until after 4PM. But my meditations have both been right and wrong before. I have the chance of a coin flip.

Jaime, Denzil, Laura, baby Phoenix and I all piled into the vehicle. We drove on a beautiful, smooth road along the cliff side. The views were beautiful. As we drove we spotted many zebras in the field and at one point saw a few giraffes in the distance. We had lunch at a restaurant surrounded by a beautiful garden.

We left the restaurant and headed to a resort that offers boat hippo tours. Laura and Jaime stayed behind with Phoenix while Denzil and I went for the boat ride. I was surprised to see so many fisherman in the water considering how deadly hippos can be.

The boat driver drove us around the lake pointing out the many bird species. We then came around a bend and saw a family of hippos all bobbing in the water, looking like they were top of each other. They kept their eyes on us the entire time, but didn't bother to investigate.

The boat tour lasted an hour and we met up with Laura, Jaime and Phoenix having tea by the pool. It was a beautiful day.

As we drove back home I stared out the window getting lost in thought. I had no idea what I was going to be doing next week. The same as all my travels, but somehow this felt different. It felt lonely.

We made it back to the compound and went for a drink at the compound bar. I stayed out for a bit, but then called it an early night. I was feeling so exhausted.

Making Decisions

Nairobi, Kenya
September 21

I was so exhausted today. I only had two beers yesterday, granted each one is 500ml, but that wouldn't be enough to make me that tired. Jaime let me know we were going to have a late morning, so there was no rush to get to their place right away. I could sleep in.

I woke up and couldn't get out of bed. I was in a sour mood. I stared at the ceiling. I meditated. I asked for clarity and direction. I need to know what to do. I took a very long shower and got dressed. I walked over to Jaime and Denzil's.

I had a lot of friends contact me over the last couple of days. Many are excited to see me. Others are giving me their words of support and encouragement. I feel loved. I am happy and excited to be back.

I still don't know what my plan is. I've tossed around a few ideas in my head, some of them being moving to Australia right away. I know that is in my bigger plan, maybe closer to a two or five-year plan as opposed to right away.

I've been thinking more about discovering my calling as soon as I'm home. I love the idea of using my skill set for fund development or communications for an NGO or charity organization. I am okay with less pay. I want to do something bigger than myself. I want my days to affect a cause or a group. I want to go home every night thinking that I did something wonderful for the world.

Maybe I get the experience of this new career change back home and I take that new experience with me somewhere else.

I do something different. Something that I would never think about doing. Living somewhere I wouldn't expect. Inner city or in an extreme suburb? Depending on the job maybe I choose to live in a small town for a bit. Experience that life.

Maybe I choose to live in Canmore for a year. That would be pretty cool. I could maybe do that. Take the idea of saying yes, experiencing life differently, extend it further into my life. I can't regret the things that I do, only the chances I didn't take.

My mind was working overtime. I chatted with Laura about life, love, and taking chances. I told her one of my biggest fears was that my ex would be with a woman that gets herself pregnant. Some women don't like the idea of waiting. They decide to make their baby dream happen, whether her partner likes it or not.

Laura said she would rather be single for life. I said that I would want to experience it at least once, but maybe decide how I do it when I get closer to 36 or 37.

I hope I will believe then that I believe today, and I always have, I want a man to choose me. He chooses me first. He loves me so much he wants to spend the rest of his life with me. We are so in love that we choose to express that in the form of a baby. That would be my perfect ending.

Surreal Safari

I was leaving for my 3-day safari this morning. The last thing I wanted to do on my trip. My finality. I finished packing my bag. I went from being accustomed to moving beds every two or three days to arriving at Jaime's, unpacking and never fully packing again.

I sent a friend a message in the morning saying I regretted taking this trip to begin with. I felt like I ruined my life. I reflected back on the last 8-months, since my breakup. Where did everything go so wrong? I held back the tears. I just didn't want to exist anymore. End my pain.

When my driver was only two minutes away from the shuttle pickup and meeting time the shuttle driver said he couldn't wait for me anymore and I would be put on another shuttle. I was loaded into a mutatu and told I would be switched over. That was fine but considering the other people on this shuttle all booked the same tour with the same company it didn't make a lot of sense. I've also learned better than to question things in Africa.

As we drove I went back my readings. I was in the middle of two different religious texts, Western versions, the Bhagavad Gita and the Dhammapada. As if I needed to hear the message at the time, the Dhammapada spoke of not committing adultery, which I had no intention, but hearing that made me think that I need to completely back away if my ex has given away his heart, fully or not.

Then it talked about releasing lesser happiness for greater happiness. In order to get greater happiness we have to release the lesser. That's where I'm at. I could be happier. I have to release what is holding me back from more happiness.

The Bhagavad Gita spoke to me on my wish to end everything. It told me that we have to picture every moment like our last. Our thoughts that are tied in this moment will determine where our afterlife could be headed. I need to be happy. I don't want to feel like I am still tied to this life if the time comes when I am truly done with it.

After several hours of driving, without the switch of vehicles that was supposed to happen, we dropped off our bags at a tented compound that my entire group, minus me, would be staying at. It was going to be "too complicated for me to stay at the same compound.

We were already on the outskirts of the Masai Mara and within minutes we started spotting impalas, zebras, and giraffes. We saw a pride of lions and shortly after a few ostriches. It was exactly everything I was hoping it would be. It felt like a surreal experience. The scenery was stunning. The animals, despite seeing them in zoos so many times before had a different element to them. The plains felt so full of life. It was breathtaking.

Coming To Conclusions

For the last few nights I have been doing a brief meditation asking for dreams that give me clarity. Show me hope. Show me something that my future holds so that I can be excited about the choices that I made. Each night I would wake up with nothing in my memory. Occasionally it would be my ex's name as soon as I woke up, which I never knew if it was the dream itself or my anxiety that I still wanted something that I couldn't have. This morning I woke up happy. I dreamed about unpacking a house. My stuff and a man's stuff. Clothing. Into a house with a mountain for a backyard.

Then I thought about my ex. Not in the same way I have, but in a way that I am ready for more. I realized that I don't want him, not where he is now anyway. For six months I have travelled the world. I have seen and done things that I would have only dreamed of a year ago.

When I left him I wanted more time with him. That was it. I was willing to quit my job to be with him. He's still working out of town. When I was here I was willing to cancel my trip two months early to be with him. He wanted to find a new girlfriend. Why am I putting myself through so much suffering for someone who isn't where I am?

The Bhagavad Gita said to give Krishna my suffering. Release it to him if I don't want it, and of course I don't. My dreams came and answered my questions for me. Find your calling. Find your home. Someone will already be there. If I live every day like it might end I will be with someone I can kiss every morning and night. They will know and accept that I love them and I feel loved every day in return. Non-negotiable.

It was a full-day game drive today. As I walked towards the mutatu the sun was just rising. It was going to be a beautiful

·

day. The mornings are very cold. I was thankful that I borrowed a jumper from Jaime. As the driver and I drove to the second camp we chatted about animals. He asked me what my favourite animal was. I said the cheetah. They are so lean and fast and ever since being a kid and watching one run on TV that was all I wanted to see.

As we entered the park there was no delay for animals. Our driver already had the roof of the van raised so we could stand up and an unlimited number of unobstructed photos.

As we drove through the park at a slow speed the radio was going off. Someone was calling our driver. Our driver started picking up speed and we all rushed back down on our seats. Whatever it was we did not want to miss it.

We drove and saw a few other vans stopped around an area. Our driver said to look for the cheetah. He was sitting in the field by himself, relaxing and scoping out the scene. Eventually he rose and although he didn't run I was able to see its lean body in its graceful walking movement.

The rest of the day we were able to spot many more animals, often times coming so close that I felt I could have reached out and touched them. It is a surreal experience seeing these animals in their natural habitat. Just before lunch we pulled along a river bank where we watched crocodiles and hippos sharing the same river banks. A live and let live relationship.

We then found a nice area in the middle of the Masai Mara where we laid out a blanket and ate our picnic lunches. We watched as the baboons made their closer and closer to our picnic, hoping to take any leftover scraps that we may be leaving behind.

After lunch we drove and saw part of the wildebeest migration. We saw more prides of lions, including a few cubs playing together. As the day came to an end we were able to see several bird species, warthogs, meerkats, elephants, a few waterbuffalo, a dik-dik, and a grouping of vultures.

When I came back to my camp I was sitting and drinking some tea, overlooking the beautiful scenery and downloading my photos onto my iPad from my camera. One of the workers from the camp asked to sit down next to me to chat. Absolutely. He asked about the animals that we have in Canada and then asked questions like "could a lion live in Canada"? I told him that it was quite cold, but I said that we do have zoos where I've seen all of these animals before. It wasn't nearly the same. It's amazing to look out on the plain and see giraffes, zebras, and wildebeests, all co-mingling with nothing but space. Then to see a lion completely unfazed by the animals that walk past her.

Although yesterday morning I was feeling regret for deciding to come on this trip, in reality I would never give it up. If I felt that my life accumulated to the moment that I had to be on the trip, then I have to assume I was also meant to finish it in the time that I did.

I've spent far too much time thinking about something that I have no control over, namely whether my love will always be unrequited to my unfinished love story, or if it could ever be returned again. I realized there are more important things to life than my petty love story problems. I wanted to explore the world. I now want to help the world, in whatever small capacity that might be. I am love. Love will find me. For now I can expand my love with the contribution I can make to the people that I help and touch.

Dear Past Kim

Nairobi, Kenya
September 24

Dear Past Kim,
Today you are driving back to Nairobi from a three day safari in the Masai Mara. The matatu is filled with people from around the world. It's an interesting take on the circle that has been this trip.

You were right. The last six months went by in a blur. There were days and weeks that seemed to last forever. There were moments that felt like they were much longer than the actual hours that they were. Sometimes three days felt like a week. Imagine that. You were actually able to put more life into the number of days. That in itself is absolutely incredible.

I am also the calmer, more patient and relaxed person that you wanted me to be. I sometimes get caught up in thoughts of the future but I can now bring myself back to this moment. To be just right here. It is a wonderful skill and will take the rest of my lifetime to work on it, but today I am so much further ahead in it than I would have been had I spent the last six months not travelling.

Past Kim, I wish I had better news for you about your heartbreak. Unfortunately it never did get better. But you put in an honest effort every day to feel healed. That's all I could have asked for. Thankfully there were days that seemed like your dreams were going to come true. You also learned that there is capacity in your heart to love again when the time is right. You did your best to not focus on your broken heart and you learned to use those moments to help focus on the right here and now. Sometimes though the thoughts and memories came without warning. You are amazingly strong. You did well. You got this and it will get better. Please believe that. You have to. You are so loved by so many, many people. People you met, people you knew from before. All of them supported you in one way or another along your journey. Some will be with you for the rest of your life. How many people in this world can literally say they have friends all over the world? Pretty cool.

Here's something you didn't consider, Past Kim, the way you did change. You asked for patience, but what your heart told you was that you needed a career change. It turns out you are greater than your days, more powerful than the hours you put in, and can make things happen quickly and with incredible precision. You were meant to help the world. You knew this in your heart. The next few months will prove it even more.

You found a religion that speaks to you. You found a new country that will one day be your home. Things that were never on your radar, but the wonders of keeping an open mind.

You still do continue to inspire, motivate and bring happiness and love into this world. Continue to do that and your life will never feel like it was wasted. There are very few people in this world that are capable of astounding and amazing things. Luckily, you are one of them. Embrace that. Use it to help everyone you touch. Your love for yourself and others will continue to grow.

I love you. I always have. I always will.

Love,
Kim

Going in Circles

Nairobi, Kenya
September 25

My last day. There is something wonderfully poetic about coming back home exactly 6 months to the date that I left. I didn't plan it that way when I decided to change my flight, but I did realize it afterwards. It was supposed to happen that way for whatever reason. I'm not going to complain about that. It's perfect.

I wasn't too excited to get the day moving. My flight back home was a late night one. I was pretty much already packed. Jaime said we weren't going to leave until about 9:30AM or so. There was plenty of time. I started every morning the same way I have every day for several months, with my meditation; a habit that I am so incredibly appreciative that I got into the practice of. It clears my head of the things I don't need it to be cluttered with. It helps me focus my energy on the things that are going to bring joy into my life. It helps me release the things that are holding me back from my full potential. I sat and felt my energy drawn so fully inward. I don't know where it came from but I broke down and started crying. A full-on ugly cry. I covered my face with my blanket. I didn't want Laura's housecleaner to hear me.

I told myself to stop it. Please, just stop. He has moved on. He wants nothing more to do with you. You do not miss him. There will be someone better. Believe that. Half a year you have been crying and hoping for something that will never happen. You should have believed him the first time he said he didn't see a future with you. There will be someone. There will be. Stop crying over him.

I cried only a couple minutes until I didn't feel the tears coming anymore. I really needed that emotional release. I have not committed to a full cry in a long time. I was releasing the things I no longer wanted in my life. I am leaving them here in Africa. As far away from me as I could possibly be again.

Maybe I was just sad about the end of this amazing experience that has brought so many mixed blessings. I would love to say that I felt better after the cry but I didn't feel any worse.

I headed over to Jaime's. We were heading to the elephant orphanage and the giraffe centre today. Jaime asked her cleaning lady, Mary, if she wanted to join us. Mary has lived her entire life in Nairobi and has never been to the elephant orphanage. She was so excited to go and she put on a beautiful dress to celebrate the occasion.

After the elephant orphanage we headed over to a lovely café and bronze sculpture gallery for lunch. We had lunch on the terrace and once I was finished eating my meal I took Phoenix from Jaime to give her a chance to eat. He is such a loveable baby. One day my future husband and I will have one of our own.

We then made our way to the giraffe centre. I saw one of the people giving a giraffe a kiss, with the giraffe getting his full, long tongue on the person's face. I thought it looked gross, but then in the nature of my animal kisses that I've given throughout my trip I thought there would never be another time to give a giraffe a kiss. I may as well make the most of it. I told Jaime to be ready with the camera because she has one shot to get this photo. I then put the pellet between my lips, and the giraffe came at it with his full, tongue. That was it for me. Time to end on a high note.

Back at Jaime and Denzil's the dark skies that were threatening rain all day deciding to finally grace us with their presence. We picked up Laura and made our way to the Windsor Golf and Country Club, where we had my first dinner; it was now all coming to an end. Before I knew it the luxury of time was finished. It was time to head back. My taxi driver was waiting. We were already late.

I packed my day bag. I locked my backpack. At this point it doesn't matter. The last flight home. I have been so lucky to not have it lost once. If it happened at this point I would be okay. Jaime and Denzil stood in the kitchen and watched me in my practiced rush go through my all too familiar routine from the last six months. I then looked up. I started to cry. I gave them both a hug. Told them I would miss them and we will see each other at Christmas. What a beautiful way to end my trip. With the love of family. With a promise of seeing each other again in the near future.

I ran downstairs, gave Laura a hug as well and told the taxi driver to go. There was no point in holding onto this moment. It was just going to make me cry even more. Then we left. The long drive to the airport. I stared out the window at the chaos that is Nairobi. People running across four-lane highways, garbage fires burning in the street, people dressed to go clubbing either by walking there or catching one of the many party mutatus. There is a saying among the ex-pats and locals: "T.I.A". This is Africa.

I made it to the airport with plenty of time. Then I waited. Waited for my midnight flight. 8 hours to London. Another 8 hours to Calgary. I will be home by noon tomorrow. I've only travelled West and will soon have completely circumnavigated the globe. Amazing.

Since Being Home

Calgary, Canada
December 26

When I came home I hoped for a lot of conclusions. I felt nothing was coming together. Then out of hope that I would receive some light of revelation I booked an appointment with a psychic.

"Your single", she says, "but your heart is still taken".

That was absolutely true.

"He is still your soulmate", she continues on, "he still sees himself marrying you and spending the rest of his life with you".

I immediately started crying. "How can that be? I asked. "He's with someone else".

"Yes, but both he and her know that something is missing from that relationship. At some point you're going to contact him again. You are going to have to drop the gauntlet. You need a commitment from him. But if he was to come forward everything would move so fast, it would make your head spin. I can see an engagement, a pregnancy, you would move to be with him".

I asked her when I would contact him and what I would say.

"You'll just know. You will not miss this sign. Be honest. He'll choose you or the other woman, but I can't even tell about anyone else unless you finish your story with him".

It was a week before Christmas. I sent him an email titled "my final love letter". I told him about some of the things that I had done since being home, I apologized for my mistakes, and then I confessed my never-ending love for him. I sent it, and expected it to go unanswered like the handful of messages I had sent him before that point.

It was a few days before Christmas and I received a response from him. "Apology accepted", he said.

427

My heart stopped beating. I replied again that if I ever saw him I would start kissing him and I would never be able to stop.

He replied a few hours later. "That is not going to happen".

I didn't know what else to say or do. I didn't want to talk with him over email. I wanted to see him, or at a minimum a phone conversation. I meditated on it, and my answer came to me. I had another email to write.

Me: I spend a lot of time meditating, especially when feeling lost and searching for answers. I pray to the universe. I pray to God. Sometimes I get answers, sometimes it's as simple as being told to wait. Tonight I was told to send you what I have been up to since coming back.

It's been a tough 3 months. Really tough. I spent probably the first month crying. Every day I was hoping to hear from you. But I tried to convince myself that was never going to happen and I carried on. However it was harder to imagine you not in my life than to imagine you were coming back. So I did. I would thank the universe every night for my soulmate. I would thank it for bringing you back. I hoped that my power of positive intention would make it so.

I started looking for jobs. I was convinced that I wanted to work in the non-for-profit sector. I applied to over 30 jobs in my first month. Only one call. For a fund development coordinator. I went through the interview process but didn't get the job, which was probably a good thing. It turns out fundraising pays really poorly.

But in the meantime I did apply for my Australian visa. Paid to have my credentials checked. That was back in November. I still haven't heard anything from it, but it could take as long as 6-12 months to really hear anything back.

I continued to apply for more jobs. I was contacted by several headhunters and went on tons of interviews. But every company, as I came close to the final stages were on hiring freezes, "going in a different direction" or need to delay other processes. One of them I didn't even pass the online personality exam. I apparently don't have sales rep personality.

I tried dating. I joined match.com. I went on one date, with a guy who ended up having terminal cancer. I would take myself off, join for about 48 hours and remove myself again. I actually came across your profile. My heart stopped. You were actively on. I decided I wasn't going to do online dating anymore and agreed to be set up. I met one guy. We had several dates in a week period and then he told me he wanted to see other girls. I cried. The pain reminded me of losing you. We continued to text a few more times then he disappeared. He reappeared several weeks later. But at this point I friend-zoned him. We would go for dinner. Chat daily. But it would never go past an evening hug. I couldn't do that to myself. I told him I wanted a serious relationship. I wanted to get married and start a family with someone that I feel is the one. He disappeared for a few days after that, reappeared but I know he is not the one. It doesn't feel right.

I decided to write a book. Keep my mind active. I need to do some serious edits though. However, I hired a publisher and the cover looks amazing. I always dreamed of writing a book.

I spent more time enjoying the outdoors. I no longer go on dog walks with my phone. I enjoy the nature for what it is. I decided to take up skiing this year. Really appreciate what Canada is. I spent a couple weekends just going to Banff, Canmore and surrounding area. I am hoping for a work from home position so I can live out there. However, I recently also decided to open myself up to more possibilities and applied to a few jobs in the Okanagan. I figure if I only had a couple of years in Canada I want to live somewhere I can truly enjoy. Calgary is no longer that city for me. I find it exhausting.

I swallowed my pride and decided it was time to go to therapy. Especially after creeping on your Facebook profile and seeing you change your relationship status. That was my rock bottom. I needed help. I started and continue to go to weekly sessions. We deal with my daddy issues. My fear of abandonment and rejection. My defense of pulling away first before getting hurt. I talk a lot about you. About my regret. About how I could possibly release you. I work really hard in therapy to heal and become better. I actually really enjoy it.

But despite all of this I still felt lost. I went to a few psychics. I needed some direction. Some type of clarification. I feel the universe is holding me in a state of limbo. It wants me to figure out a big piece. The piece that keeps pushing my heart and mind back to you. This week I felt like there were several messages telling me to call you. I tried. Every day for a week. Right to voicemail. Maybe you're on vacation.

But this is where I am: I have just been completely vulnerable with you. I held nothing back, and I never, ever would with you. I still love you. I would literally do anything for you. When I picture my soulmate it feels like you. If there was even a glimmer, a small chance you could see yourself with me I would hold onto that. Years if it took. But if not, I need to know. Truly. I am holding onto you. I need to know that either I was wrong. You don't think we are soulmates. I will accept that. I will never contact you ever again. I promise. There are so many couples that breakup and find each other again. We have both grown and changed. I am ready for your love. I know now what true love feels like and I will fight to the death for it. I'm here. I will do whatever it takes. I will wait, I will work on us, I will just provide you with my company. I don't know what you need. But I am here for you. Lee, I wanted to call you and have this conversation. Or please call me and give me your answer. I would so much rather hear it in your voice than over email. Please love me enough to do that.

I need to know that I am your soulmate and we can work it out or I never was and I can live with the idea of what I thought we had was false and I will continue my search for the person my heart is calling out to.

I love you. I hope to hear from you soon. I hope to hear your call even more.

He replied the following morning. He told me that I changed and he wasn't going what I put him through. Then, "I know now that you're home you think it can all be the way it was but it won't be".

I read his response and somehow in those few words I received all the answers I was looking for. He missed the point. I didn't break up with him because I was happy with our situation. I didn't go on a mission to search for deeper meaning in my life because I felt my soul was satisfied with the status quo. I wanted to grow and expand. I wanted a partner that was going to grow with me, or at least support me as I searched for more. I wanted things to be better. Better than ever. I wanted to find the authentic version of myself. I want to live in a city that serves my active, outdoorsy lifestyle. I want a career that makes my heart feel as full as my paycheque. I wanted a commitment with the man I loved. I wanted a marriage and family with him. I didn't want what I had, that's why I had to change. I wanted someone that was going to say "I pick you". He would offer to do anything in the world for me, because I would do the exact same for him.

I realized in that moment he still was my soulmate, but with a different definition. A soulmate is someone that makes you search deep inside yourself. This person inspires us to heal, to change, grow and expand. If we are lucky they will be with us through the process, but if not, it was not meant to be. Their contribution isn't anything less to the amazing impact they have in our lives. Thankfully I also believe we have more than one.

I wasn't originally going to respond to his last email, but then I did: "I'm sure one day we'll be friends again. And thank you for hoping the best for me. I hope the best for you. But for now I will change my prayers from wanting you to wanting someone who wants me in return. Please send out a pray of love for me too. I want to find my soulmate and have him love me for the rest of my life. I won't settle for less".

I closed off the email: "I send you love, happiness and light. I hope your life is better than it ever was".

Then I realized as much as he missed the point I did too. I was still proving my worth to someone else. I read the email I sent to him over again. In a year I have accomplished so much. So much! I did it by myself. I went and focused on making myself a better person and I'm still wasting my time replying to six line emails?

I didn't just grow on the trip, I grew even more when I came back home. I now know how to love myself unconditionally and I am fully prepared to love someone else the same way. I do still want to be married and start a family, but only because that will be my next adventure, not something that will complete me or define me. I love myself too much to give my heart away to someone that isn't going to be fully invested in us. I am a full vessel of love. I know how to keep myself feeling full and I am now spilling over. And the last time I felt this way I met a man in the queue.

This is still my story. I am open to amazing possibilities.

Acknowledgements

Thank you, the reader. My only dream for this book was to inspire people to travel, travel solo, slow-down in your life and to know that no matter how dark the day, or heartbreak, things always get better.

Thank you so much to my mom who encouraged me to finally live out many of my dreams. Thank you for taking Tila and allowing my only concern to be lifted making it easier for me to fly and soar. Thank you to my family, Tom, and Taylor. Thank you, Joanne for listening and being there for me before, during and after I returned. This has been the hardest year of my life and your support, your love, and your calm rationality, has meant the world to me. Thank you, Blair for always giving me brotherly advice. Thank you, Sarah for your honest opinion. Thank you, Aliza for reading my book twice and giving me your amazing and critical feedback. The dream I had for what I wanted it to become was done through your labour of love. I cannot thank you enough! Thank you to Candace for also reading and helping me where I needed it. I am so grateful for your time and energy. Thank you, Brittany for being available for a chat or a tea as I struggled with my healing. Thank you, Mandi for talking me through and being my virtual company on some of my darkest days. I found myself looking forward to receiving messages from you and then my days would become so bright.

Thank you to everyone on my journey. The people I met, the impact you had on my heart, none of it will ever be forgotten. Thank you to my Dharma sister, Ange. You challenged me and kept me having fun throughout the process. You were always following up with me and I felt my journey was helping your through your own soul search. Thank you, Shaune for meeting me and following along with your advice. Thank you, Tara for responding back to me when I had nothing left. Thank you, Kim and Darren for your love, your tough love, but always constant. Thank you, Jaime and Denzil for your graciousness. You are both beautiful people. Thank you, Laura for allowing me to stay in your flat and our conversations. Thank you, Dan, meeting you was incredible and our short time together had such a long impact on my life. Thank you to everyone else, Claire and my Australian tour group, Carmen, Kayla, Peemore, Sean and my Indian tour group, Bruce, Liz and my Egyptian tour group, and the people I met on Kilimanjaro and my Masai Mara safari. Thank you to everyone I met on every day trip, those that added me on Facebook, or I just had a brief conversation with. You all made my life feel so incredibly full.

Thank you to everyone that read my blog every day. It's because of your comments that you all loved reading and following my personal journey that I decided to write this book. Thank you to those that recommended a publisher to make my dream come true.

Finally, thank you to my former rockstar, my muse. You were my driving force. This book was often times difficult to write because of the emotion and love that I still felt. I know one day I will find love that amazing again. One day my love story will become complete with someone who makes me feel like that and chooses me, chooses us. You inspired that dream.